Exploring Education at Postgraduate Level

There is a growing demand for educational professionals to develop a more critical understanding of the key and emerging debates in education so that they can better meet the challenges and demands placed upon them. *Exploring Education at Postgraduate Level* represents a range of perspectives from educational experts to academic researchers and highlights the key issues surrounding contemporary education.

Organised into three parts and drawing on key issues in education theory, policy and practice, the book considers areas such as special educational needs (SEN), evaluating learning, comparative education and gender. Featuring reflective questions, case studies and summaries of core ideas, the chapters explore:

- The troublesome learning journey
- Applying educational thinkers to contemporary educational practice
- Values production through social and emotional learning
- Policy research: in defence of *ad hocery?*
- The politics of critical reflection in higher education and the workplace
- Developing critical thought about SEN
- The refuge of relativism.

Aimed at supporting students on Masters–level courses, this accessible but critically provocative text is an essential resource for those wishing to develop a more critical understanding of the role, purpose and function of educational systems and practices.

Anne O'Grady is Principal Lecturer and Partnership Manager for the School of Education at Nottingham Trent University, UK.

Vanessa Cottle is Senior Lecturer and Programme Leader for the MA Education at the University of Derby, UK.

Exploring Education at Postgraduate Level

Policy, theory and practice

Edited by Anne O'Grady and Vanessa Cottle

Routledge
Taylor & Francis Group

LONDON AND NEW YORK

First published 2016
by Routledge
2 Park Square, Milton Park, Abingdon, Oxon OX14 4RN

and by Routledge
711 Third Avenue, New York, NY 10017

Routledge is an imprint of the Taylor & Francis Group, an informa business

© 2016 Anne O'Grady and Vanessa Cottle

British Library Cataloguing in Publication Data
A catalogue record for this book is available from the British Library

Library of Congress Cataloging in Publication Data
O'Grady, Anne (Educator)
Exploring education at postgraduate level : policy, theory and
practice / Anne O'Grady and Vanessa Cottle.
pages cm
Includes bibliographical references.
1. Universities and colleges—Graduate work I. Cottle, Vanessa.
II. Title.
LB2371.O37 2016
378.1'55—dc23
2015009249

ISBN: 978-1-138-81407-3 (hbk)
ISBN: 978-1-138-81408-0 (pbk)
ISBN: 978-1-315-74775-0 (ebk)

Typeset in Bembo
by Swales & Willis Ltd, Exeter, Devon, UK

Contents

Contributors

Editors

Anne O'Grady has an established record in educational researching and teaching. Her research focuses on adult learners who experience marginalisation, within a framework of social justice, exploring social inclusion and exclusion dichotomies.

Vanessa Cottle is Senior Lecturer and Programme Leader for the MA Education at the University of Derby, UK. She has a broad range of teaching expertise. Her research explores postgraduate teaching and learning. Her doctoral study focuses on postgraduate identity and self-esteem.

Contributors

Joanne Byrd is a member of the teacher education team at the University of Derby. Her research interest is in partnership development, and recognising the value of inter-professional dialogue.

Tina Byrom is an established academic, teaching across both compulsory and higher education provision. Tina's research focuses on social justice. She has published in the fields of transition, widening participation and non-traditional learners.

Nicole Chavaudra is an expert in children's service provision, leading on major change projects and innovations in Children's Services. Her current doctoral thesis explores social pedagogy as a model for service providers supporting looked-after children.

Andrew Clapham is an experienced teacher, researcher and academic. His research interests include the role of inspection, professional accountability and postgraduate study.

Trevor Cotterill is an expert in further education teacher training, and specialises particularly in learners with learning difficulties and disabilities.

Ang Davey has worked across further and higher education in senior leadership positions. Her academic interests consider peer observation and behaviour management.

Mike Flay is an expert in special educational needs and has published widely in this field. He currently supervises a number of doctoral students.

Melody Harrogate has a background in lifelong learning, with expertise in leadership and management and teacher education. Her research has focused on quality leadership and management and needs analysis in education.

Dennis Hayes is an internationally recognised academic in the field of education, and describes himself as a philosopher manqué.

Nic Lightfoot is a Principal Lecturer at Sheffield Hallam University. Her professional interests explore educational policy and issues of widening participation.

Jennifer Marshall is an educational expert in the field of Comparative Education and English for Speakers of Other Languages (ESOL). Her recent research projects have centred on the internationalisation of higher education.

Ruth Mieschbuehler works as an Educational Researcher. Her PhD, *The Minoritisation of Higher Education Students*, was a study of philosophical and pedagogical approaches to student educational experiences.

Ruby Oates is an expert in early childhood studies. Her research interests include professionalism, power and the politics of the childhood worker, as well as reflective practice and pedagogy.

Deborah Outhwaite is an educational expert in the field of Leadership and Management, and social policy. Her current doctoral study examines how leadership teams introduce non-mandatory policy in education.

Claire Pass is an Advanced Skills Teacher with a responsibility for ensuring the quality of teaching and learning at Saint Benedict Catholic Voluntary Academy, an 11–18 school in Derby.

Fiona Shelton is an expert in primary education, and is widely published in the topics of behaviour management, curricula and gender. Her current doctoral thesis considers teacher autonomy in education.

Vivienne Walkup is a renowned educational academic who has published widely in the field of education and psychology. Her doctoral thesis considered mothers in higher education.

Jon White is an expert in the field of early years education. His professional interests revolve around the process of transition, and its relationship with resilience, for children between home and nursery.

Peter Wood has published widely in the field of education. His doctoral thesis considered the role of SEAL (Social and Emotional Aspects of Learning) as an intervention strategy in primary education.

Preface

Anne O'Grady and Vanessa Cottle

Education is a concept that has been experienced by each and every one of us in one way or another, but as individuals with our own unique context we experience it in a distinctive way. Education can be thought of as a prism of perspectives, ever changing depending on which direction it is experienced and viewed from. These perspectives deserve not only to be explored, as suggested by the title of this book, but also questioned, challenged, discussed, compared and embraced.

This book commences with two chapters which act as a framework for critically considering educational issues beyond the undergraduate level. The first chapter by Vanessa Cottle draws from literature and her own experience in a bid to alert potential and actual postgraduate students to the challenges ahead, whilst the second chapter takes a broader, more philosophical view of being critical. Being critical is something we are constantly being asked to do – but Dennis Hayes challenges us to think about what being critical actually is.

The sections of this book are represented by what might be viewed as the three pillars of the field of education – theory, policy and practice. It will become clear as you read through that each 'pillar' inevitably relates to, or underpins, aspects of the others' content. In this respect the book should not be seen as a suggestion that education is a linear process from theory to policy to practice, or a cyclical process where practice informs theory. Rather, we encourage you to see education as a process of dynamic interactions between diverse perspectives of education. This demands a commitment from the reader for a deeply critical approach to engaging in its study. Each of the contributing authors – who range from experienced researchers to novice writers – have taken a position, in many cases a contentious one, to offer the reader. It will be up to the reader to determine the authenticity of these positions. Each author has their own style of writing: some have adopted a personal and reflexive approach; others demonstrate a skilful literature review; some have shared insights of their doctoral research. This book offers you the challenge to recognise these styles, to embrace the arguments and contentions that are proposed and to read the content of the chapters with an enquiring, questioning and critical mind.

Within each section, too, the chapters relate to each other – there are connections and disconnections, ambiguities and contradictions – as well as many common themes for you to elicit. The prism analogy also reflects the different lenses through which each of the authors views their particular focus; the focus addressed in each chapter demonstrates the particular passions of the contributors. Together these are of interest and importance to practitioners and would-be practitioners alike in all fields of education.

The theory section begins by questioning the importance of educational theory within teacher education by asking if knowing how to teach is more important than understanding the importance of education, whilst the next chapter challenges the concept of employing psychological principles in teaching practice without a full understanding of theoretical frameworks. The implications of a child's identity in terms of gender and its relationship to achievement are contested in Chapter 5. This gives rise in the next chapter to a discussion around the implications of social control with a particular view of social and emotional learning. This chapter draws from Bourdieu, as do other chapters in the book, to bring attention to the importance of sociological as well as psychological aspects in teaching, learning and broader educational issues. It is practitioners themselves who are challenged to think about their own learning and development in Chapter 7, where curriculum perspectives are discussed from sociological and psychological thinking about teaching and learning as well as schooling and education. The theme of practitioners also appears in the final chapter of the theory section where the consequences of assessment, now accepted as a crucial part of the learning process, are examined as a tool for judging practice.

The focus of the chapters in the policy section ranges from higher education to early years settings, but underpinning all chapters is the notion that education is not just about teaching and learning, but rather could be an opportunity to address social disadvantage and improve social mobility. A range of contentious issues are identified from the 'big picture' concerns of social justice as exemplified in Chapters 10 and 13 to the more specific concerns such as whether a more highly qualified practitioner is more effective than one who has sufficient confidence in their own professionalism to effect change based on their own experience, as considered in Chapter 14. This bottom–up approach to management is contrasted with the influence of the top–down approach, i.e. Government to institution to practitioner, a theme that is also discussed in Chapters 15 and 16. Chapters 11 and 12 focus on specific educational policies, i.e. the pupil premium and policies related to those for whom English is not their native language. The contrast between a caring, social justice policy approach and an ethos of accountability is strongly drawn within the policy section of the book.

The third section of this collection of essays relates much more to practice. An account of critical reflection begins this section, and whilst this discussion is based within the context of higher education, the underlying messages apply to all sectors. The early years are clearly a significant time for building on a child's natural inclination to be interested in their world. It is in these years that transitions between the different places that children find themselves in may be most challenging – the second chapter of this section considers these places and how practitioners can help build the required resilience in an ever-changing world. The borderline between poorly behaved (a socially constructed term) children and those with special educational needs is often blurred, and Chapters 19 and 20 explore each of these concepts in turn. In all sectors of education the planning of teaching and learning needs to be effective for learners, practitioners and the institution. However, within the constraints of the curriculum and awarding body requirements, this can be challenging, and Chapter 21 provides a consideration of a range of leadership styles which may be used to mould an organisation in shapes that meet the needs of all stakeholders. The final chapter of the collection takes another 'big picture' view of educational practice from a philosophical viewpoint, by inviting us to stake a claim in our contribution to the practice of education.

We hope that you find this book stimulating; if it is successful, it will raise more questions than provide answers.

Acknowledgements

With thanks to all the students and educational practitioners who have enlightened our own educational journey.

Introduction

1 Troublesome learning journey

Vanessa Cottle

Introduction

Students new to masterly learning (referred to as level 7 by Ofqual 2014) in education derive from a range of contexts and perspectives. Examples of these contexts and perspectives include: their current professional context; professional standing and maturity; academic discipline and prowess; and personal characteristics and motivations. According to Morris and Wisker (2010) this heterogeneity leads to implications for student wellbeing and, therefore, achievement. Whilst Morris and Wisker (2010) recognise that the process of learning naturally, even necessarily, brings with it troublesome experiences, they feel that it is important for students to be supported by their higher education institutions (HEIs) to deal with these experiences. Their research (2010: 4–5) identifies 'a sense of community belonging'; a 'culture which nurture[s] confidence', 'successful supervisory relationships' and equitability for these diverse students as elements in preparing them for dealing with the challenging experiences of postgraduate study.

Other recent research (Wellington 2010; Turner and Simon 2013; Tobbell et al. 2010) concurs with Morris and Wisker (2010) in suggesting that HEIs should help students in developing the skills required to overcome those unforeseen barriers to attainment and progression. However, I contend that students do need to be pro-active in: recognising their own limitations and difficulties; identifying what provision is available; and discussing their needs with appropriate persons where support is not available.

The journey begins

Whatever the motivations for starting a postgraduate learning journey, for most there will be an expectation that, as Hulse and Hulme (2012) found, opportunities for learning and engaging in critical explorations of practice will be encountered. The degree to which individuals embrace and engage with these opportunities will vary and be dependent on personal motivations, life priorities and circumstances. Additionally, each participant brings their own personal profile of skills, qualities and experience which will have implications for their experience of postgraduate study. Furthermore, individuals have preconceived ideas that influence their approach to study; for example, practitioners with a healthy record of continuing professional development (CPD) training events may believe that study at masterly level will be a similar experience in furthering their professional status. However, CPD training events and education at masters level offer different types of learning and, whilst both are valuable to a lesser or greater degree, Turner and Simon (2013) draw on Aubusson et al. (2009) to make a distinction between teacher learning and professional learning. They explain that teacher learning concerns training teachers about their role in practice and that professional learning concerns teachers developing the degree of autonomy which enables them to take responsibility for their own decisions.

The above array of elements is integral to an individual's personal and professional lifelong learning journey and suggests that the knowledge anticipated as an outcome from study will be highly situational; that is, particular to the context in which it grows and is used. Capable learners sustain their journey by commanding a range of academic literacies to enable reinterpretation of new ideas and concepts (yet not the misinterpretation of them) in the light of understandings developed in their professional context. Negotiating the journey towards proficient scholarship requires a willingness and openness to embark on a process of deconstruction and reconstruction of practice by employing innovative and creative approaches, and applying sometimes unfamiliar theoretical and conceptual frameworks. This synthesis of theory and practice is usually militated by tacit knowledge emerging from previous internalisations and embedded understandings of practice, thus the importance of the situational context.

Engaging in study

The reconsiderations and new meaning-makings of knowledge, understanding and often practice mentioned above can only be achieved by engagement in study and commitment to practice together with the type of autonomy and independence that comes with confidence in one's own decisions and actions. However, overwhelmingly, literature that researches and considers postgraduate study (for example Lahiff 2005; Wellington 2010; Dickson 2011; Hulse and Hume 2012; Tobbell et al. 2010) identifies confidence as a particular concern for students. This issue can be seen from two perspectives. One perspective highlights students' claims that, as a result of completing postgraduate studies, their confidence levels increase. However, the literature offers no indication by how much or at what level of confidence students started their journey – the distance travelled is very much for the individual student to measure and this reflects the personal development gains to be achieved during postgraduate study. The other perspective reflects students' concerns about their inadequate levels of academic competency and some literature, for example Conway (2011) and Butler (2009) certainly suggest that there is a percentage (again not quantified) of students for whom these self-doubts are well placed. Lea and Street's (1998) work is drawn on by Hallett (2010) and Strauss and Mooney (2011) to identify different dimensions of postgraduate students' academic competency needs. These were, first, skills such as grammar and spelling, developing appropriate search terms to source relevant reading sources and structuring writing for different purposes. Second, they identified academic socialisation, which implies forging relationships to become part of the academy. Then, third, academic literacies were identified, for example how to reference, ethical expectations, using evidence to support arguments and how to be critical. It is the second of these dimensions that can cause the most difficulty when each HEI, and indeed programme within the institution, brings to bear its own cultural expectations. The institutional culture can potentially have a negative effect on confidence levels by exacerbating students' difficulty in grasping what is required.

Personally, I have always assumed that postgraduate students would have a competent command of academic literacies and I believe this assumption is shared by my colleagues and others outside higher education. Indeed Strauss and Mooney (2011: 541) champion a good command of English as 'essential' for postgraduate study, yet Hallett (2010) has identified that masters students have difficulty with basics like spelling, grammar and referencing. This gives rise to a concern about achieving a balance between what I think of as process over content. An overemphasis on process has the potential to detract the student from what is likely to be at the heart of the desire to learn, the content; i.e. the knowledge to be gained from study which will inform and improve practice. However, Strauss and Mooney (2011) consider that without the ability to write well, achievement cannot be demonstrated. My experience supports the notion that for masterly study academic literacies are essential – it is inconceivable to me that a practitioner in any form of education might not be able to construct a sentence, paragraph or argument using sound English underpinned with appropriate and authoritative sources. To me, without this foundation subject matter cannot be grasped through reading, nor can it be articulated through writing with any degree of confidence (which as we have seen above is the subject of much discussion in the literature) and, therefore, cannot be transformed into the new meanings which students aim to gain from their study.

Learning to read

McCulloch (2013: 145) gave some insights into what it is to develop reading skills for the purpose of writing. Her study of students who thought aloud as they read revealed strategies which included 'drawing inferences', 'checking authors' credentials' and the 'drawing of comparisons across multiple sources'. The better the command of and use of English, the more efficiently students would be able to access reading sources that go to the heart of their writing needs; it would also aid in understanding author perspectives and help penetrate seemingly impenetrable theories. Accessing, reading and understanding sources, however, can be overwhelming and confidence is required to reject those sources unsuitable for purpose. According to McCulloch (2013: 142), having sufficient confidence to 'view sources as holding potentially conflicting positions' rather than 'see[ing] them as the accepted authority' is another essential in the repertoire of literacies.

This ability to recognise authority in academic writing, or lack of it, is identified by Turner and Simon (2012) as taking a critical stance. They suggest developing a critical stance with the literature enables a deconstruction of one's beliefs and values, for example one research participant in their work reported experiencing a 'significant shift' in her practice from a focus on teaching to a focus on teacher and pupil learning. This participant's developing autonomy based on growing understanding of the concepts behind her own actions gave her the confidence and ability to successfully defend her new innovative teaching and learning strategies with Ofsted inspectors. This suggests that students need to face their postgraduate studies with an openness to meet challenges which might demand a change of mind, or even heart, knowing that this may have implications for their core values and beliefs.

Facing the blank page

As reading is transformed into writing, students are expected to engage in an exhausting list of activities to enable them to defend or refute confidently their current and future practice. For example, they should be able to justify the relevance of their sources, offer a consideration of the author's and their own positionality and offer an interrogation of the author's research design. Wellington (2010) suggests that time has elastic properties; his research participants found that writing seemed to slow their thinking down and this probably helps to explain why the business of writing can draw out ideas and tacit knowledge. It is clear then, to me, that it is through the process of writing that students demonstrate not only their knowledge and understanding, but also their level of critical analysis and evaluation.

And after the reading and writing

There is a further point to developing masterly reading and writing skills, and that is the submission of assignments or the sitting of examinations. Work submitted is usually returned to students having been assessed in accordance with the HEI's marking guidance and with feedback from an academic with expertise in the field. The process of credible feedback and feed forward is a fundamental part of any learning. Studies in postgraduate contexts (Kumar and Stracke 2011; Boud and Molloy 2013; Dijksterhuis et al. 2013) confirm that, whilst feedback is significant, to be fully effective it should be a two-way activity in which students lead in its initiation. Feedback should be about sharing ideas, meanings and implications – about becoming a pedagogic discourse (O'Grady and Cottle 2014).

The process of receiving, engaging with and acting on feedback received involves the postgraduate student in a determination to reflect; a preparedness to revisit thinking and the confidence to challenge others' thinking. Hallett (2010) sees academic support as both addressing deficit and planning for development: feedback can be pivotal in achieving both. Feedback and feed forward is viewed as a professional pedagogic dialogue by O'Grady and Cottle (2014) and as such can be seen as part of the developing relationship between student and academy and, therefore, goes some way to alleviate students' feelings of isolation identified by Morris and Wisker (2010).

The theme of confidence discussed earlier in relation to feedback is explored by Strauss and Mooney (2011: 541) when their participants demonstrated low confidence by frequently asking whether they were on the 'right track' rather than being able to make their own judgement. Certainly, students frequently appear at my tutorials unprepared to engage in discussion about their work, to simply ask 'is my work okay?' This approach suggests poor levels of independent thought and autonomy, both noted by Quality Assurance Agency for Higher Education (QAA) benchmarks as being characteristics of masterly achievement, and could suggest a desire on the student's part to adopt a tick-box or hoop-jumping approach to study. It is unclear whether this is due to pressures from other life priorities, a learned approach to study emanating from their own practices in teaching and learning or feelings of isolation resulting from poor academic literacy and consequent low confidence levels. Further research is required here and is a consideration of my doctoral thesis on Becoming an Education Masters Student. Over-supportive tutors who are more than willing to adopt the least line of resistance by taking too much responsibility for the student's work could also contribute to this dependency. Such an approach to supporting learning could exacerbate or even feed students' low confidence by increasing their dependency on the 'tutor-crutch', particularly at postgraduate level.

Where the above student–tutor dependency model develops, allowing students to scrape through their learning journey, there can be dramatic and irretrievable implications when, at the dissertation stage, there is finally an overt expectation on the part of the supervisor, and a realisation on the part of the student that there is no alternative but for the student to demonstrate independence and for the tutor to withdraw. I am proposing here that whilst the student–tutor relationship might overcome student isolation, relationships, as with other aspects of study, have a purpose and should be cultivated to enhance independent learning, not replace it.

Wellington's (2010) concern with student emotions led him to an alternative perspective on the feedback process. He suggests that students anticipate feedback with trepidation as a result of, amongst other things, the emotion invested during the process of writing. This may not be surprising when, from the student viewpoint, time and energy is committed to recording their thoughts, and sometimes feelings, in print or verbally for a judgement, which the student may feel takes no account of them as an individual, may be disparaging and may not grasp the intended meaning and argument.

What did it really mean?

The professional pedagogical dialogue (O'Grady and Cottle 2014) mentioned earlier demands an element of self-reflection. A consideration of Gibbs' (1988) model of reflection reveals that seeking comment from others is part of this process. Therefore, reflection, whilst ultimately a personal experience, does not need to be a lonely part of the learning journey and may diminish feelings of isolation. Wellington (2010) perceives reflections as confessions which are an essential and positive part of reflexivity and a feature of the criticality required (QAA 2010) of postgraduate students. Such reflexivity is about facing oneself, one's actions and motives, a process which may be neither easy nor pleasant. Going further, I argue that reflexivity is about taking action on what has been learned and about making sense of experiences. According to Gadsby and Cronin (2012: 2), for the purpose of their discussion on reflective journaling as a mechanism to support masters-level writing skills, reflexivity is achieved through

> a consideration of, and possible change in, [students'] own personal skills, knowledge and disposition in light of personal, professional and wider social contexts in which [students] as practitioners operate.

It is clear that progressing through the postgraduate learning journey successfully requires sufficient confidence in one's own independence of thought and autonomy to be able to take account of new learning in context and by planning and taking appropriate action.

Nearly there

The part of being reflective that is about talking and sharing with others is also the first step on the journey to becoming part of a masterly community. Wenger (1998: 7) explains that communities of practice arise when groups of individuals 'count on each other to cope with intricacies of obscure systems'. Such a core community includes those who have become expert, with those more novice individuals on the periphery moving to the core as they learn through talking, sharing, questioning and contributing. Study with others certainly gives rise to dialogue through argument and discussion and Reeves (2011: 964) sees this 'extracting and carrying' as leading to the mobilisation of knowledge and that by

> making distinctions in practice and recombining the knowledge of one person, or of
> a group, with the knowledge of others

synthesis of theory and practice can occur. Discussion with others means that there is
an imperative to 'think through and articulate . . . thoughts . . . it forces you to examine
the strength of your argument' (Hallett 2010: 232). Hallett's (2010) and Reeves' (2011)
comments mirror Wenger's (1998) concept of a community of practice and strongly
suggest that learning and application of new concepts is neither linear nor straightforward.
I have observed the very gradual process where students, particularly those who study
part-time, are absorbed into the culture of their programme and consequently cast off
feelings of isolation as they grow in confidence.

Consequences of daring to learn

It can be confusing for an otherwise successful individual to realise that they have a gap in
their academic literacy repertoire. Morris and Wisker (2010) found that this could lead to
feelings of being deskilled and create conditions which are challenging to well-established
professional identities. An example might be a successful school teacher, although expert
in a subject discipline, say geography, who struggles with academic literacies appropriate
for studying education at masterly level and is exacerbated by a tutor who comes from
yet a different discipline. Understanding how the variety of identities and contexts of
those involved in the learning journey, i.e. tutors, students and institutions, dynamically
interact is seen by Hallett (2010) as being a central factor in facilitating academic literacy
development. I would urge students embarking on this journey to be alert to this and
suggest that their insights and reflections on their own and others' positions will be helpful
in spotting and addressing barriers to their academic development.

Illeris (2014), who draws from a range of other authors' definitions, claims that learning is about change and transformation resulting from experiencing and assimilating new
ideas and concepts. The outcome of masterly education can, therefore, be transformational and for Illeris (2014) identity is what is transformed in the learning process. Wilson
and Deaney (2010) ascertain that tensions arise as one's identities compete with each
other according to the different contexts in which they are played out. It can then be
seen how the mindset for masterly learning needs to bridge the divide between teacher
learning and professional learning discussed earlier in this chapter. Professional identity
for many who work within educational contexts is developed within a culture that often
'requires a high degree of unquestioning conformity' (Gleeson and Husbands 2001: 314
cited by Hulse and Hulme 2012) to meet the demands of accountability. This culture
of performativity tends to drive the technicism that becomes central in a practitioner's
life, challenging the risk-taking that will, almost certainly, be the tempting outcome for
those who do embrace the opportunities to engage in the deconstruction of current
practice as they absorb new concepts and ideas. This challenging journey and the offer of
transformation may feel somewhat intimidating for some who may choose to resist the
consequences by retreating into the comparative safety of liminality (Land et al. 2014) and
remain on the threshold of transformation and new identity. Postgraduate learning may
offer an opportunity for students to risk stepping through this threshold by embracing
their own growing independence and their developing identity as a postgraduate who has
authority to engage in critical debate and make new meanings.

The final leg?

Resistance to transformation is reflected in a recent discussion I had with some students. I was particularly struck by the fact that they struggled to see the relevance of a core module of their MA Education programme. The module, on research methodology, is essential to the Independent Study – the final piece of work in which a year of time is invested and outcomes are usually significant in terms of effect on individuals' practice and even career; certainly without passing this module they will not achieve the qualification. To me, the apparent reticence of this small group of students suggested that they had not fully embraced the mantel of postgraduate-level study; that is, they were rejecting or resisting a developing academic identity and had chosen to remain in a state of liminality on the threshold of transformation. To some extent this is understandable where the practitioner or professional identity foregrounds that of the postgraduate student. However, I wonder to what extent an individual will derive benefit from such study if they resist developing knowledge and understanding of research methodology. It is, after all, this that underpins the competence required for the development of new knowledge which must be critiqued to be applied in practice and is a stated characteristic required for accreditation of a master's qualification (QAA 2010). Furthermore, a grasp of research methodology is indispensable in making judgements about the ethicality, validity and reliability of increasingly available sources used to substantiate claims.

Postgraduate students are often involved in informal research in action as they reflect on, evaluate and adjust their own practice. Postgraduate students quickly become aware that the term *research* suggests all manner of mysteries in the guise of epistemology, ontology and paradigms and are exposed to a wider range of research approaches and data collection tools than undergraduates. As an educationalist, the methodologies employed can present a further trouble to contend with as the qualitative approaches often adopted may seem alien when compared to those quantitative paradigms adopted during undergraduate years. Indeed, educational decision makers often expect quantitative research, rather than qualitative, to justify why funding should be committed to proposed projects and this can seem counter-intuitive for many educationalists. Then there are the implications and consequences of being an insider researcher where the demands on the researcher to remain objective and unbiased may be testing. An employing organisation's values and agendas could create further tensions for a researcher. For example, an organisation which funds, or simply gives consent for, research could exert power to influence how research findings are interpreted. Drake and Heath's claim (2011: 23) that practitioner research cannot be 'clean, neutral or objective' and that it carries ethical challenges for which the student has to take responsibility demands a research design that is exhaustively considered and systematically executed by the postgraduate student at the culmination of their learning journey.

This final leg of the journey then is no less troublesome than the earlier stages; in spite of all the hurdles overcome, the challenges of learning continue. If the learning journey progresses successfully, questions raised within the process of meaning-making are deeper and they demand more attention to get closer to an answer.

Arrival

Underlying much of the research, and my own experience of working with masters students, is a sense that postgraduate students lack preparedness for the journey to come and, in some cases, they have unrealistic expectations of themselves and the HEI at which they study. The requirements of postgraduate courses in terms of time, energy and implications for emotional wellbeing and professional identity can come as a shock. Whilst all institutions aim to support their learners through their troubles, the required postgraduate competencies of independence and autonomy demand that students also support themselves. It is, however, also very clear that by recognising and addressing the pitfalls to be faced during this potentially troublesome journey, the outcome can be rewarding and transformational for students as their confidence rises, their academic relationships are shaped and their practice emerges in creative and innovative ways. The reader is invited to reflect on whether the risks and demands are worth the reward.

References

Aubusson, P., Ewing, R. and Hoban, G. (2009) *Action learning in school: reframing teachers' professional learning and development.* London: Routledge.

Boud, D. and Molloy, E. (2013) Rethinking models of feedback for learning: the challenge of design, assessment and evaluation. *Higher Education* 38:6, 698–712.

Butler, G. (2009) The design of a postgraduate test of academic literacy: accommodating student and supervisor perceptions. *Southern African Linguistics and Applied Language Studies* 27:3, 291–300.

Conway, K. (2011) How prepared are students for postgraduate study? A comparison of the information literacy skills of commencing undergraduate and postgraduate information studies at Curtin University. *Australian Academic & Research Libraries* 42:2, 121–135.

Dickson, B. (2011) Beginning teachers as enquirers: m-level work in initial teacher education. *European Journal of Teacher Education* 34:3, 259–276.

Dijksterhuis, M. G. K., Schuwirth, L. W. T., Braat, D. D. M., Teunissen, L. W. T. and Scheele, F. (2013) A qualitative study on trainees' and supervisors' perceptions of assessment for learning. *Postgraduate Medical Education* 35:8, E1396–E1402.

Drake, P. and Heath, L. (2011) *Practitioner research at doctoral level.* London: Routledge.

Gadsby, H. and Cronin, S. (2012) To what extent can reflective journaling help beginning teachers develop masters level writing skills? *Reflective Practice: International and Multidisciplinary Perspectives* 13:1, 1–12.

Gibb, G. (1988) *Learning by doing: a guide to teaching and learning methods.* London: Further Education Unit.

Hallett, F. (2010) The postgraduate student experience of study support: a phenomenographic analysis. *Studies in Higher Education* 35:2, 225–238.

Hulse, B. and Hulme, R. (2012) Engaging with research through practitioner enquiry: the perceptions of beginning teachers on a postgraduate initial teacher education programme. *Educational Action Research* 20:2, 313–329.

Illeris, K. (2014) *Transformative learning and identity.* London: Routledge.

Kumar, V. and Stracke, E. (2011) Examiners' reports on theses: feedback or assessment? *Journal of English for Academic Purposes* 10, 211–222.

Lahiff, A. (2005) Developing academic writing: a case study of post-compulsory practitioners' personal and professional development. *Journal of Vocational Education and Training* 57:3, 275–290.

Land, R., Rattray, J. and Vivian, P. (2014) Learning in the liminal space: a semiotic approach to threshold concepts. *Higher Education* 67, 199–217.

Lea, M. and Street, B. (1998) Student writing in higher education: an academic literacies approach. *Studies in Higher Education* 23:2, 157–172.

McCulloch, S. (2013) Investigating the reading-to-write processes and source use of L2 postgraduate students in real-life academic tasks: an exploratory study. *Journal of English for Academic Purposes* 12, 136–147.

Morris, C. and Wisker, G. (2010) *Troublesome encounters: strategies for managing the wellbeing of masters and doctoral education student during their learning process.* York: Higher Education Academy.

Ofqual (2014) *Comparing qualification levels,* available at http://ofqual.gov.uk/help-and-advice/comparing-qualifications, accessed November 2014.

O'Grady, A. and Cottle, V. (2014) *PAAR for the course: making a difference,* conference paper presented at HECU 7 Conference, Lancaster University.

Quality Assurance Agency for Higher Education (2010) *Masters degrees characteristics,* available at http://www.qaa.ac.uk/en/Publications/Documents/Masters-degree-characteristics.pdf, accessed November 2014.

Reeves, J. (2011) Investigating knowledge exchange and creation on a practice-based master's programme. *Studies in Higher Education* 36:8, 953–967.

Strauss, P. and Mooney, S. (2011) Painting the bigger picture: academic literacy in postgraduate vocational education. *Journal of Vocational Education and Training* 63:4, 539–550.

Turner, K. and Simon, S. (2013) In what ways does studying at M-level contribute to teachers' professional learning? Research set in an English university. *Professional Development in Education* 39:1, 6–22.

Tobbell, J., O'Donnell, V. L. and Zammitt, M. (2010) Exploring transition to postgraduate study: shifting identities in interaction with communities, practice and participation. *British Educational Research Journal* 36:2, 261–278.

Wellington, J. (2010) More than a matter of cognition: an exploration of affective writing problems of post-graduate students and their possible solutions. *Teaching in Higher Education* 15:2, 135–150.

Wenger, E. (1998) *Communities of practice, learning, meaning and identity.* Cambridge: Cambridge University Press.

Wilson, E. and Deaney, R. (2010) Changing career and changing identity: how do teacher career changers exercise agency in identity construction? *Social Psychology of Education* 13, 169–183.

2   Is everyone a Socrates now?

A critical look at critical thinking

Dennis Hayes

Introduction

Many teachers say they try to teach school or university students to be critical thinkers. They even pride themselves on this; after all, who wants children just to take in knowledge passively? There is a problem with this widespread belief that makes it a bit of a delusion for most teachers. The truth is that you can't teach people to be critical unless you are critical yourself. This involves more than asking students to 'look critically at X, Y or Z' as if criticism was a mechanical task. As a teacher you have to have the critical spirit, which does not mean moaning endlessly about education policies you dislike or telling students what they should think. It means, first and foremost, that you are capable of engaging in *conversation*. This does not mean chatting but a constant engagement in debate and discussion based on considerable knowledge. Today this is something that is almost entirely absent not only in the educational world but in wider society.

Debate and discussion must take place in public if they are to constitute anything like a conversation. By 'public' this means beyond the classroom in which there is a cosy and essentially private relationship between the teacher and students. The doors are shut and ideas are kept locked in. Debate may sometimes take place in an open lecture if discussion is allowed but essentially it requires engagement with the public outside of school, college or university. Formal debates may hint at what could be a conversation and there is some interest in providing them, whether in schools through initiatives like *Debating Matters*, or in festivals like the *Battle of Ideas* or at high-profile events organized by *Intelligence Squared*. That formal initiatives are needed shows how little debate and discussion now occurs spontaneously.

These observations may seem to imply that teachers and lecturers should become 'public intellectuals' and take their ideas beyond the ivory tower. But the problem of the lack of wider engagement is not merely the result of the narrow professionalism of academic life with academics increasingly talking and writing for themselves and their peers. There is a greater problem. There is no clear 'public' for intellectuals to engage with as there may have been in the past. A public now has to be created but this cannot be done without first convincing people that debate is necessary. The lack of debate means there has to be a debate about debate before we can have other debates and discussions (see Hayes 2004; 2005; 2008; 2012).

There are two broad cultural changes that make public engagement harder today. The first is the existence of a 'therapeutic' or 'therapy' culture (Furedi 2004; Ecclestone and Hayes 2008). At its heart this new culture sees everyone, but particularly young people and students, as vulnerable, as potential victims. Not only are they seen as vulnerable to physical harm but they are psychologically and emotionally fragile. Discussion in therapy culture is no longer robust. It takes place in 'safe' spaces where people have the 'confidence' to be 'open' and 'voices' are listened to with 'respect' and all possible 'offence' is avoided. Therapeutic self-expression has replaced the robust intellectual challenge that debate requires. The second cultural change that re-enforces therapy culture is the climate of fear created by the 'Rushdie affair'. Although the impact on academic life is often ignored, the publication of *The Satanic Verses* on 25 September 1988 and the subsequent fatwa issued by Ayatollah Ruhollah Khomeini on 14 February 1989 calling for the death of Salman Rushdie has had a major effect on intellectual and cultural life. Author Kenan Malik summarized these changes in this way:

> What both the literary and the academic worlds have internalised is a culture of fear which is dominated by the fear of giving offence. In universities there are codes of conduct which expect academics and students to conduct themselves, to write and discuss and debate and criticise in inoffensive ways. The etiquette of inoffensiveness means that differing beliefs are not being taken seriously. Taking them seriously means recognising that they may come into conflict and this means we have to write and argue about them.
>
> (quoted in Hayes 2013b: 35)

In a therapy culture the avoidance of offence seems natural and the outcome is quietism. No one challenges others' beliefs and ideas and if a teacher or a student does, they are likely to be seen as bitter and difficult rather than as someone who takes ideas seriously.

Being 'critical' is now a synonym for being 'offensive'. What Malik, in his statement above, calls the 'etiquette of inoffensiveness' is not merely a matter of style or approach. It often means just being silent. To give an example, it is hard to see how statements like 'I don't believe there is any basis for a belief in God' will not offend, no matter how pleasantly put. It can easily be said to show 'disrespect' for people's devoutly held beliefs. Silence is the safe and respectful option in the contemporary university where showing 'disrespect' to a 'viewpoint' may lead not only to condemnation but to unemployment (Leiter 2014).

To challenge this culture it is necessary to defend the right to say what you think, whether or not it is deemed 'offensive' (AFAF 2006). Understanding therapy culture and how it diminishes people by not taking them or their ideas seriously enough is essential if 'criticism' in its proper sense is to be restored.

'Criticism', according to the nineteenth-century educationalist and poet Matthew Arnold, is 'a disinterested endeavour to learn and propagate the best that is known and thought in the world' ([1864] 2003: 50) and all academics should be as 'bound' by that definition as he was. To engage in criticism in this way is to develop our knowledge and understanding and this will naturally lead to engagement outside of the university. The Australian philosopher John Anderson, who defended Arnold's concept of criticism, saw just this consequence:

> The work of the academic, qua academic, is criticism; and, whatever his special field may be, his development of independent views will bring him into conflict with prevailing opinions and customary attitudes in the public arena and not merely among his fellow-professionals.
>
> (Anderson [1960] 1980: 214)

'Criticism', as Arnold defined it, is more like a character trait; the development of a critical spirit and a willingness to engage in the give and take of discussion. By developing 'independent views' you will have something to say and you will want to engage with others in a conversation about your ideas. Criticism then becomes part of your way of life but is never just self-assertion or therapeutic self-expression. Criticism is always about the world and not about you.

'Critical thinking' as therapy

There is something absurd about wanting to be 'critical'; about wanting to be a 'critical thinker' or wanting others to be 'critical thinkers'. If you want to know all about art and understand painting, this makes sense. But to want to be 'critical' can only be about you and your needs. There is a market ready to meet those needs. There is a vast literature and many courses that offer to teach people to be critical thinkers. The titles of some of the hundreds of books offer inspiration and 'quick-fix' success: *The Power of Critical Thinking*; *Think Well and Prosper*; *Critical Thinking for the Discerning SEO*; *Critical Thinking Skills: Success in 20 Minutes a Day*; and *Critical Thinking for Students*. It is not an exaggeration to say that there is a 'critical thinking' industry. There is even a community of critical thinkers which wants to help people survive in an increasingly complex world by making 'critical thinking' a social value (see www.criticalthinking.org). Almost every university has a 'checklist' of critical thinking advice and skills for students from any discipline to use, because although we 'could say that critical thinking is at the heart of academic study, it's more of a process, a way of thinking, understanding and expressing ourselves, than a single definable skill' (University of Sussex 2014).

The difficulty with the critical thinking industry is that critical thinking is not a skill, or a set of skills, or a 'process'. Another Australian philosopher, John Passmore, criticized this idea nearly fifty years ago:

> If being critical consisted simply in the application of a skill then it could in principle be taught by teachers who never engaged in it except as a game or defensive device, somewhat as a crack rifle shot who happened to be a pacifist might nevertheless be able to teach rifle-shooting to soldiers. But in fact being critical can be taught only by men who can themselves freely partake in critical discussion.
>
> (Passmore 1967: 198)

The critical thinking industry was only in its beginning when Passmore (1967) wrote his paper and repeating the straightforward refutations he makes provokes outrage from vested interests and criticizing 'critical thinking' can itself be challenging (see Hayes 2014b). But what is unacceptable to the industry must be said. Divorcing 'critical thinking' from subject content reduces it to a checklist of skills that aims to give people the flattering pretence of being 'critical' without having to do the hard intellectual work of developing their knowledge and understanding of their subject. To that extent it is a therapeutic approach.

Worse still, the application of the skills-based checklist approach to various 'isms' reduces them to a flattering pretence of criticality. If a feminist or Marxist teacher demands a certain perspective be adopted, their views might be held to be 'critical' but what they actually offer is training in Marxism or feminism which could be done through tick-box techniques. It almost acquires the character of a drill – like learning your times tables – or being able to spot what arguments are fallacious following a guide to elementary argument. You look for set features of class or gender oppression and denounce them. Tick, tick!

The skills-based approach to critical thinking flatters individuals into thinking they are critical. It makes them feel better. It makes them feel that they have unique abilities. They are *critical people*. Their self-esteem is increased without the knowledge and understanding required for true criticism. In the 'critical thinking community' this is just vanity, but in the university it damages students' abilities to become independent thinkers, partly by wasting their time away from their studies, but also by misleading them about what being critical actually means. This approach seems to offer a shortcut to criticism.

Although some universities put a copyright on their lists of 'critical thinking skills', it is pointless and ineffective restriction because they are much the same throughout the UK university sector and globally. Take the example of these statements or 'tips' that summarize Edinburgh Napier University's advice on critical thinking (2014):

1   Keep an open and enquiring mind.
2   Ask yourself:

- What am I being asked to think or believe?
- Does the author have anything to gain by it?
- What evidence is being produced to convince me?
- How is that evidence interpreted?
- Are there other interpretations of the evidence?
- What further evidence do I need?
- On reflection, what is it reasonable to conclude?

This sort of thing is trivial and utterly useless. Why the moral injunction to be 'open' minded? Open to viewpoints that involve witchcraft and superstition when studying medicine? More importantly, terms like 'evidence' only make sense in a particular subject context. What would it mean in philosophy? Again, what do 'interpretation' and 'reasonable' mean outside of any particular subject? We may think up answers to these questions but this whole approach is wrong. Some of these checklists are very lengthy and would require a degree in bureaucracy to apply them. One thing we know is that anyone using them would be a mechanical and not a critical thinker.

Similarly, if 'critical thinking' was not this sort of cobbled together advice but was instruction in informal and some informal logic, would it help produce critical thinkers? It may produce some clever people who could go around spotting fallacies and mistakes in argument but, as with experts at crossword puzzles, we would describe such people as clever rather than critical.

A new variant on the skills approach to critical thinking is Philosophy For Children (P4C). This essentially introduces children to 'philosophical' arguments and problems without doing any real philosophy. It is another 'feel-good' activity for teachers and pupils (Ecclestone and Hayes 2008; Hayes 2014a). There is a tendency to think that children have some pure approach to thinking unsullied by adult prejudice and bias. In reality they are literally ignorant of philosophy and this approach leaves them in a state of ignorance which they, and the often very nice and well-intentioned people who teach P4C, believe is philosophical when it is a therapeutic state.

Reducing 'critical thinking' to skills seems to offer an instrumental 'philosophical' shortcut to understanding and surviving in a changing world and across the changing world of education, from the primary school to the university. The 'critical thinking' industry that uses this approach is based on the assumption that everyone needs 'critical thinking skills' to cope and to succeed. In fact, what is being sold, and what many buy into, is a therapeutic illusion.

Critical thinking as 'conformist therapy'

In the management of educational institutions and even in real-world businesses, a different sort of therapeutic critical thinking has become dominant.

Many people will have heard the statement, particularly from managers, that 'positive criticism' of plans and ideas is 'welcomed'. Although this sounds like an invitation to engage in criticism it is actually an instruction to abandon criticism and accept what is on offer and try to improve it. The trade-off is that you will be accepted as part of a team 'going forward' and not be seen as 'negative'. In reality all criticism is negative criticism.

To ensure that everyone is 'on side' and no one is negative, institutions offer staff development which is almost universally therapeutic. Exercises in team building and in developing communication and listening skills take a therapeutic form. The presence of a flip chart is often an indication that you are in amateur therapy and learning to think as management wants you to think. Hardly ever are such activities seen as the actions of an authoritarian and controlling management because they take place in a therapeutic culture in which we are all expected to be nice to one another and not to offend or upset anyone by challenging their deeply held beliefs.

All this gentle conformity through therapy may be familiar but the latest turn is required conformity to the ideas and beliefs of the institution. Employees are required to hold certain views about the values of equality: inclusion, diversity and multiculturalism, despite these being contested concepts (see Hayes 2013).

In a university, being counselled to accept and hold certain beliefs undermines, and is in contradiction to, the basis of the university. The university is based upon criticism and if lecturers are told what to believe and go along with the university-imposed values and beliefs they cannot be said to be academics and cannot teach students to be critical when they are no longer critical themselves.

Again this is rarely seen as managerial authoritarianism because the imposition of many of these beliefs is undertaken in therapeutic awareness-raising activities which do not allow any intellectual examination of these beliefs. Management ensures that, through positive criticism in these therapeutic forms, you become more 'open' and adopt their beliefs.

This process of critical therapeutic examination of your personal 'assumptions' and 'reviewing your beliefs' is reinforced through the exercises required to succeed in most professional programmes which require students to engage in various processes of 'reflection', writing 'reflective logs' or 'personal reflections' on their experiences. Without relating these experiences to any discussion of theory, which may once have been the intention, these 'reflective' activities are self-indulgent forms of therapy which can undermine the idea that you need to know anything. Navel-gazing replaces the hard work necessary to master professional knowledge and understanding. In a therapeutic culture critical reflection spontaneously becomes critical therapy.

Critical theory as critical therapy

The critical thinking industry and the new forms of management and professional control through therapeutic criticism may seem like easy targets for criticism. There are, however, more theoretical and academic examples of 'critical' approaches and ways of thinking.

Consider the various 'radical' approaches that self-consciously adopt the label 'critical' as a prefix – critical theory, critical race theory, critical race philosophy, critical realism, critical reflective practice and so forth. When something has the prefix 'critical' in this way it is an indication that what is being promoted is a political position which is often presented or takes, in a therapeutic culture, a therapeutic form. One of the features of the therapeutic culture is that it has come into being after the collapse of politics and constitutes our contemporary post-political state (see Ecclestone and Hayes 2008: Ch. 7). The promotion of 'political' views in our current emotional state requires therapy. Critical race theorists, for example, promote the view that if you are white you are racist and if you are black you are oppressed. If you deny that you are white and therefore racist you need therapy to understand yourself and your racism. If you are black and deny that you are oppressed you also need therapy to understand your oppression. This subjective psychologizing of racism is a long way from traditional anti-racism which was based upon the possibility of a unified struggle against capitalism as the cause of racial oppression (see Hayes 2013a). In a therapeutic culture, it seems the politically correct approach, which indeed it is, and it is hard to openly challenge without facing the charge of 'racism'.

In the not-too-distant past, the demand that you adopt the political perspectives of these 'critical' approaches would have been seen as indoctrination. The proponents of these theories are quite explicit and even celebrate their political objectives. One champion of 'critical pedagogy' argues that rather than teach 'core knowledge' teachers should aim to '[provoke] students to fight against the corridors of power and enforce equality for themselves and others' (Coles 2014). Outside of any wider political struggles in society, this approach is not merely substitutionalism, it is a pretend politics and a feel-good activity for teachers. The consequence for the pupils is that they will be indoctrinated rather than educated.

The major influence on all these politicized and therapeutic 'critical' approaches is 'critical theory'. An examination of critical theory in more depth will show how it develops a therapeutic form in therapy culture which was potentially an aspect of critical theory from the outset. Critical theory is built on an assumption that it should be 'emancipatory' and is therefore political. It has an easy appeal because it criticizes capitalist power relations from a philosophical standpoint that focuses on communication. Money and bureaucratic power 'threaten the communicative achievements of the lifeworld' and have invaded everyday culture to the extent that 'the human potential for reaching understanding in language is beginning to dissolve' (Honneth 1999: 325–326). To challenge power, therefore, we must regain communicative achievements. The moralistic appeal of this banality – for that's what it is – to middle-class academics is that the emancipatory challenge is one they can deal with. We can't communicate: is there a therapist in the house?

'Critical theorists' are a loose political grouping of academics with nothing that connects them other than their 'inter-subjectivity'. The strength of their commitment to 'critical theory' satisfies their emotional desire not to appear reactionary. This is a great benefit to former radicals who flock to conferences with titles like 'Discourse, Power and Resistance' and think they are a movement!

The commonplace academic critique of critical theory sees it as weakened by its own 'cognitive dependence on a "pre-theoretical instance", an existing interest in emancipation which it seeks to articulate' (Dews 1999: 320). The political aim to 'emancipate' people drives the desire for communication and 'communicative action' rather than communication creating the desire for emancipatory action. It is essentially a sleight of hand.

All this may seem academic and irrelevant to practitioners but one of the leading influences on critical theory is Jürgen Habermas whose extensive writings, particularly about the idea of 'communicative action', have influenced many works in education such as the best-seller by Harkin, Turner and Dawn: *Teaching Young Adults* (2000). To show that Habermas's work has a therapeutic rather than a liberatory or emancipatory consequence, let's consider how it differs from the older 'critical theory' of the Frankfurt School and try to explain its current vogue. The Marxist sociologist Göran Therborn makes a useful distinction between 'classical' critical theory and that of Habermas:

> Classical critical theory was sociologically determined . . . however thin and fragile the actual bonds may have been, it was linked to a definite social force, the working class. Habermas's theory is linked only to his own view of the 'functions' of the human ego. This is more clearly formulated in another article: 'Reflection must go further back than any historically determined class interest and lay bare the complex of interests of a self-constituting species as such.'
>
> (Therborn 1977: 124–125, citing Habermas 1971: 119)

The aim is to enhance our individual moral sensibility rather than develop class consciousness. All well and good, we may think, but only if we have no sense of history or of the political and economic world we inhabit and live entirely in a world of ideas. The original retreat of the Frankfurt School intellectuals, in the face of the defeat of communist and socialist struggles, the weakening of the labour movement, the rise to power of fascists and the corrupting influence of international Stalinism, was a retreat into the intellectual world. The Frankfurt School opted out of real politics for an idealist Hegelian philosophy. Habermas's retreat is more contradictory and deeper. He looks towards a pre-theoretical understanding that is just assumed to connect with critical theory in some way. We are with Habermas's 'theory' taken out of the real world of struggle.

What we have in his approach to critical theory is an early but explicit adoption of a therapeutic approach. His notion of 'communicative action' is explicitly connected with therapy:

> 'genuine confirmation of critique remains unattainable' unless we enter into 'communication of the type of the therapeutic "discourse" 'that is, precisely in successful process of education [*Bildung*] voluntarily agreed to by the participants themselves' (Habermas 1972: 31) and in which each learning level is confirmed in the individual's own experience, after the model of psychoanalytic therapy.
>
> (Young 2000: 536)

Habermas sees the moment of interaction as all. His aim is not revolution or social change but 'communication free of domination'. An idea that is idealistic, vague and appealing to academics. If all we have is a critique of ideas rather than a struggle for state power, then this critique can 'be harmoniously settled through criticism of the structures of public opinion by the enlightened efforts of critical students and scholars' (Therborn 1977: 139). The appeal is simple – chatter can bring about change.

What the attempt to focus on communication reveals is the end point of the retreat from real engagement with the world of politics. It presents a flattering illusion of academic subversion. Therborn, describing 'Habermas's popularity among young Anglo-Saxon reformist academics', explains it this way:

> He combines an apparently left-wing pedigree, conventional humanism and a notion that the basic political problems are problems of communication. The blandness of these ideas is evident. Since, however, it is a law of ideological gravitation that eclecticism attracts empiricism, British and Scandinavian sociology incipiently feels strongly drawn towards him. A vogue for Habermas is a predictable product of its own horizons.
>
> (Therborn 1977: 139)

We can go further and recognize that this focus is perfectly in tune with contemporary therapeutic culture. Hence Habermas's 'critical therapy' goes from strength to strength in academia.

In a therapeutic culture the idea of 'criticism' as requiring engagement in a public and deep conversation has become debased. It has been replaced by a therapeutic training in the use of 'critical thinking' skills and with managerial and professional therapeutic activities that promote conformism to institutional goals. Even once radical theories of social and political engagement, with their origins in class struggle, have been transformed into a therapeutic pretend politics. The future for criticism looks bleak as it just seems normal that that these things take a therapeutic form. In a therapy culture the promotion and experience of therapy leads to a desire for more therapy and calls for a return to a traditional sense of being both critical and creative have no impact (cf: Dent 2007). But need things continue to be so bleak?

The future of criticism in therapy culture

I once gave a talk about critical thinking to a large group of first-year students and one girl in the class said that the lecturers she most disliked were the ones who 'banged on and on about the importance of being critical'. What she longed for was one of them to assert or say something that could then be discussed and debated, even challenged. As Passmore (1967) argued, the disciplines are debased and distorted if they are used to inculcate 'critical thinking' – they must not be thought of as the means to something else – the acquisition of critical thinking skills. Training pupils or students to say 'I don't agree' or 'I question that' is training in cynicism.

What the foregoing arguments mean for any lecturer or student is that you cannot choose to be 'critical'. You cannot be trained to think critically. You cannot order someone to be critical through putting the word 'critical' in statements of aims, objectives or in university 'mission statements'. Nor can you become critical because a programme team write 'critically analyse' or 'critically evaluate' in the learning outcomes or marking criteria of a course.

The person most associated with criticism and who was put to death for it was Socrates. I often quote Anderson describing Socrates' view of education in this way: 'The

Socratic education begins . . . with the awakening of the mind to the need for criticism' but I often miss out the concluding part of Anderson's description which expresses this awakening as one 'to the uncertainty of the principles by which it supposed itself to be guided' ([1930] 1980: 69).

This is my practice as my usual audience of teachers, teacher trainers and educationalists will immediate assume that this means question those bad ideas you have and get the right ones i.e. conform, or they will be taken as an appeal to the openness that is really just one step towards freeing the mind from 'absolutist' principles and beliefs in favour of continuous therapy.

If the Socratic approach of rigorous and unremitting questioning can be given a therapeutic twist, and even the elenchus seen as therapeutic, there can only be one way forward. It is best not to try to reverse the new therapies of 'critical thinking' but to return to Arnold's definition of criticism as 'a disinterested endeavour to learn and propagate the best that is known and thought in the world'. If we seek knowledge and understanding in this way, it is a noble, moral and demanding enterprise, and if we bind ourselves to it, 'critical thinking' will take care of itself.

References

AFAF (2006) Statement of Academic Freedom: www.afaf.org.uk (accessed on 23 August 2014).

Anderson, J. ([1930] 1980) Socrates as an Educator, in *Education and Inquiry*. Oxford: Basil Blackwell, 64–80.

Anderson, J. ([1960] 1980) The Place of the Academic in Modern Society, in *Education and Inquiry*. Oxford: Basil Blackwell, 214–221.

Arnold, M. ([1864] 2003) The Function of Criticism at the Present Time, in Collini, S. (Ed) *Culture and Anarchy and Other Writings*. Cambridge: Cambridge University Press, 26–51.

Coles, T. (2014) Critical Pedagogy: Schools Must Equip Students to Challenge the Status Quo, *The Guardian*. 25 February 2014: http://www.theguardian.com/teacher-network/teacher-blog/2014/feb/25/critical-pedagogy-schools-students-challenge (accessed on 23 August 2014).

Dent, S. (2007) We Need Creative Critics and Critical Creators, *The Guardian*. 27 September 2007: http://www.theguardian.com/books/booksblog/2007/sep/27/inanarticleforthe (accessed on 23 August 2014).

Ecclestone, K. and Hayes, D. (2008) *The Dangerous Rise of Therapeutic Education*. London and New York: Routledge.

Edinburgh Napier University (2014) Critical Thinking Tips, *Critical Thinking*: http://www2.napier.ac.uk/getready/managing_information/critical_thinking.html#critical_thinking_tips (accessed on 23 August 2014).

Furedi, F. (2004) *Therapy Culture: Cultivating Vulnerability in an Uncertain Age*. London and New York: Routledge.

Habermas, J. (1971) *Towards a Rational Society: Student Protest, Science and Society*. Boston: Beacon Press.

Habermas, J. (1972) *Knowledge and Human Interests*. London: Heinemann.

Harkin, J., Turner, G. and Dawn, T. (2000) *Teaching Young Adults: A Handbook for Teachers in Post-Compulsory Education*. London and New York: Routledge.

Hayes, D. (Ed) (2004) *The Routledge Guide to Key Debates in Education*. London and New York: Routledge.

Hayes, D. (2005) Take a Few Tips From Socrates, *Times Educational Supplement*. 16 September 2005: http://www.tes.co.uk/article.aspx?storycode=2134212 (accessed on 23 August 2014).

Hayes, D. (2007) Everybody is a Socrates Now, *Times Educational Supplement*. 22 June 2007: http://www.tes.co.uk/article.aspx?storycode=2401209 (accessed on 23 August 2014).

Hayes, D. (2008) Forget the Evidence: A Real Debate with the Public is What We Need, *Times Higher Education*. 18 September 2008: http://www.timeshighereducation.co.uk/news/forget-the-evidence-a-real-debate-with-the-public-is-what-we-need/403609.article (accessed on 23 August 2014).

Hayes, D. (2012) Time for a Good Old-Fashioned Debate about Education, *The Huffington Post.* 24 September 2012: http://www.huffingtonpost.co.uk/dennis-hayes/education-gove-debate_b_1899857.html (accessed on 23 August 2014).

Hayes, D. (2013a) Teaching Students to Think Racially, *Spiked*, 19 March 2013: http://www.spiked-online.com/newsite/article/13459#.U_isUfmwI-g (accessed on 23 August 2014).

Hayes, D. (2013b) After the Rushdie Affair It's Naughty Not to be Nice, *Times Higher Education*, 26 September 2013: 34–35: http://www.timeshighereducation.co.uk/twenty-five-years-on-therushdie-affair-is-still-having-a-stifling-effect-on-academic-freedom-argues-dennis-hayes/2007660.article (accessed on 23 August 2014).

Hayes, D. (2014a) Can Kids do Kant? *The Conversation.* 13 February 2014: https://theconversation.com/can-kids-do-kant-22623 (accessed on 23 August 2014).

Hayes, D. (2014b) Let's Stop Trying to Teach Students Critical Thinking, *The Conversation.* 8 August 2014: https://theconversation.com/lets-stop-trying-to-teach-students-critical-thinking-30321 (accessed on 23 August 2014).

Honneth, A. (1999) The Social Dynamics of Disrespect: Situating Critical Theory Today, in Dews, P. (Ed) *Habermas: A Critical Reader.* Oxford: Blackwell, 320–327.

Leiter, B. (2014) University of Illinois Repeals the Frist Amendment for Its Faculty, *The Huffington Post.* 23 August 2014: http://www.huffingtonpost.com/brian-leiter/university-of-illinois-re_1_b_5703038.html (accessed on 23 August 2014).

Marsh, J. (2000) What's Critical about Critical Theory?, in Hahn, L.E. (Ed) *Perspectives on Habermas.* Chicago and La Salle: Open Court, 555–567.

Passmore, J. (1967) On Teaching to be Critical, in Peters, R. S. (Ed) *The Concept of Education.* London: Routledge and Kegan Paul, 192–211.

Therborn, G. (1977) The Frankfurt School, in New Left Review (Ed) *Western Marxism: A Critical Reader.* London: Verso, 83–139.

University of Sussex (2014) Critical Thinking, *Study Success at Sussex S.3*: http://www.sussex.ac.uk/s3/?id=87 (accessed on 24 August 2014).

Young, R. (2000) Habermas and Education, in Hahn, L.E. (Ed) *Perspectives on Habermas.* Chicago and La Salle: Open Court, 531–552.

Part I

Theory

3 Applying educational thinkers to contemporary educational practice

Anne O'Grady

The need to consider educational theory in contemporary pedagogy seems somewhat redundant. It sees little attention in teacher education programmes, which appear to increasingly focus on 'how' to engage people in learning, rather than 'why' people might engage in learning (other than the requirement to do so by law!), and what the purpose of education might be for contemporary society. Having a working knowledge of educational thinkers informs one's philosophy as an educational practitioner, and whether you view the role of learners as recipients or partners of an educational interaction, but this cannot happen if you are not introduced to their work. In this chapter I introduce a few of the most influential theoretical thinkers that have informed my work. In introducing the thinking of Bourdieu, Freire, and Wenger, I present brief overviews of their arguments and demonstrate, with examples from my own practice, how they have been useful in informing my thinking and actions as an educational practitioner.

Locating myself in educational theory

I started my journey of engagement with educational thinkers in 2002 when I enrolled on a MA Research degree at a Russell Group university. At this time I was not interested in developing a career in academia; I wanted a space to explore how a policy at the time – the *Skills for Life* policy (DfEE, 2001) – was influencing the ways in which adults were enabled and supported to engage in learning opportunities. In trying to find out how and why adults were undertaking these learning experiences, I was advised to read the work of some key (although I did not know it at the time!) theorists – first Foucault (1989, 1991), then Bourdieu (1977, 1990, 1993, 1997, 2003), and Freire (1993, 1994). These theorists' works were difficult to read, never mind understand, and I struggled to see their value or purpose – particularly in relation to the research I was carrying out. However, through discussion, re-reading and interpretation, they helped me to develop a way of exploring and understanding adults' learning experiences – and importantly, how I saw myself as an educator and my contribution to the educational exchange.

The doctoral study I conducted explored the learning experiences of socially constructed groups: people identified as *offenders, long-term unemployed*, and *adults with low levels of literacy and numeracy*. Foucault's discussions on power, Bourdieu's conceptualisation of symbolic violence and its use in (re)producing societies, along with his concepts of *habitus* and *field*, and Freire's work on education for *emancipation*, collectively helped me to explore from differing perspectives my research participants' experiences of, and participation in, education.

Since completing my PhD, I have gone on to teach across undergraduate and postgraduate programmes, and always introduce my students to theory to frame our discussions and develop our critical understanding of the topic of the debate. What is particularly interesting here is that, as a practitioner, I had not encountered educational theory prior to my PhD study, and I certainly did not see the value or merits of it; or how it could be so informative and useful to my educational thinking and practice. Perhaps it could reasonably be argued, therefore, that educational theory only has a place, or value, in educational research, and no place in the real work of pedagogy. Anecdotally, it seems that the role of theoretical thinking is increasingly compromised when providing courses to support the development of the future workforce of educationalists. The English policy direction for teacher education (often titled *training*) is ambitiously re-directing it to a more practically driven, 'apprenticeship'-type model of pedagogy, where trainees learn 'on the job' alongside their qualified colleagues (DfE 2010, 2011). There seems limited space within the new direction for teacher education to consider the role, purpose, and function of education; or to consider an educator's professional autonomy or agency within their growing professional identity and their contribution to the educational land-scape going forward. The question of why government policy seems to be deliberately driving initial teacher education in this direction needs to be considered. Is this because a dominant minority do not want educators in a classroom who make independent profes-sional judgements and decisions about how to engage people in learning, or perhaps it is because educators are not regarded as professionals who are able to provide an educational experience that is valuable?

By introducing you to a very small selection of some educational thinkers who have informed and influenced my practice in this chapter, I argue that providing space for educators, both existing and developing, to consider, discuss, and explore the thinking of educational theorists can significantly contribute to a more coherent and meaningful understanding of education – its role and position in society. Exploring theory can, and should, inform how educators engage with, deliver, and practise education. At a time when education is increasingly prescribed and imposed – through initiatives such as curriculum revisions, assessment and examination strategies, national student surveys, and inspection regimes – I contend that it is even more important for an educational practitioner to develop professional agency, informed by engagement with the work of educational thinkers, to better understand not just how to deliver education but also to become consciously aware of our actions within that educational interaction.

Exploring the pedagogic application of some educational thinkers: Pierre Bourdieu

Bourdieu's *conceptual tools* are 'good to think with' (Jenkins 2002: 176). His work has been used and applied across a broad range of disciplines and provides a set of concepts through which educational policies and practices can be explored. Grenfell (2004) suggests Bourdieu defended his work as a collection of concepts, rather than one overarching theoretical approach, and this is perhaps why his work has been so widely applied to modern-day thinking, across a range of perspectives. Bourdieu (1990, 1993, 1997, 1998, 2003) developed a set of concepts to promote the consideration of *situational awareness*. Amongst his significant body of work, he explored how educational institutions – as social spaces – informed, influenced, and determined social reproduction. Particularly, Bourdieu observed how positions of people in a society were constructed and maintained by a dominant few upon a dominated majority through key structural systems of, for example, family, community, and school. Bourdieu explored the relationship between an individual: *habitus*, and a context: *field* (Grenfell 2004), asserting that an individual is shaped by the position they occupy within a social *field*, which is intricately linked to *capital* (*cultural*, *social*, and *economic*) (Bourdieu 1997).

Using the concepts of Bourdieu, my own work has allowed me to explore the extent to which marginalised groups are *situationally aware* (Bourdieu 1993). Working with offenders and unemployed adults, for example, I explored how their *habitus* was constructed through their lived experiences and context – their *fields*, and how they developed a *feel for the game* to understand their current situation. I used Bourdieu's conceptual tools to explore to what extent research participants were *situationally aware*.

Habitus and field

The extract below represents an unemployed research participant's power within the social space, or *field*. The extract exemplifies the limited amount of agency he felt within the *field*. Even though he did not want to attend a training programme, he was directed to do so – he felt he had no power or authority to influence the situation and if he did reject the decision that was being made for him, the consequences would have been too great to accept.

40.J   No, I didn't want to come. I wanted to stop at home. It were dole what sent me up here.

41.A   Right. So, why did you come if you didn't want to come?

42.J   Er, I couldn't tell you. I don't know why they sent me up here. I tried to tell the dole I couldn't read and write. They said 'oh, give it a try'. I give it a try and after 26 weeks I still couldn't pick now't up.

(TP 8, O'Grady 2008: 285)

When Bourdieu thought about how an individual develops a sense of self, he used the term *habitus*. *Habitus* describes a system of dispositions, and combines (a) how an individual *becomes* as result of an organising action, (b) a way of being, and (c) a pre-disposition, which Bourdieu (1977) regarded as a tendency, a propensity, or an inclination. Importantly, Bourdieu (1977) determined that *habitus* only exists in, through, and because of the practices of actors (individuals), their interactions with each other, and their environment. The *social game* is inscribed in individuals because of their *habitus* and ensures they meet various situations in specific ways, thereby creating consistency in behavioural response and choices. Such models of behaviour – dispositions – are produced by *habitus*. Bourdieu (1977) asserted that *habitus* can be passed on through generations, is inculcated from an early age, and is often socially reinforced through education and culture, rather than by explicit teaching.

In the quote below it can be observed how the offender research participants developed their *habitus*; particularly how they learnt particular behaviours and how they met situations. For the first individual, he was exposed to a teacher who he felt singled him out. His *habitus* developed a way of being because of the interaction with both the teacher and the educational environment.

> 8.M   Yeah, a normal ordinary comprehensive, yeah. And, I felt a teacher used to single me out, particularly in English, like; used to make me stand up and read my work out and read out of books and that and I'm not very good at spelling.
>
> 9.A   So how did that make you feel?
>
> 10.M   [pause] I think the right word is rebellious. Yeah, I rebelled against the system and I was extremely disruptive there. I got expelled at the end of my first year.
>
> (HMP 2, O'Grady 2008: 264)

In the following quote, one can see how the offender research participant developed a disposition – a learnt behaviour – to the educational system he was interacting with which ultimately led to a rejection of that social situation, explained by Bourdieu (1977) as a *field* (context).

> 68.C   Umm. And then I got expelled from school, went to another school, got expelled from that school, went to another school, got expelled from that one, went to another school, and then in the end they just gave up and said no, no we're not, we're not taking him.
>
> (HMP 4, O'Grady 2008: 265)

Bourdieu's concept of *field* enables us to understand how an individual's *habitus* is informed and developed, perhaps changed or presented differently, within varying social *fields*. Bourdieu (2003) outlined such social arrangements as social *fields* (a structured system of social positions) with their own *logics of practice* (ways of working), each with varying degrees of autonomy from other *fields* (Lingard et al. 2005). The operation of social *fields* is overarched and structured by power. This determines the relationships of individuals within a *field* – and the constraints and opportunities determined by the structure of the *field* (Bourdieu 1993). *Fields*, then, not only shape *habitus* but are also the products and producers of *habitus*. Within each *field*, a competitive marketplace exists in which positions are constantly being played out and reinforced by actions of encounters between actors within the *field* and between actors in differing *fields* (Bourdieu 1993). Individuals develop a *feel for the game* as they become familiar with that particular social context – *field*.

Bourdieu provides the following explanation of how these relationships exist within a social structure:

> In a field, agents and institutions are engaged in struggle, with unequal strengths, and in accordance with the rules constituting that field of play, to appropriate the specific profits at stake in the game. Those who dominate the field have the means to make it function to their advantage; but they have to reckon with the resistance of the dominated agents.
>
> (Bourdieu 1993: 88)

In the set of quotes below from unemployed adult research participants, it can be observed how they have come to develop a *feel for the game* within the *field* of unemployment. As someone who relies on the government welfare state system for financial support, they have limited agency or power within that social context – *field* – and become united as both products and producers of their *habitus:*

153.An   No, I think it was mainly coming here, because last time I came, you get friendly with a group of lads out there and you want to come back and see them and things like that.

(TP 2, O'Grady 2008: 281)

78.D   And I started looking at Jobcentre for jobs and that like, and ever since I've been going on these schemes and that, you know.

(TP 4, O'Grady 2008: 281)

54.M   The only jobs I have had is when the benefit office here send me like on placements and that but they've never ended up in jobs.

(TP6, O'Grady 2008: 282)

The relationship between *field*, education in this instance, and the *habitus* of an individual – either as a learner or practitioner – can provide a useful space for understanding educational experiences.

Symbolic violence and pedagogy

Bourdieu and Passeron's (1990) concept of *symbolic violence* specifically considers the relationship between education and social reproduction. Through *symbolic violence* they attempt to demonstrate that, through the system of education, processes of social order and restraint are continually (re)produced through indirect cultural mechanisms. Bourdieu and Passeron (1990) characterise *symbolic violence* as an imposition of a system of symbolism and meaning ('culture') upon groups in such a way that they are likely to be experienced as legitimate (Bourdieu and Passeron 1990). Such *legitimacy*, they assert, obscures power relations, thus allowing such impositions to be successful. *Culture* reinforces power relations, further enabling a systematic reproduction of society, achieved through a process of misrecognition. *Pedagogic action*, according to Bourdieu and Passeron (1990), is the primary socially constructed mechanism for the operationalisation of *symbolic violence* through pedagogic work, as *pedagogic action* works to reproduce power relations, thereby ensuring the interests of dominant groups or classes in society prevail:

Pedagogic action involves the exclusion of ideas as unthinkable, as well as their positive inculcation (depending, of course, upon the nature of the ideas). Exclusion or censorship may in fact be the most effective mode of pedagogic action.

(Jenkins 2002: 105)

Such *pedagogic action* can be readily observed being practised in classrooms. Whilst I was undertaking a piece of research in a large socio–economically deprived county of England, I was asked to explore the literacy practices of practitioners across all the primary schools in the county. What became apparent through my discussions with practitioners was that their pedagogic approach – and actions – reinforced and reproduced a social order and hierarchy. Quite subconsciously, practitioners were developing literacy lessons that were out of the scope of experience of the young people in receipt of those lessons – notions of holiday, international travel, and experiences of airports were legitimately seen as appropriate areas of focus, but reinforced the idea that some groups are excluded from such practices, retaining a reinforcement of social order.

We are all, as practitioners, involved in pedagogic action through pedagogic work. To varying degrees we direct what is being taught, and what information is privileged over other information. In the construction of this chapter, it could readily be argued that I am directing you to read particular theorists over others, and that by not selecting others I am influencing your thinking. By understanding the concept of *symbolic violence*, operationalised through *pedagogic action*, I argue we have stronger agency in determining the educational interactions we engage in.

Capital and pedagogy

Bourdieu (1997) also used the concept of *capital* to further understand the structures and mechanisms that underpin the order of things in a society. He argued that the unequal academic achievements of individuals were as a direct result of *cultural capital*: 'a weapon and a stake in the struggles which goes on in the field of cultural production' (Bourdieu 1997: 50). *Social capital*, he argued, further contributed to the establishment and reproduction of social relationships (Bourdieu 1990) that could be directly useable, either in the short or long term, to influence social order (Bourdieu 1997). *Economic capital*, however, is presented by Bourdieu as 'the root of all the other types of capital' (Bourdieu 1997: 53).

Using Bourdieu's concepts 'to think with', Jenkins (2002) allows educationalists to consider their role in how cultures construct societal norms, rules, and regulations; and how individuals acquire *habitus* through their interactions with and between *fields*. According to Bourdieu (1993), each *field* within society is structured according to what is at stake within it (educational, cultural, economic, and political). Once various forms of capital and their associated representative credentials are widely accepted and acknowledged within a society as relations of power, *symbolic violence* can be said to be in action, as domination no longer exists directly between individuals but they become a mechanism through which relations of domination exist (Bourdieu 1998).

By engaging with Bourdieu's concepts, we, as educational practitioners, can develop a considered analysis of an experience as exemplified above in my work with research participants undertaking adult literacy and numeracy courses. And this can act to influence and inform the ways in which we adapt our professional practice. As educators we can reflect on how systems, places, and curricula could be understood as mechanisms of *symbolic violence*, or how one's *habitus* can be influenced by an individual's *fields* of experience, and consider the degree to which education could be identified as a societal institution for role allocation. Bourdieu's thinking can allow us to become more *situationally aware* of how we are part of a society, and how we contribute to its production and reproduction. But he is only one example of how different educational thinkers, with different philosophical perspectives, can inform our practice.

Paulo Freire

Using the theoretical principles of Freire (1993) allows educationalists to consider their role and contribution in education – to develop what Freire terms a *critical consciousness*.

Freire (1921–1997) is a well-known educational activist within educational thinkers. He developed his philosophy of education – a philosophy of *critical pedagogy* – whilst working with adults, developing literacy programmes. For Freire, education should be seen as an opportunity – a mechanism through which people can move themselves out of poverty by recognising the oppressive nature of the structures under which they live. Education, Freire (1993) argued, has the potential to liberate people, and to allow transformative activity. His view was that students should be co–constructors of their own education experience through a cycle of theory, application, evaluation, and reflection. Through this cycle, a process of new meaning-making can take place through this student–teacher dualistic experience, facilitated by a real pedagogic partnership based on dialogue and sharing of information (O'Grady and Cottle 2014). Through this model of education individuals, he argued, can build and develop a *critical consciousness*, rather than a rather pedestrian model of education which he descried as a *banking model* (Freire 1993) where learners are seen simply as recipients of knowledge, and educators as intermediaries delivering the knowledge seen as appropriate and valuable by a powerful minority, thus ensuring a population are allocated to a pre-determined role in society. By developing an educational opportunity that encourages people to become conscious of their own situation, learners could become active readers of their world as well as of words. Freire (1993) asserted that individuals would then be able to recognise their subjugation by a dominant minority, creating a space for conscious emancipation and liberation, rather than continuing to live under oppression. Education, for Freire, should provide opportunities for freedom; it should enable people to develop agency and result in individuals taking action against their oppressors by challenging the imposed social order. Ultimately, his philosophy advocates that education should offer *hope*, and should be the only reason for an education offer. Without this, he argued, we exist in a *state of hopelessness* (Freire 1994).

As an example of how an understanding of educational theory can transform an individual pedagogical ontology, I have an example. In my work with postgraduate students, I lead a module: exploring educational thinkers and how they might be applied to practice. Students are invited to select theorists, research the theorist's work, and present their findings for discussion. In this way I hope to demonstrate the value of a shared discourse to develop understanding of theoretical principles and their value for thinking about the type of practitioner they either have been, want to be, or are. Following the module, one student reflecting on the discussions stated that for her it was a critical moment in her career planning; that she could clearly see her role and contribution as an educator going forward. This young lady is now ambitious to research the learning experiences of Asian women and work with them within a Freireian framework of critical pedagogy.

Etienne Wenger: communities of practice

A further thinker I want to introduce here is Etienne Wenger. He, and his colleagues, have provided a framework for us, as educational practitioners, to explore our ways of working, both in terms of our peers, educator–educator, and in terms of our learners. Based on a set of principles around learning in constructing identity, Lave and Wenger (1991) introduced a model of learning termed *communities of practice* in which they outline a range of *communities* through which a learning experience can be engaged:

Communities of practice are groups of people who share a concern or a passion for something they do, and learn how to do it better as they interact regularly.

(Wenger 2012: online)

Wenger (1998) identifies four components for meaningful learning: *community*, *identity*, *meaning*, and *practice*. Crucially, for this theoretical model, Wenger (1998) argues that because we, as humans, are social beings, learning is best achieved through a shared learning structure which combines engagement, imagination, alignment of interest, and a shared language. *Community* is the term Wenger applies to this process. Through a community approach to learning, he posits that one's identity can be negotiated and renegotiated and a personal history of *becoming* is created. As social beings, we already belong to what Wenger has coined *communities of practice*, to a greater or lesser extent. The degrees to which we become involved in these, however, vary. In their work, Lave and Wenger (1991) observed individuals acting as either: *core, active, occasional, peripheral*, or *transactional participants*. *Core participants* are described as individuals who are at the centre of a community and considered expert in that domain of interest; *active participants* are closely involved with the focus of the community; *occasional participants* are seen as individuals who *dip in and out* of an area of interest; *peripheral participants* are those who have minimum engagement with the community but are aware of it; and finally, *transactional participants* are individuals becoming aware of, or seeking information around, a new area of interest.

You may well be able to locate yourself in a range of *communities of practice* without having previously giving them a name, and Wenger acknowledges this. Critically, though, now that you are able to do this you may be able to consider cultivating a *community of practice* (Wenger et al. 2002) within your learning environment.

Over the last decade, for example, communities of curriculum practice have been widely adopted by adult literacy and numeracy practitioners. This approach to learning (increasingly seen as virtual communities) as a shared, co-constructed enterprise, Wenger (1998) argues, is a useful space for sharing ideas, where societal norms can be challenged. What makes these communities of practice unique for learning is their active participation. Communities of practice should not be considered simply as a collection of people who have a shared interest in phenomena. It is the interaction with others within such communities, Wenger argues, where learning takes place and new meaning and understanding is created.

Conclusions

Space does not allow me to introduce to you the work of others who I think have provided valuable ways for us to explore and understand the practices associated with education – why we do what we do in the way that we do, and how, but I would encourage you to read theorists widely: the work of Dewey (1963), for example, and his ideas of modelling education based on the principles of democracy, pragmatism, and experience. For Dewey (1963) education was responsible for the development of a civic society in which values were clearly understood, with a democratic and shared interest in personal growth, resulting in progressive opportunities for the development of equitable relations. Dewey's 'pedagogic creed' (1966) was based on self-action, interaction, and transaction. Framed within a curriculum of critical citizenship, he argued that teachers should act as facilitators for interactive student enquiry, which is student–led and flexible. This model, he asserted, would enable knowledge acquisition across disciplines.

The work of Foucault (1989, 1991) and how a person's subjection to power creates *docile bodies* which manage one's life on a microscale through a network of moral codes provides a useful alternative model for exploring education. Teachers, using a Foucauldian frame, could be regarded as 'technicians of behaviour' as they are charged with approving and implementing appropriate moral codes adopted by a society. Our education system, examined through this theoretical lens, could be seen as a mechanism for social manipulation or engineering, leading to the subordination of the mass populous into docile beings. To work against this, Foucault suggests, individuals should become *critical agitators*. However, to be able to do this you do of course have to be aware of the influences of power imposed by social structures and systems!

Your views of education – your decisions around why you are engaged in the *vocation* of education (and that is another discussion regarding the key principles of education as a vocation, art, science, or practice which we can't have here) – are crucial to understanding your practice, and the role of policy and research in informing practice. The argument I put forward here is not to advocate for one particular theorist or another, or assert a particular position or view, but that developing an understanding of a range of educational theorists and thinkers – whoever they are – adds value to you as an agent of your own practice within the structures of education in which we work, whether in a formal or informal context, vocational or academic.

Murphy (2013), introducing the work of some key social theorists, provides a nice framing of the value of theory: 'social theorists are analytical frameworks or paradigms used to examine social phenomena' (Murphy 2013: 4).

Education, and our role in and of it, does not come without a history and our future is built on lessons from our history. I argue that education is not an objective process. It is wholly subjective, based on the experiences and knowledge we have been exposed to during our lives. Engaging with educational thinkers and theorists provides us, as educational practitioners, with a great opportunity to be exposed to a range of ways in which education can be and is experienced and negotiated. This can only be a good thing when we are trying to develop our understanding of education for contemporary society – and our role in shaping that educational experience. Theorists are often studied, or advocated for, as the right perspective or the best perspective. I would strongly argue against this. My argument is that we should be exposed to as many thinkers as possible – so that we can come to an informed view of education and the roles of, for example, power, culture, capital, and self, in influencing and determining the type of education that is either provided or practised. Whilst each theorist will provide their own unique perspective on how the structures of education are constructed in a society, and we as agents engage with it, it is important to note that they themselves have been influenced by the theorists who pre-date them and their own personal experiences of 'becoming' (Wenger 1998), providing 'hope' (Freire 1994), the influence of power in these experiences (Foucault 1991) and developing our 'situational awareness' (Bourdieu 1993). Engagement in thinking should be a lifelong activity, in which our experiences allow us to become 'critical citizens' (Schilpp and Hahn 1989).

These theories have not been presented in a particular order, taxonomy, or hierarchy, and have not been selected because they are representative of the key thinkers or theorists. Rather, they exemplify my own engagement with them as thinkers and their influence on me – as a practitioner, as a researcher, and importantly as a citizen of modern western society. Theory matters!

References

Bourdieu, P. (1977) *Outline of a Theory of Practice* (Nice, R., Trans.), Cambridge: Cambridge University Press.

Bourdieu, P. (1990) *The Logic of Practice*, Cambridge: Polity Press.

Bourdieu, P. (1993) *Sociology in Question*, London: Sage.

Bourdieu, P. (1997) 'The Forms of Capital' (Nice, R., Trans.), in Halsey, A. H., Lauder, H., Brown, P., and Wells, A. S. (eds.) *Education, Culture, Economy and Society* (46–58), Oxford: Oxford University Press.

Bourdieu, P. (1998) *Acts of Resistance*, Cambridge: Polity Press.

Bourdieu, P. (2003) *The Social Structures of the Economy*, Oxford: Polity Press.

Bourdieu, P., and Passeron, J-C. (1990) *Reproduction in Education, Society and Culture* (Nice, R., Trans.) (2nd ed), London: Sage.

Bourdieu, P., and Wacquant, L. (1992) *An Invitation to Reflexive Sociology*, Cambridge: Polity Press.

Department for Education and Employment (2001) *Skills for Life: The National Strategy for Improving Adult Literacy and Numeracy Skills*, London: Department for Education and Employment.

Department for Education (2010) *The Importance of Teaching: The Schools' White Paper*, London: Department for Education.

Department for Education (2011) *Training our Next Generation of Outstanding Teachers: An Improvement Strategy for Discussion*, London: Department for Education.

Dewey, J. (1963) *Experience and Education*, London: Collier Macmillian.

Dewey, J. (1966) *Democracy and Education: An Introduction to the Philosophy of Education*, London: Collier Macmillian.

Foucault, M. (1989) *The Archaeology of Knowledge*, London: Routledge.

Foucault, M. (1991) *Discipline and Punish*, London: Penguin Books.

Freire, P. (1993). *Pedagogy of the Oppressed*, New York: Continuum.

Freire, P. (1994) *Pedagogy of Hope: Reliving Pedagogy of the Oppressed*, New York: Continuum.

Grenfell, M. (2004) *Pierre Bourdieu: Agent Provocateur*, London: Continuum.

Jenkins, R. (2002) *Pierre Bourdieu, Revised edition*, London: Routledge.

Lave, J., and Wenger, E. (1991) *Situated Learning: Legitimate Peripheral Participation*, Cambridge: Cambridge University Press.

Lingard, B., Taylor, S., and Rawolle, S. (2005) 'Bourdieu and the study of educational policy: introduction', *Journal of Education Policy*, 20, 6: 663–669.

Mackie, R. (ed) (1980) *Literacy and Revolution: The Pedagogy of Paulo Freire*, London: Pluto Press Limited.

Murphy, M. (ed) (2013) *Understanding Foucault, Habermas, Bourdieu and Derrida*. London: Routledge.

O'Grady, A. (2008) *Choosing to Learn or Chosen to Learn: A Qualitative Case Study of Skills for Life Learners*, University of Nottingham: Unpublished Thesis.

O'Grady, A., and Cottle, V. (2014) *PAAR for the Course: Supporting Postgraduate Level 7 Students through a Taught Programme*, Higher Education Close Up Research Conference, Making A Difference, Lancaster University, UK.

Schilpp, P. A., and Hahn, L. E. (eds) (1989) *The Philosophy of John Dewey* (3rd ed), Carbondale: Southern Illinois University.

Taylor, P. V. (1993) *The Texts of Paulo Freire*, Buckingham: Open University Press.

Wenger, E. (1998) *Communities of Practice: Learning, Meaning and Identity*, Cambridge: Cambridge University Press.

Wenger, E., McDermott, R., and Snyder, W. M. (2002) *Cultivating Communities of Practice*, Boston: Harvard Business School Press.

4 The application of psychological principles within education

Appliance of science or pick-n-mix?

Vivienne Walkup

Introduction

Assumptions are made about psychology and education providing sound foundations for driving improvements in formal learning situations, but whilst psychology and education may go hand in hand, they are nevertheless subject to debate and change and related to political and social context. This chapter considers ways in which the psychological approaches and principles rooted in humanistic, cognitive and behavioural theories are applied to educational contexts and how the focus of these shifts depending upon political and social influences. Thus epistemological positioning concerning the nature and value of knowledge changes without any clear acknowledgement of such influence. Beginning with my own experiences of teacher training in the early 1970s, the chapter considers the move to non-selective secondary education in the UK and ways in which psychometric testing such as blanket IQ tests for 11-year-olds gave way to other forms of establishing learning. The way in which the learner/student/child/pupil is viewed is at the centre of the changing approaches to education and learning and this chapter will critically discuss how these differing views (from active learner to passive recipient of knowledge) link with epistemological positioning and how they influence and are influenced by current educational thinking. The value and application of educational research related to learning will be debated in the light of the above and the differences between sound research findings and marketable 'quick-fix' packages aimed at busy practitioners will be examined. Some of these will be drawn upon and questions will be raised about the negative impact they may have upon those at the receiving end of educational research.

Training (and it was called training then rather than education) as a teacher in the UK in the 1970s was all about facilitating project work and encouraging individual interests. The Newsom Report (1963) and the Plowden Report (1967) were held up as the cornerstones which supported our approaches to teaching. There was an emphasis on putting the child at the centre of learning and allowing him/her to follow their interests and learn through discovery. The psychology we were taught was based upon the ideas of Piaget (1963, 1964, 1969) and Bruner (1960, 1966, 1973). Clearly the view of learning we were expected to adopt was of individuals actively constructing their own knowledge through the processes of 'assimilation' and 'accommodation' to expand and change their existing 'blocks' of knowledge (schemas). Whilst behaviourism was considered during this time as informing an understanding of rewards and punishments within the classroom, it was viewed as a mechanistic and incomplete approach which did not take the whole person into account. At this time the UK was in the process of rejecting its system of selective education at the age of 11 years and introducing Comprehensive Schools to replace Grammar Schools, Secondary Modern and Technical Schools. Thus the emphasis on psychometrics and intelligence testing which prevailed at the beginning of the 1960s was fading and being replaced in the 1970s by views of 'whole-child' development which included discovery learning (Bruner, 1961) and social and emotional factors as suggested by Carl Rogers (1969). At the time, somewhat naively, I thought that we had arrived at 'the truth' about learning and went forward with missionary zeal to encourage ex-Grammar School boys (newly reconfigured into a Comprehensive School over the summer of 1974) to write creatively about things they were interested in and worry about the grammar afterwards. Forty years later it is easy to see that psychology and education have moved on and been subject to changes and 'fashions' related to social and political contexts. In this chapter I will select some of these changes and examine them critically in terms of their integrity and impact and argue that they have been used to shore up ideological assumptions rather than enhance education.

Measuring intelligence – the selected child

Before the introduction of comprehensive education, all children attending state schools had to take the 11-plus tests. These tests, which used Spearman's General Intelligence factor or 'G' (1904), were promoted by Cyril Burt, a renowned psychologist who was an advisor on the committee which developed the 11-plus tests. Burt's (1917) research on identical twins was used as a basis for the argument that intelligence is inherited and thus measurable and quantifiable:

> Parental intelligence, therefore, may be inherited, individual intelligence measured, and general intelligence analysed; and they can be analysed, measured and inherited to a degree which few psychologists have hitherto legitimately ventured to maintain.
>
> (Burt, 1909: 166)

Therefore the assessed children should be separated according to ability so that they could receive appropriate education (in Grammar Schools for the most able, Secondary Modern Schools for the less able and Technical Schools for those with technical or scientific skills). Burt's work was very well received with remarkably little critical examination at the time but was subsequently found to be at worst fraudulent and at best unreliable (Hearnshaw, 1979; Tucker, 1994, 1997) after his death in 1971. It is easy to see how the right-wing views of Burt and other psychologists such as Charles Spearman (1927) and Francis Galton (1883) chimed in with the existing social and political views about class and career expectations and despite issues around the validity of intelligence testing such as those raised by Philip Vernon (1960). The reliance upon quantitative measures (such as IQ) gave these views an apparent objectivity which removed any suggestions of bias or elitism, but they in fact were fraught with social and cultural assumptions about the sort of knowledge a child should have. For example, questions might include concepts and experiences which were outside of a child's experience but they would be recorded as a lack of intelligence. I remember being dumbfounded on my first teaching practice (with 11-year-olds from a range of ethnic backgrounds in an inner-city school) to discover that a third of the pupils did not know what sand was. As the project work I had planned was based around the seaside, this caused me to have a deep rethink about the assumptions I had made and the similar assumptions which were made in intelligence testing.

Of course the good old 'nature–nurture' debate looms large here. The vast majority of current psychologists would agree that both inherited characteristics and the environmental experiences of human beings influence a person's ability to learn, although some would emphasise one over the other. Looking at the notion of intelligence testing, as it was in standard use before the move to comprehensive education, makes us acutely aware of that underlying view that people are born with varying degrees of intelligence. Adopting that view meant that children's capacity for learning was more or less fixed and so they should be educated accordingly.

It is a clear example of science (in this case, psychology) being used selectively to shore up particular educational initiatives rooted in social and political discourses.

The curious child and active learning

Calls for an approach which acknowledged the role of child development and the environment evolved in the 1960s as society became more progressive and Piaget's work, which emphasised the way that children construct their worlds and build knowledge as they develop cognitively, became central to the psychology of education field. Piaget's ideas of human cognitive development included the assumption that there are certain universal stages (sensory–motor, pre-operational, concrete operational and formal operational) that are influenced by interactions with the environment as children build up their knowledge of the world. Thus children add to and adapt their knowledge 'schemas' by processes Piaget named 'assimilation' and 'accommodation': this involves active engagement and learning on the part of the child, rather than the traditional assumptions that children are passive recipients of knowledge. Putting the child at the centre of her/his own learning was a very different way of looking at education which had traditionally relied upon the teacher 'teaching' rather than the child learning. Thus teachers were encouraged to facilitate learning, taking into account the idea of encouraging progression from one stage of cognitive development to another by providing an appropriately challenging environment. Teachers would then encourage new learning by presenting tasks which necessitated grasping new ideas when the child was ready to progress to the next stage. Piaget named this concept 'equilibration' or balance which occurs when children are comfortable with what they know but this needs to be upset to 'disequiliberate' or oblige children to actively learn and progress to the next stage. From this perspective, the teacher's role is to support or 'scaffold' this learning when required rather than to deliver it to them wholesale (Wood et al., 1976) and to allow children to develop their interests. In the process of doing this it was argued that they would acquire the necessary literacy and numeracy skills. Vygotsky's social constructivist views of cognitive development chimed in with this and added the notion of a zone of proximal development (an area within which children are capable of learning certain things) and stressed the importance of language and culture in the development of cognitive abilities (1978, 1987).

Carl Rogers' humanistic views of education (drawing upon therapeutic approaches) added to the argument of people as individuals who are at the centre of their own worlds; they are affected by the world around them but how they perceive and react to that will vary from individual to individual. Rogers contended that learning should be 'person' or 'student'-centred to allow them the 'freedom to learn' and achieve self-actualisation (Rogers, 1969). Thus a learner needed to be considered as a whole person rather than a set of abilities and Rogers stressed the importance of understanding the barriers which people might put in place (such as low self-esteem) which might affect their motivation and prevent them becoming a fully developed or 'actualised' person and thus having the 'freedom to learn'. Views such as those of Piaget, Vygotsky, Bruner and Rogers meant that children and young people within the education system were seen as having individual learning needs which meant that teachers with perhaps up to 40 students in a class were expected to provide learning opportunities suitable for these individuals within that group. Whilst this is clearly desirable from a humanistic perspective, it made life hard for teachers who were working with mixed-ability groups and had to take all ability ranges into account in their planning.

Measuring progress – the tested child

Whilst these progressive ideas fitted well with the 'permissive society' atmosphere of the 1960s and early 1970s (particularly for primary education), they became increasingly unpopular as the country moved into a recession. Calls for teachers to be more accountable and claims that formal whole-class teaching were needed to improve pupils' progress with regular testing and competition (Bennett, 1976) found favour (although the research this was based upon was by no means as scientifically rigorous as was assumed). Thatcher's views in the early 1980s, that education should be regulated, resulted in the disempowerment of teachers and Local Education Authorities (LEAs) with moves towards a National Curriculum, control over teacher training/education and a gradual return to central government. The increased focus on attainment, testing and competition meant that psychological research on cognitive processes such as individual differences in the ways people learn went onto the backburner. The 1980s saw the notion of learning styles and preferences flourish. This was rooted in the theory of 'multiple intelligences' proposed by Howard Gardner (Gardner, 1983) which suggested that humans possess different forms of intelligence such as logical-mathematical, linguistic, musical, bodily kinaesthetic, spatial, interpersonal and intrapersonal. Gardner's view of intelligence differed from Spearman's general ability 'G' mentioned earlier and suggested that whilst there was a genetic, innate basis for intelligence, this could be developed through experience and learning.

This notion of intelligences consisting of a number of different abilities was popular with educationalists. Kolb's work on experiential learning throughout this period provided a model and inventory (1971, 1981, 1984) which formed the basis for many later theories. Kolb's research identified four fundamental learning styles associated with different approaches to learning (diverging, assimilating, converging and accommodating). He suggested that these develop as the person moves from infancy to adulthood (Kolb, 1984). This view of both 'natural' and 'nurtural' influences was well received and stood up quite well to robust critical review. However, some of the work which followed this was less rigorous and over-simplified, raising issues about appropriating selective elements of research for the purposes of providing marketable strategies to help teachers and support learning. The reduction of multiple intelligences to what became popularised as the VAK (visual, auditory and kinaesthetic model) was promoted widely and teachers were encouraged to determine the learning styles of their individual pupils. Not only is the notion of VAK a misconstruction of Gardner's multiple intelligences, it is likely to lead to teachers labelling pupils as certain types of learner. Some schools even provided badges for pupils which announced their learning style (Franklin, 2006), thus limiting the types of learning they were exposed to and producing a self-fulfilling policy. Hindsight is a wonderful thing and there were many scorching criticisms of VAK subsequently (Coffield et al., 2004; Franklin, 2006; Sharp et al., 2008), but at the time educationalists were caught up in the need to demonstrate that they were taking psychological theories into account in their teaching. I remember feeling extremely uncomfortable with the notion of presenting staff development based on VAK and learning styles – it all seemed rather like a quick-fix sort of party game – and I am sure many others shared my discomfort. Unfortunately, though, when these 'trends' take off it is difficult to be a dissenting voice and hang onto your job until there is enough evidence to support the argument.

Brain Gym was another trend which had a similar lack of rigour in terms of its scientific origins but nevertheless became very popular in schools. Based upon an approach called Educational Kinesiology (Edu-K) presented by the Dennisons in the 1980s (Dennison and Dennison, 1989), Brain Gym was marketed as a way to improve learning through the use of movement. The scientific underpinnings are questionable to say the least, borrowing from alternative chiropractice which is itself pseudoscientific and claiming to use neuroscience research to substantiate the use of Brain Gym. The claims of Brain Gym (a commercial package) are bold and include assertions such as helping people to 'learn ANYTHING faster and more easily' and 'reach new levels of excellence' (Brain Gym website). Teachers are told that they can use Brain Gym to unlock the potential of students through movement activities such as 'crawling, drawing, tracing symbols in the air, yawning and drinking water' (Hyatt, 2007). Whilst few would argue that exercise and water are beneficial to all human beings, many strident critics of this approach condemn its use of pseudoscientific jargon to underpin simple movements:

> They teach that rubbing your ribcage will stimulate the carotid arteries beneath and increase blood flow to the brain and 'activate the brain for an increased flow of electromagnetic energy.'

> (Goldacre, 2006: online)

Both VAK and Brain Gym have made mileage from the actual scientific research carried out into cognitive neuroscience but most scientists would condemn the rush to operationalise findings into educational packages which claim to be rooted in neuroscience (Goswami, 2006). Similarly, the courses aimed at teachers which encourage identifying children as 'left-brained' or 'right-brained' learners have little basis in scientific research and it is worrying that such 'neuromyths' are so easily accepted into the world of education. Again, it is worth asking the question about epistemological assumptions and how the shift of these provides opportunities not only for desirable additions to knowledge and the improvement of education but also for the dilution and exploitation of such knowledge to suit market and political purposes.

Managing behaviour – the manipulated child

Alongside some of these initiatives to improve learning came the drive to 'manage' pupil behaviour more effectively. This became a key issue largely because of the need for schools to publish test results (Standard Assessment Tests/SATs) and be placed on a league table. Introduced as part of the Citizens' Charter in the early 1990s by John Major's

Conservative government, this strategy was supposedly to encourage a free market and allow parents free choice but in fact resulted in additional stress for teachers and pupils as 'teaching to test' and focus upon improving statistics took over. With more emphasis upon classroom behaviour to ensure efficient, measurable learning, behavioural techniques were dusted off and underwent some varnishing. As with VAK and Brain Gym, there was a flurry of publications offering strategies to improve behaviour and raise the achievements of pupils such as those by Bill Rogers (1995, 2000) and Sue Cowley (2001) which became favoured texts for teachers going into many editions.

It is easy to see why behavioural techniques of managing behaviour moved once more to the forefront of school agendas and publications. Again, the ideas of earlier writers were resurrected to market behaviour management strategies and therefore raise the results. It is worth remembering though that however it is presented, behaviourism is based upon operant conditioning drawn from the work of Skinner (1953) with pigeons and rats and is about manipulation. The teacher/child relationship then is assumed to be one which involves moulding students' behaviour through the application of behavioural techniques such as positive and negative reinforcement and punishment. Identifying areas for change, introducing these strategies and measuring the changes fits neatly into the current focus on measuring progress and the claims of behaviour management; therefore, to offer a scientific, quantifiable solution is seen as useful and desirable. The use of rewards to reinforce desired behaviour makes perfect sense, although obviously it is not as straightforward with humans as rewarding a rat for pressing a level with a food pellet (Skinner, 1953) because of the complexity of human needs, desires and motivators. So, for example, the 'rewards' have to be meaningful to those receiving them and so providing such rewards as praise, stars, team points or certificates will not be effective if it is meaningless to the student. Too often those pupils who are least motivated to learn will be unimpressed with these types of reward and consequently the reward becomes useless. Whilst no-one would argue with the notion of a learning environment which allows effective learning to take place and this would involve organisation and order, the idea of a child/learner as a passive creature who can be conditioned to behave appropriately is disconcerting. Further, evidence of the effectiveness of such methods is mixed as they seem to increase reliance on external drives to encourage learning (extrinsic motivation) rather than fostering the desire to learn and satisfy curiosity (intrinsic motivation) (Deci et al., 1999).

Humanistic ideas of providing 'freedom to learn' and understanding how children construct their own understanding seem to have disappeared along with Piagetian notions of the naturally curious child, and regimentation and quantification of learning has become the focus (disempowering both students and teachers). Interestingly, Gardner's multiple intelligences (which contain intrapersonal and interpersonal intelligences or intelligence about self and others) were drawn upon to form the basis of 'emotional education' which includes the concept of 'emotional intelligence' and began to appear in the 1990s. This at least acknowledged that people are more than what Bannister (1966) termed 'ping-pong balls with memories' (behaviourism) and a number of initiatives were introduced by the government. Emotional development was promoted within the Foundation Stage (3–5-year-olds) of the National Curriculum and in Personal, Social and Health Education/PSHE for older children and young people. In 2007 Social and Emotional Aspects of Learning/SEAL was introduced by the Department for Children, Schools and Families (DCSF):

[SEAL is] a comprehensive, whole-school approach to promoting the social and emotional skills that underpin effective learning, positive behaviour, regular attendance, staff effectiveness and the emotional health and wellbeing of all who learn and work in schools.

(DCSF, 2007: 4)

Attempts to encourage children to become more emotionally intelligent (which consists of four broad abilities: perceiving, integrating, understanding and managing emotions: Mayer and Cobb, 2000) were introduced in the 1990s and included activities such as 'circle time' and the use of emoticons to show recognition of appropriate emotions. These initiatives sit uneasily alongside strict expectations about results on tests and the assessment of SEAL in terms of pupils' social and emotional skills, mental health difficulties, pro-social behaviour and behaviour problems, and many concluded that it had 'failed to make a significant impact' (Humphrey et al., 2009: 31) which resulted in it being removed from the curriculum. Humphrey himself concluded that:

We've got a lot of whip-cracking about standards, a lot of stress on the three Rs. But government needs to get the right balance between the academic, the social and the psychological aspects of education. Kids don't just need their five A★s at GCSE, they need to be able to get on with other people.

(*The Guardian*, 2012: 28)

Conclusion

As noted throughout this chapter, part of the issue with the use of psychological theories and research within education is the way that they are used and misused according to the needs of those in power. They are also often misrepresented or used inaccurately in the media and therefore become vague and misunderstood. Certainly, the terminology related to emotional intelligence is a case in point as this is often loosely used and so impossible to pin down.

It is worth reflecting upon the role of the teacher too who is seen as incapable of making professional choices and providing appropriate learning opportunities and support for students. My own view is that if presented with a new 'wonder cure' or trend sold as 'psychological research shows . . .', it is always wise to look at the research evidence itself rather than at summaries or promotions based upon the research. Science reporting like any other tends to concentrate on positive findings and neglect inconclusive or negative ones, so it is important to go back to original research articles to establish that this is a legitimate appliance of science. Being armed with the first-hand information allows teachers to challenge initiatives based upon tenuous, selected findings and to avoid some of the facile, pick-n-mix solutions that are sometimes offered.

References

Bannister D. (1966) Psychology as an exercise in paradox. *Bulletin of the British Psychological Society*, 19, 21.
Bennett, N. (1976) *Teaching Styles and Pupil Progress*. London: Open Books.
Bradley, P. (2003) Emotional intelligence, Report to Executive Member for Education and Lifelong Learning. Available at www.portsmouth.gov.uk/media. Accessed June 2014.

Bruner, J. S. (1960) *The Process of Education*. Cambridge, MA: Harvard University Press.

Bruner, J. S. (1961) The act of discovery. *Harvard Educational Review* 31 (1): 21.

Bruner, J. S. (1966) *Toward a Theory of Instruction*. Cambridge, MA: Belknap Press.

Bruner, J. S. (1973) *Going Beyond the Information Given*. New York: Norton.

Burt, C. L. (1909) Experimental tests of general intelligence. *The British Journal of Psychology*, 3, 94–177.

Burt, C. l. (1917) *The Distribution and Relations of Educational Abilities*. London: The Campfield Press.

Burt, C. L. (1921) *Mental and Scholastic Tests*. London: P. S. King. Republished and revised (4th ed.). London: Staples (1962).

Burt, C. L. (1923) *Handbook of Tests for Use in Schools*. London: P. S. King. Republished (2nd ed.). London: Staples.

Coffield, F., Moseley, D., Hall, E., Ecclestone, K. (2004). *Learning Styles and Pedagogy in Post-16 Learning. A Systematic and Critical Review*. London: Learning and Skills Research Centre.

Cowley, S. (2001) *Getting the Buggers to Behave*. London: Continuum International Publishing Group.

DCSF (2007) *Social and Emotional Aspects of Learning for Secondary Schools*. Nottingham: DCSF Publications.

Deci, E. L., Koestner, R. and Ryan, R. M. (1999). A meta-analytic review of experiments examining the effects of extrinsic rewards on intrinsic motivation. *Psychological Bulletin*, 125, 627–668.

Dennison, P. and Dennison, G. (1989) *Brain Gym* (teachers' edition, revised). Ventura, CA: Hearts at Play Inc.

Franklin, S. (2006) VAKing out learning styles: Why the notion of 'learning styles' is unhelpful to teachers. *Education*, 34, 1, 3–13.

Galton, F. (1883) Inquiries into human faculty and its development. London: Macmillan. Available at http://galton.org/books/human-faculty/text/galton-1883-human-faculty-v4.pdf. Accessed August 2014.

Gardner, H. (1983) Frames of Mind: The Theory of Multiple Intelligences. New York: Basic Books.

Goldacre, B. (2006) *Brain Gym (educational kinesiology)* http://www.badscience.net/2006/03/the-brain-drain.

Goswami, U. (2006) Neuroscience and education: From research to practice. *Nature Reviews Neuroscience*, 7, 406–413. doi: 10.1038/nrn1907

Hearnshaw, L. S. (1979) *Cyril Burt: Psychologist*. Ithaca, NY: Cornell University Press.

Humphrey, N., Kalambouka, A., Lendrum, A., Wigelsworth, M., Samad, M., Farrelly, N., Wolpert, M, Aitken, J., Fonagy, P., Frederickson, N., Day, C., Rutter, M., Vostanis, P., Meadows, P., Tymms, P. and Croudace, T. (2009) *A Systematic Review of Social and Emotional Skills Measures for Children and Young People*. London: Department for Children, Schools and Families. eScholarID:10840

Hyatt, K. (2007) Brain Gym: Building stronger brains or wishful thinking? *Remedial and Special Education*, 28, 2, 117–124.

Kolb, D. A. (1971) *Individual Learning Styles and the Learning Process*. Working Paper #535–71, Sloan School of Management, Massachusetts Institute of Technology.

Kolb, D. A. (1981) Experiential learning theory and the learning style inventory: A reply to Freedman and Stumpf. *Academy of Management Review*, 6(2): 289–296.

Kolb, D. A. (1984) *Experiential Learning: Experience as the Source of Learning and Development*. Englewood Cliffs, NJ: Prentice-Hall.

Mayer, J. and Cobb, C. (2000) Educational policy on emotional intelligence: Does it make sense? *Educational Psychology Review*, 12 (2), 163–183.

Northen, S. (2012) Schools strive for pupils' happiness. *The Guardian*, Monday 16 January 2012. Available at *The Guardian* (2012) http://www.theguardian.com/education/2012/jan/16/children-wellbeing-schools-ofsted. Accessed August 2014.

Piaget, J. (1963) *Origins of Intelligence in Children*. New York: Norton.

Piaget, J. (1964) Development and learning. In R. Ripple and V. Rockcastle (Eds.), *Piaget Rediscovered* (pp. 7–20). Ithaca, NY: Cornell University Press.

Piaget, J. (1969) *Science of Education and the Psychology of the Child*. New York: Viking.

The Plowden Report (1967) *Children and their Primary Schools: A Report of the Central Advisory Council for Education (England)*. London: Her Majesty's Stationery Office. Available online at http://www. educationengland.org.uk/documents/plowden/plowden1967-1.html.

Rogers, B. (1995) *Behaviour Management: A Whole-School Approach*. Lisarow, Australia: Scholastic Australia.

Rogers, B. (2000) *Cracking the Hard Class: Strategies for Managing the Harder than Average Class*. London: Paul Chapman.

Rogers, C. (1969) *Freedom to Learn: A View of What Education Might Become* (1st ed.). Columbus, OH: Charles Merrill.

Sharp, J. G., Bowker, R. and Byrne, J. (2008) VAK or VAK-uous? Towards the trivialisation of learning and the death of scholarship. *Research Papers in Education*, 23(3), 293–314. doi:10.1080/02671520701755416

Skinner, B. F. (1953) *Science and Human Behavior*. New York: Macmillan.

Spearman, C. (1904) General intelligence, objectively determined and measured. *The American Journal of Psychology*, 15(2): 201–292.

Spearman, C. (1927) *The Abilities of Man: Their Nature and Measurement*. Retrieved August 2014 from http://www.questia.com/PM.qst?a=o&d=88815427. The Newsom Report (1963) *Half our future: A Report of the Central Advisory Council for Education (England)*. London: Her Majesty's Stationery Office. Available online at http://www.educationengland.org.uk/documents/newsom/newsom1963.html. Accessed August 2014.

Tucker, W. H. (1994) Fact and fiction in the discovery of Sir Cyril Burt's flaws. *Journal of the History of the Behavioral Sciences*, 30, 335–347.

Tucker, W. H. (1997) Re-reconsidering Burt: Beyond a reasonable doubt. *Journal of the History of the Behavioral Sciences*, 33(2): 145–162.

Vernon, P. E. (1960) *Intelligence and Attainment Tests*. London: University of London Press.

Vygotsky, L. S. (1978) *Mind in Society: The Development of Higher Mental Process*. Cambridge, MA: Harvard University Press.

Vygotsky, L. S. (1987) The genetic roots of thinking and speech. In R. W. Rieber and A. S. Carton (Eds.), *Problems of General Psychology, Vol. 1. Collected Works* (pp. 101–120). New York: Plenum. (Work originally published in 1934.)

Wood, D. J., Bruner, J. S. and Ross, G. (1976) The role of tutoring in problem solving. *Journal of Child Psychiatry and Psychology*, 17(2), 89–100.

5 Gender: stories and lies

Debunking myth and determining reality

Fiona Shelton

Introduction

> What are little boys made of?
> Slugs and snails, and puppy dogs' tails
> That's what little boys are made of.
> What are little girls made of?
> Sugar and spice and all things nice
> That's what little girls are made of.
>
> (Traditional rhyme)

Above is a popular, traditional rhyme, familiar to most of us, epitomising attitudes to boys and girls which can still be seen to prevail today in the 21st century, with the pink revolution and so called laddish subculture seen in schools. Whilst this rhyme can be perceived as humorous, it demonstrates a particular way of depicting both boys and girls; an attitude we should explore to address the myths and realities that exist around boys' and girls' educational achievements and employment choices in later life. Describing boys and girls in these terms can lead to the development of identities which are potentially destructive and can have a negative effect on the perceptions that young people hold about each other and themselves. Despite shifts in attitudes, there are still cases where gender divides exist in homes, families and societies, which teach children about the domestic roles of males and females.

In this chapter I will explore the attitudes we see in everyday life in relation to male and female identity. Additionally I will consider some of the myths and realities relating to the educational achievement of boys and girls and present some ideas for reflection to address attitudes to gender that are often not challenged. By gender I refer to the socially constructed roles, behaviours, activities and attributes that a society considers appropriate for men and women. The sex of a person, whether they are male or female, a boy or a girl, refers to the biological and physiological characteristics that define men and women (World Health Organisation, 2015).

It might be useful to begin by drawing from a particular campaign to demonstrate attitudes to gender. A controversial clothing range developed by the American company David and Goliath founded in 2000 by Todd Harris Goldman flooded the market worldwide: T-shirts, calendars, games and books depicting a boy running away from flying rocks, with the slogan 'Boys are stupid, throw rocks at them', and others such as 'Boys come from the stupid factory' and 'Boys are pretty much smelly and useless', drew attention a decade ago. Glenn Sacks (American talk-show host and men's and fathers' issues columnist) gained a huge amount of support and attention for his campaign against Goldman's products, with thousands of outlets withdrawing clothing and other items (HEqual, 2014). To suggest that stupidity is somehow intrinsic to boys can be seen as troubling to the gender education gap and the underachievement of boys in school because it is simply not true: boys are not born less intelligent than girls.

In fact, research undertaken by Francis (2010) highlighted the possible impact of gender stereotypical play on children's future subject preferences and job prospects. She found that although girls have closed the gap with boys when it comes to achievement, in maths and science they are still less likely to be high achievers in these subjects or to study them beyond GCSE. What is interesting is that they continue to excel in literacy and humanities subjects. Early play is considered to have a crucial impact on these trends (Francis, 2010). The study highlighted how the toys manufactured, packaged and intended for boys demonstrated a greater range of learning opportunity than toys created for and aimed at girls. Boys' toys tended to be far more diverse than girls' toys, and included toys which were technical, construction-based, propelling boys into a world of technology. Play of this manner was seen to be much more exciting, adventurous and educational. Of the girls' choices, however, learning potential was much more limited; there was little that could be related to skills development or to the curriculum, although Francis (2010) did note how the baby doll used in the study provided well-developed information on the needs of a baby and how to meet those needs. The potential learning opportunities from the girls' toys were focused around imaginative and creative play, which goes some way to explain the 'sugar and spice and all things nice' sentiments directed towards girls in the traditional rhyme above.

As in the 1970s when the first studies of gender, play and toys were conducted by researchers (e.g., Thompson, 1975; Kacerguis and Adams, 1979), they concluded that girls' play developed their communication skills and emotional literacy, while boys' play encouraged them to grow up with better technical knowledge. It is only more recently that toy manufacturers such as Lego have created more construction sets specifically for girls. The range is known as Belville and includes themes such as horse jumping and a royal summer palace, although the unisex range affords interest to girls too. The concern I would raise here is still around the depiction of girls' and boys' interests, and how toys become gender-assigned due to their context and the longstanding stereotypical perceptions held of boys and girls. Boys build spaceships while girls build a palace. So when a palaeontologist, an astronomer and a chemist, all female, made their debut in the toy market in 2014 (de Castella, 2014), the range 'Lego Friends' was a sell-out hit in the first week. These female scientists are seen to be undertaking highly intellectual, complex and demanding roles, which may begin to redress some of the balance in subject choice and employment preference in the future. More importantly, they demonstrate to girls that women choose these job roles as well as men and as they require instructions to be read and constructions to be created, they can further develop girls' technical and intellectual abilities.

But there still remains the concern that boys' language ability is less advanced than that of girls', and this is believed to be a key factor in boys' underachievement. According to Wilson (2007), boys are often significantly less independent than girls prior to starting school and differences in language development are evident right from the early years. It is particularly white working-class boys who lack the essential language skills needed to be successful in education (Demie and Lewis, 2010; House of Commons Education Committee, 2014).

Improving this deficiency in language development, Sommers (2014) claims, is a key factor for improving boys' achievements in school. She states that if boys come to school 'reading ready', they are more likely to achieve well across the curriculum. Ensuring they can make choices about their reading material and that the right reading material is available can make a big difference to boys' reading preferences. She additionally argues that boys should be allowed to be boys and that we should work harder to understand boys' approaches to learning. Being allowed to play more often and being encouraged to use their imaginations, unleashing their adventure stories, can help improve boys' writing. The 'circle time', 'tell us how you feel' culture that pervades primary education moves further away from the needs of boys (Sommers, 2014); she claims that there is a need to reverse these boy-averse trends. However, this sustains and maintains the stereotypes often held about boys and girls. The zero-tolerance approach to behaviour in schools, whilst laudable in some respects, also sees more boys expelled from schools than girls, whereas some tolerance and understanding about boys' development might see an improvement in educational outcomes (Sommers, 2014). Consequently, whilst we might not use the terms 'slugs' and 'snails' as in the aforementioned rhyme, we might consider how to ignite boys' imagination and allow more boisterous behaviour, if it is managed effectively.

On the other side of the coin is the rise of the 'Girly-Girl World', the 'Pink Attitude' and the 'Princess Culture'. The rise in pink and fluffiness are media and consumer-based factors which contribute to the girly world. The problem with pink is not with the colour itself. The problem lies in the way pink is used as a singular representation of girls' interests and identities. Flicking through a contemporary mail order catalogue recently, I was fascinated by the bedding section. The girls' bedding included a quilt cover with a life-size photograph of a ballerina in a pink tutu and a pink princess dress printed on the quilt; the child's head when they are in bed makes up the full picture. In contrast, the boys' bedding showed photographs of an astronaut and a pirate. I have nothing against these but it might have been useful to show boys and girls in some gender-neutral roles rather than simply taking this longstanding stereotypical approach.

Gender parity is important across the consumer market, because children read the market and packaging through cultural lenses presented to them by the companies selling children's goods. Children can make their own choices about which toys to play with and need not be judged because they choose a gender-defined toy that is deemed to be in opposition to their own gender. In fact there has been a call to end the gender divide in toy manufacturing. The 'Let Toys Be Toys' campaign is asking the toy and publishing industries to stop limiting children's interests by promoting some toys and books as only suitable for girls, and others only for boys (Let Toys Be Toys, 2014). Some shops have already ceased promoting the pink and blue aisles of children's toys and have replaced signage with gender-neutral designs and labelling to provide opportunities for girls and boys to simply choose toys they would like to play with.

Reports on boys' underachievement have dominated educational discussions since the 1990s (Murphy and Elwood, 1996; Gallagher, 1997; Martino et al., 2009). Boys' underachievement has caused somewhat of a moral panic within politics and in the media. This frequently expressed propensity in education, that girls' overachievement is a cause for concern, is in itself a cause for concern. According to Paule (2008), an implication of this is that by 'overachieving' girls are somehow being seen as disrupting a perceived natural order, that this is a social problem and that it is the cause of boys' underachievement.

Faludi (2000) explored this moral panic in her research with men regarding the underachievement agenda. She refers to an old model of masculinity, which she believed showed men how to be part of a larger social system. She stated that this model provided men with a context in which they could understand and navigate their masculine role; the societal context has now changed and men might need to reconstruct their understanding of masculine identity. So perhaps the moral panic should be less about boys' underachievement and girls' overachievement, and more about restructuring societal attitudes to boys and girls (Holz and Shelton, 2013).

Whilst boys' underachievement has dominated educational news in recent times, it is not new. According to Robinson (1998, online), a 1966 survey of 11,000 7-year-olds found that girls were better readers than boys in all aspects of reading ability.

> It [the report] found that in maths there were more high achieving boys than girls, but otherwise achievement was comparable. A survey of 5,000 primary pupils in 1971 found that the girls on average make rather higher scores than the boys in all tests, except vocabulary at 8 and 11 years.
>
> (Robinson, 1998: online)

Girls now dominate the exam leagues in all phases and subjects except mathematics and have consistently achieved higher grades than boys since the introduction of GCSEs. Smithers (in the *Telegraph*, 2014) stated that boys had marginally overtaken girls in GCSE maths since the switch to end-of-course exams five years ago. In 2014 girls were seen to pull further ahead than boys again, despite the move to end-of-term exams. According to Smithers, the redesign of GCSEs should have seen an end to a generation of 'discrimination' against boys in which girls benefited from coursework and modular exams (Paton, 2014: online). He further stated that it might take time to embed the new exam system to demonstrate a difference.

> The other side of the coin is that the way GCSEs have been structured in the recent past might have been discriminating against boys. It is nonsense, and indeed illegal, to deliberately design an examination to favour one gender over another, or one social group over another.
>
> (Schools Improvement Net, 2014: online)

As reported by Paton (2014), GCSE results in 2014 confirmed that 72.3 per cent of girls were awarded GCSE grades of A* to C, with only 63.7 per cent of these awarded to boys, demonstrating a gap of 8.6 percentage points. Grades A or A* were awarded to 24.8 per cent of girls and 17.6 per cent of boys. These trends have been broadly consistent since 1989 (Paton, 2014), which coincides with the point at which the National Curriculum was introduced when the education system offered greater parity for boys and girls.

Interestingly, in the 1960s and 1970s, it was the underachievement of girls, not boys, that was highlighted and explained in a number of ways. First, there were spurious arguments relating to IQ theories, which claimed that females are innately less intelligent than males, and second, there was research into gender socialisation throughout society, such as the work of Sharpe (1972 and 1994). Her research suggested that in societies such as the UK, the socialisation process as it operated, at least up to the 1970s, meant that many parents socialised their daughters to show dependence, obedience, conformity and domesticity. Boys, on the other hand, were more likely to be encouraged to be dominant, competitive and self-reliant. Sharpe (1972) argued that girls had been socialised to focus on the importance of romance, being a wife and becoming a mother rather than on the importance of their education and following a career. Sharpe later replicated her study in the 1990s. Girls were then more focused on their education and career prospects, thus demonstrating a shift in perceptions about their own role in society as well as in their socialisation as young women. The school system has additionally changed, with more attention paid to personal, social and emotional education than in the past, a system that Sommers (2014) believes is detrimental to boys' educational achievements.

In general, until the 1980s, girls were usually offered a school curriculum that prepared them for life in the home, for example studying home economics, housewifery, needlecraft and cookery; whereas boys were offered practical subjects such as woodwork and metalwork or were encouraged to study academic subjects (National Grid for Learning, 2010). It was not compulsory for girls to study the sciences and their subject choices narrowed their options in the employment market. The introduction of a common examination system in 1984, a compulsory National Curriculum in the Education Reform Act of 1988 and national targets based on standardised tests of pupils' abilities in core subjects at various ages in part began to address the problem of gender-differentiated subject choices in secondary education (Holz and Shelton, 2013). It became compulsory for boys to study modern languages and for girls to study mathematics, science and technology. However, Arnott et al. (1999) noticed that this did not prevent young men and women choosing gender-stereotyped subjects and later post-16 vocational and academic courses.

So girls' achievements can be attributed to the changing factors in socialisation and in wider society, with greater opportunities being available to women and to the changing curriculum. Curriculum 2000 opened up greater choice for girls in terms of their subject choices at GCSE and Advanced Level examinations, which in turn has created greater opportunities in the workplace. According to the Office for National Statistics (2008), women represent almost half of the workforce in the United Kingdom and whilst they increasingly hold influential positions, evidence suggests that the labour market is still failing women. Pay levels are improving but they still do not reflect the qualification levels of women, and women in some occupations are still fighting for equal pay and positions in the workplace (Perfect, 2011). The double burden, experienced by the majority of women, would suggest that women's lives are still largely constrained by childcare and domestic responsibilities in addition to paid employment (Holz and Shelton, 2013).

Because boys' educational attainment has dominated the debate for over 20 years, there has been little literature published since the 1970s and 1980s in terms of what is meant by educational work for girls in contemporary schools. Renold (2012) identifies that this is not the case in relation to boys, as there is a range of guidance documents which clearly focus on working with boys and ways to raise their achievement, with the government commissioning reports to help raise the achievement of boys. Jackson et al. (2010) propose that many girls' and young women's lives are not reflected in popular stereotypes and efforts to address this are often lost in the continued debate about boys' educational attainment. According to Mendick (2012), the boys' underachievement debate controls how we understand gender and education, making us focus more on some factors and forget about others. She reminds us that the debate turns achievement into an issue of girls versus boys, and we then overlook the problems girls face in education including, amongst others, teenage pregnancy and sexualisation. The debate around boys' and girls' education is complex; it is not as simple as developing female-focused programmes and materials for use in schools, because as suggested by Renold (2012), much of the literature which targets girls' educational needs may be contributing to reinforcing gender stereotypes of what it means to be a girl learner.

The challenge for schools, teachers and those working with young people is to think critically about educational materials, practice and information aimed at working in a non-discriminatory way, and to consider how such programmes might unintentionally reinforce and sustain rather than challenge existing gender stereotypes (Shelton, 2013).

Adding to the difficulties with gender equality are curriculum areas which are associated with one gender or the other. Paechter (2012) states that in most western countries, mathematics, science and technology are seen as masculine subject areas, whereas humanities and languages tend to be associated with femininity. The result is that young people often feel uncomfortable studying a gender-defined subject when they are not of that assigned gender or they simply do not choose subjects they feel are not assigned to them. In other cases young people often find themselves in inadvertent single-sex classes simply because of the implicit nature of gender marking of subjects. The ensuing problem is that girls are less likely to study the higher-status subjects of mathematics, science and technology, and therefore they are not in a position to pursue high-status and better-paid careers later on. Similarly, boys are more likely to opt out of the humanities and modern foreign languages, closing down other options which may be more beneficial to them. Holden's research discusses children's 'avowed commitment to gender conformity' (2002: 107), which means that encouraging children to make specific curriculum choices may not work.

Out-of-school activities are often open to both boys and girls but the implicit gender-marked activities often prevent boys and girls from joining in with activities which are aligned to the opposite sex. This relates to the previous discussion around how comfortable girls and boys feel in participating in gender-marked activities and how they themselves conform to gender-specific activities. In the UK, the Scout Association (formerly the Boy Scout Association) and the Girl Guide Association are probably the most popular groups that children and young people join outside of school. Until 2007 only boys could join the Scout Association and only girls, the Guides. Girls were first admitted in 1976 to the Scouts through the Venture Scouts, a section for older children, and the rest of the sections on an optional basis in 1991. In 2007 when ruling changed, 'Scouting' became co-educational and all Scout Groups in Britain must now accept girls as well as boys.

Scouting is the largest co-educational youth movement in the UK with a combined adult/young person membership of over half a million people. More girls than boys became Scouts in 2011, a first in the movement's history. Some 4,330 girls and 3,796 boys joined between January 2010 and January 2011 (BBC, 2011: online). Despite this growth, boys in the Scouts still outnumber girls by over five to one.

Girl Guiding UK is a separate organisation; it has about half a million members, including about 100,000 adult volunteers. It is for girls and young women only and has come under condemnation for maintaining a single-sex group. Whilst girls have been invited to join Scouts, boys are still prohibited from joining the Guides. The main reason according to some Girl Guides (Saner, 2009) is that girls want to be part of a girl-only group. It could be argued, however, that whilst Girl Guides conduct research to highlight the issues girls and young women face, the association sustains and contributes to gender stereotyping and reinforces gender-assigned activities and subjects, whilst Scouting has taken steps to embrace both genders.

Gender is one of the most interesting dimensions of social change (Ruspini, 2007); but it is also currently less investigated in the field of education and a shroud of silence has fallen over discussions around gender identity construction in recent years (Shelton, 2013). In early childhood, children tend to have rigid perceptions of gender, which shape their initial ideas of what it means to be a boy or a girl. The different ways in which gender identity is constructed are actively maintained and re-constructed throughout life. Francis (2000) highlights that gender-appropriate identities and behaviours are fluid, and some children challenge or ignore them. Children work hard to construct and maintain their gender identities whilst recognising that the behaviours typical of masculine and feminine roles are not binding.

Young people draw on their knowledge of norms and stereotypes to enact their social identities, including their gender identities, and therefore essentialist thinking can be challenged to ensure that young people are able to negotiate their personal identity in more fluid ways. What constitutes feminine and masculine ways-of-being are constantly reinforced in everyday interactions, and the process of 'gendering' individuals is ongoing and dynamic. Because the emphasis on boys' underachievement can marginalise and downgrade the achievements of girls, in education we should cease to propagate the boys' underachievement agenda and do more to understand and meet the needs of all children, regardless of gender. We should look to the creation of gender-equitable school cultures and talk openly to boys and girls about gender stereotyping, so that we continue to challenge and change essentialist and traditional attitudes towards gender.

References

Arnott, M., David, M. and Weiner, G. (1999) *Closing the Gender Gap: Postwar Education and Social Change*, Cambridge: Polity Press.

British Broadcasting Corporation (2011) *Scouts: Girls Overtake Boys in Admissions*, BBC News, available from: http://www.bbc.co.uk/news/uk-13082946, accessed November 2014.

Castella, T. de (2014) *How did Lego Become a Gender Battleground?* BBC News, 6 August 2014, available from: http://www.bbc.co.uk/news/magazine-28660069, accessed December 2014.

Demie, F. and Lewis, K. (2010) *Raising Achievement of White Working Class Pupils: Barriers to Learning,* London: Research and Statistics Unit.

Faludi, S. (2000) *Stiffed: The Betrayal of the American Man,* New York: Harper Perennial.

Francis, B. (2000) *Boys and Girls' Achievement: Addressing the Classroom Issues,* London: Routledge Falmer.

Francis, B. (2010) Gender toys and learning, *Oxford Review of Learning,* 36:3, 325–344.

Gallagher, A. (1997) *Educational Achievement and Gender: A Review of Research Evidence on the Apparent Underachievement of Boys.* DENI Research Report Series No. 6.

HEqual (2014) *Book Retailers Promote the Stoning of Boys: HEqual Takes a Stand,* available from: https://hequal.wordpress.com/2014/01/15/book-retailers-promote-the-stoning-of-boys-hequal-takes-a-stand, accessed December 2014.

Holden, C. (2002) Contributing to the debate: The perspectives of children on gender, achievement and literacy, *Journal of Educational Enquiry,* 3:1, 97–110.

Holz, O. and Shelton, F. (2013) *EDucation and GEnder: Gender-Specific Education in Different Countries, Historical Aspects - Current Trends,* Munich: Waxmann.

House of Commons Education Committee (2014) *Underachievement in Education by White Working Class Children,* London: The Stationery Office.

Jackson, C., Paechter, C. and Renold, E. (Ed.) (2010) *Girls and Education 3–16: Continuing Concerns, New Agendas,* Maidenhead: Open University Press.

Kacerguis, M. and Adams, G. (1979) Implications of sex typed child rearing practices, toys, and mass media materials in restricting occupational choices of women, *The Family Coordinator,* 28:3, 369–375.

Martino, W., Kehler, M. and Weaver-Hightower, M. (Eds) (2009) *The Problem with Boys' Education: Beyond the Backlash*, London: Routledge.

Mendick, H. (2012) *Boys' 'Underachievement'*, available from: http://www.genderandeducation.com/resources/contexts/the-boys-underachievement-debate, accessed October 2014.

Murphy, P. and Elwood, J. (1996) *Gendered Experiences, Choices and Achievement: Exploring the Links*, ESRC seminar series: Gender and Schooling, University of London Institute of Education.

National Grid for Learning (2010) *What are the Patterns of Achievement for Students of Different Genders?* Cardiff: NGFL.

Office for National Statistics (2008) *Focus on Gender,* available from: http://www .ons.gov.uk/ons/rel/social-trends-rd/focus-on-gender/september-2008/index.html, accessed October 2014.

Paechter, C. (2012) *Curriculum*, available from: http://www.genderandeducation.com/resources/pedagogies/curriculum, accessed November 2014.

Paton, C. (2014) GCSE results 2014: girls pulling further ahead of boys, *The Telegraph,* 21 August 2014.

Paule, M. (2008) *Achieving Gender Equality in Teaching and Learning,* available from: http://www.teachingexpertise.com/articles/achieving-gender-equality-teaching-and-learning-3643, accessed October 2014.

Perfect, D. (2011) *Gender Pay Gaps*, Manchester: Equality and Human Rights Commission.

Renold, E. (2012) *Working with Girls in Schools*, available from: http://www.genderand education.com/resources/pedagogies/working-with-girls-in-schools, accessed April 2012.

Robinson, J. (1998) Girls on top? *Socialist Review,* Issue 216, available from: http://pubs.socialistreviewindex.org.uk/sr216/robinson.htm, accessed October 2014.

Ruspini, E. (2007) Changing femininities, changing masculinities, social change, gender identities and sexual orientations, *Sociological Research Online*, 12:1.

Saner, E. (2009). Keep the Campfires Burning: 100 Years of the Girl Guides, *Guardian online,* 21 August, available from: http://www.guardian.co.uk/lifeandstyle/2009/aug/21/brownies-girl-guides, accessed December 2014.

Schools Improvement Net (2014) GCSE results 2014: girls pulling further ahead of boys, available from: http://schoolsimprovement.net/tag/alan-smithers, accessed December 2014.

Sharpe, S. (1972 and 1994) *Just Like a Girl*, Harlow: Penguin.

Shelton, F. (2013) Upsetting the apple cart: overachieving girls, underachieving boys, in Holz, O. and Shelton, F. (eds) *EDucation and GEnder: Gender-Specific Education in Different Countries, Historical Aspects-Current Trends,* Munich: Waxmann.

Sommers, C. (2014) *War on Boys*, Prager University, available from: http://www. prageruniversity.com/Political-Science/War-on-Boys.html#.VKGD8DyBGA, accessed December 2014.

Thompson, S. (1975) Gender labels and early sex role development, *Child Development*, 46:2, 339–347.

Wilson, G. (2007) *Pocket PAL: Raising Boys' Achievement*, London: Continuum International Publishing Group.

World Health Organisation (2015) *Gender, Women and Health,* available from: http://www.who.int/gender/whatisgender/en, accessed December 2014.

6 Values production through social and emotional learning

Peter Wood

Introduction

Across the world, in countries such as Canada, Singapore, Japan, New Zealand and Germany, social and emotional learning (SEL) is deemed as an integral aspect of an individual's education. Similar views influenced the formation and use of the Social and Emotional Aspects of Learning (SEAL) scheme in primary and secondary schools in the UK (Hallam et al. 2006). Whilst such schemes have been positively appraised by researchers, others have argued that these initiatives are a form of social control, as they endorse specific values and behaviours, outlining 'the type of person a child should become' (Craig 2007: 11). Drawing on such opinion, and empirical data gathered for a study that investigated the interpretation and use of SEAL in primary schools in the UK, I make the case that SEL schemes are being operationalised as a form of values education to exercise 'disciplinary power' (Foucault 1977). The Nanny State approach of the existing and past governments, to interfere in the family's role of shaping values (Gewirtz 2001; Gillies 2005b; Parr 2009), will be discussed to rationalise the belief that schools and SEL schemes are prime sites of intervention, with both being exploited to encourage children to behave and act in specific ways. With reference to Bourdieu's (1986) notion of cultural capital and in keeping with the views of Apple (2004) and Ball (2008) – that education helps to produce and maintain cultural hegemony – this chapter will consider if SEL schemes have the potential to marginalise and/or promote certain values, norms and behaviours, to guard against 'cultural pollution' (Apple 2006). First, I explore the historical underpinnings of values education before highlighting concerns regarding values production via the national and hidden curriculum. Second, I provide an overview of SEL, and in doing so explore opinion offered by its proponents and critics. Third, I present empirical data which, in addition to the views offered by Bourdieu (1986), Apple (2004) and Ball (2008), elucidates how SEL schemes are 'amenable to exploitation' (Burman 2009: 137) by schools. Finally, I evaluate the implications of my arguments before offering recommendations for future directions.

Education and values

An unresolved and constant dilemma for educators relates to their role in developing values amongst their pupils (Cairns 2000). Indeed, academic opinion pertaining to this quandary has been ongoing for centuries. During the 18th century, educationalists such as Jean-Jacques Rousseau declared that 'the noblest work in education is to make a reasoning man' (Rousseau 1762: 256), whilst in 1885, Emile Durkheim argued that we should:

never lose sight of what is the aim of public education. It is not a matter of training workers for the factory or accountants for the warehouse, but citizens for society.

(Durkheim 1885: 449)

For Durkheim, education serves a function for society as it should 'shape social beings by instilling shared moral traditions, practices and ideals' (Cladis 1998: 20). John Dewey maintained this stance in his writings throughout the 20th century where his progressive model and heuristic approach to schooling clarified a need to educate the 'democratic citizen' (Wilkins 2000: 17). Such opinion is also demonstrable in the terminology of various acts of parliament in the UK, such as the 1944 Education Act and the Education Reform Act 1988, which both identified the central role of the education system in values production. The National Curriculum, which stemmed from the latter of these acts, was the first step in explicitly recognising the integral tenet of schooling in shaping the values of pupils, by making it compulsory for schools to promote the physical, mental, cultural, spiritual and moral development of pupils and of society. Since, the view that 'values . . . lie at the heart of the school's vision' (Cairns 2000: 6) has been demonstrated in a range of government Green papers that emphasise the need for pupils to access education to gain 'flexible attitudes and enduring values' (DfEE 1998: 12), and in reports that clarify how the introduction of values education will inevitably lead to positive changes in young people's attitudes, behaviours and dispositions (see Crick Report 1998). Indeed, more recently, in high-profile recommendations for education made within the Review of Primary Education carried out by Jim Rose in 2009, the Cambridge Primary Review by Robin Alexander and colleagues in 2009, and in a report regarding early intervention techniques in schools by Graham Allen in 2011, the preference for values-based education has continued. Whilst the association between education and values has undoubted historical and contemporary support, it would be foolish to assume that values education is exempt from opposition and in the next section of the chapter I share some of these critiques.

Problematising values education

To contextualise the critiques that follow I first need to introduce aspects of a philosophical debate between those who promote monism and those who endorse pluralism. In short, the debate focuses on 'whether the values of a society can work harmoniously together or whether by nature they are destined to conflict with one another' (Robbins 2013: 100). Value monists, such as Plaw (2004: 109), maintain the values of society are 'harmoniously integrated' and that this is plausible as each value supports the realisation of all others (Dworkin 2011), or because our perception of competing 'values' may in fact be reduced to a 'supervalue' such as pleasure (Chang 2001). On the other hand, value pluralists, like Weber (1946), assert that more than one worthy value exists, and that often these values contrast and conflict with one another. Drawing on this debate, authors such as Pierre Bourdieu, Michel Foucault, Michael Apple and Stephen Ball point out some fundamental flaws with values education, emphasising the notion of power as a particularly problematic concept in this arena. As society is organised into those who lead and those who are led, ultimately those who hold the power can affect the lives of others. With reference to values education, I argue that one question is worthy of exploration: whose values are being promoted?

For Apple (2004), the school, supported by both the national and hidden curriculum, adopts the role of a 'reproductive force in an unequal society' (p. 25). As a mechanism of cultural and social reproduction (Bourdieu and Passeron 1990), the school acts as a socialising agent transferring 'appropriate' attitudes and values to students. However, whilst this may seem favourable at first glance, the education system has been declared as a tool that only re-affirms the values of the dominant groups in society (see Apple 2004, 2006; Ball 2006, 2008). In this sense, the education system reproduces and maintains the cultural capital of the dominant host culture. Even though the education system assumes the possession of cultural capital (Bourdieu 1977), such assets vary as a result of social class, creating an unequal playing field that makes 'it difficult for lower class pupils to succeed in the education system' (Sullivan 2002: 145). According to Bourdieu (1986), as the more affluent middle and upper-class groups dominate society with regards to wealth and power, they, through education, are able to impose their own values and behaviours as the normative culture (Apple 2006). The imposition of such cultural hegemony estab-lishes the values and behaviours of the dominant culture as the societal norm and ensures that the 'others' (Paechter 1998) in society are assessed in terms of their conformity to these norms.

The normalisation process in education, whereby actions and behaviours become accepted as normal and taken-for-granted within society, is also a cause for concern for proponents of values education. Foucault (1977) argued that the process of normalisation – the construction of idealised codes of conduct and behaviours whereby various techniques encourage individuals to conform to these norms – became increasingly popular within many establishments, including the education system, in the 19th century. The aim of this process, which uses a minimal amount of force, or what Foucault termed 'disciplinary power', is to create a '[body] that may be subjected, used, transformed and improved' (Foucault 1979: 136). As I assert later in this chapter, researchers are now using such ideas in their critiques of social and emotional learning, as they argue this form of values education aims only to socialise children to transform them to behave in specific ways, by legitimising specific behaviours whilst marginalising others (Craig 2007; Ecclestone and Hayes 2008). Before discussing these views, I will first introduce the concept of social and emotional learning.

Social and emotional learning in schools

As subjects such as numeracy and literacy are intended to enhance mathematical and linguistic intelligence respectively (Gardner 1983), schemes popularly known as 'social and emotional learning' (SEL) aim to develop social, emotional and behavioural skills, and intra and interpersonal intelligence (Gardner 1983). According to Weare (2007), SEL helps people to 'form positive relationships with other people', to 'understand themselves and their own emotions' and to 'respond to the emotions of others in helpful ways' (p. 240). Many US-based SEL programmes concentrate on teaching 'social awareness, empathy and healthy communication' (Ciarrochi and Mayer 2007: 14). In Canada, under what is referred to as 'social responsibility', children receive lessons which aim to promote peaceful problem solving and which encourage greater self-awareness, whilst in Israel it is now compulsory for children to be educated in *Life Skills*. Similar initiatives are also used in countries such as Singapore, Japan, New Zealand and Germany to name a small minority. Amongst the leading countries in identifying the importance of promoting well-being through SEL is Australia. Their *Kids Matter* initiative's primary aim is to 'improve the mental health and well-being of primary school students' (DfHA 2007: 2), and to enhance levels of intra and interpersonal intelligence amongst children by encouraging emotional control and self-awareness. In a review of the SEL schemes mentioned, Cohen and Sandy (2007) argue that teaching children to self-reflect, to be self-aware, to be empathetic, to control impulses, and to handle relationships are essential if such schemes are to be effective. Many authors, including Elias (2000), Gadre (2004) and Kroeger et al. (2007), have highlighted the benefits of SEL in schools, citing improvements in anger management strategies, social skills and ability to resolve conflict amongst children as justification for their claims.

Such findings, however, should be interpreted with caution as opposition is also offered. Research by Maag (1992) and Mistry et al. (2004) demonstrates that the success of such initiatives is far from inevitable as the use of these schemes is varied and complex. Furthermore, others have offered disapproval and highlighted meaningful criticism. The Foucauldian notions of 'normalisation' through 'disciplinary power', discussed earlier, are particularly useful when analysing how such criticism has been formulated, as it has been maintained that SEL is merely a tool of socialisation. Applying Foucault's (1977) concepts to their criticism of SEL, authors such as Craig (2007) and Ecclestone and Hayes (2008) contend that these schemes are a form of values education that endorse specific behaviours, with the aim of socialising children so that they adhere to the values deemed appropriate by the 'dominant culture' (Bottery 2000: 3). Craig (2007), for example, feels that SEL is a psychological intervention which may be harmful, arguing it forces children to conform as it 'outlines the type of person they should become. This is in effect a form of social control/compliance' (p. 11). In response to this process of social control, she claims that 'children will become more rebellious' (Craig 2007: 11), which will lead to an increase in negative behaviours and a decrease in levels of emotional well-being. Ecclestone and Hayes (2008; 2009) echo Craig's (2007) sentiments, and re-affirm that SEL schemes are forms of social engineering which not only coach but coerce children to feel they should experience specific constructions of emotional well-being. I offer support for this stance in the next section of this chapter, where I present some of my own empirical findings gathered during a four-year ESRC-funded study that explored how the UK-based Social and Emotional Aspects of Learning (SEAL) initiative was being interpreted and used in primary schools.

The interpretation and use of SEAL

The SEAL initiative, introduced under New Labour in June 2005, is a curriculum-based resource with the aim of 'developing all children's social, emotional and behavioural skills' (DfES 2005: 6). Whilst numerous evaluations of the scheme have been undertaken (see Hallam et al. 2006; Humphrey et al. 2008; Banerjee 2010), few have acknowledged the claims of authors such as Craig (2007) and Ecclestone and Hayes (2008), who advocate the stance that the initiative is a form of social control. We offered a degree of support for these claims in Wood and Warin (2013) where we illustrated how school staff interpreted and used SEAL in response to their perceptions of pupils' parents, and maintained that where parents were positively appraised, the scheme was used to complement what was perceived to occur in the home; whilst in schools where parents were negatively appraised, SEAL was used to counter their endeavours by highlighting and endorsing alternative values and behaviours. In the remainder of this chapter I focus specifically on the latter of these findings and illustrate how school staff members interpreted and used SEAL as a scheme to promote specific behaviours and values whilst marginalising others.

One common assumption held by staff was that pupils should make eye contact with the individuals with whom they are communicating to be assertive. Many staff members were of the view that those failing to make eye contact with others displayed 'inappropriate social skills' (Samantha – Teaching Assistant) and this belief was particularly prevalent when staff discussed the values and behaviours of 'Asian children' and their 'issue of lowering their gaze' (Bob – Learning Mentor). However, assertiveness, perceivably exemplified by eye contact when speaking with adults, was a value and behaviour appreciated in schools but not necessarily in the home. This culture clash is well represented in the following staff comment:

> *Jane (Teacher):*   You'll find that with Asian children, when they go to the mosque if they look at the Imam, that's disrespectful, he'll say straight away 'lower your eyes, lower your gaze'. . . . Even with parents, if children get told off and you look at your parent that's disrespectful, you're supposed to lower your gaze. . . . It's what they've been taught at home and in the mosque . . . they aren't encouraged to be . . . forthcoming with their ideas.

As this values-based behaviour was uncommon amongst some Asian pupils, staff members within my sample perceived these children to not only display inappropriate behaviours but to also lack assertiveness skills, which, at times, prompted teachers such as Jane to ask: 'why are you not looking at me when I'm talking to you?' Consequently, SEAL was used as a vehicle to advocate eye contact and to teach Asian children this skill. Indeed, others claimed that such behaviours were expected of pupils so that they conform to 'the rules' (Lilian – TA) 'in this country' (Alice – Head Teacher). Further examples of the emphasis and importance placed upon this behaviour is encapsulated in the extracts below:

> *Charlotte (TA):*   An Asian girl can't come into a school like this and put their head down; it's the rules, you've got to behave by them.
>
> *Alice (Head Teacher):*   Those Asian children are going to have to learn that in this country, if you want something, you have to look somebody in the eye, because it's expected.

In response, schools made use of SEAL to advocate eye contact, based on the belief that this behaviour exemplified typical assertiveness and social skills. Elements of 'cultural violence' (Galtung 1990) were a common theme within the comments offered by the staff members, where they often legitimated certain cultural norms and outlawed others. Below is an extract that not only captures such thought but also illustrates how SEAL was interpreted and operationalised as a scheme to 'other' (Paechter 1998) such values and behaviours.

Samantha (TA):   (SEAL) is to help the poorer children or of a lower class, we shouldn't call them that, but of the Asian community . . . (Asian parents) don't teach the children, they don't play games with them like we did. I mean obviously they do but in their own language and in their own way. They just don't do the things that English parents do . . . they don't teach them the manners the same.

By constructing minority ethnic values as belonging to 'they' or those of 'others', school staff members operationalised SEAL as a form of values education to encourage behaviours they felt Asian pupils should display. Hartley's (2003: 6) assertion that SEL schemes are being 'managed for instrumental purposes' as they 'produce' and help to 'construct an identity' for children was evidenced in the views expressed by the participants in my study. Although 'effective SEL explores skills with pupils in order to help them to . . . work in the contexts they encounter', the data gathered illustrates how staff are ignoring such advice by imposing a normative model of 'the one right way to do things' (Weare 2007: 247).

SEL as a form of cultural imperialism

Although family, parents (Bowlby 1969) and peers (Harris 1995) have long been viewed as influential agents of values production and socialisation, schools have consistently been regarded as close rivals in this domain (Sigel 1970; Apple 2004). Indeed recently, under consecutive governments, education is one area where the state has legitimately and persistently intervened in family life, particularly in the early years of education. Although New Labour placed emphasis on state intervention, whilst the Coalition government presented a guise of valuing self-responsibility and individuality, critics maintain that both are examples of a 'neo–liberal agenda' that has 'increased regulation and surveillance of certain kinds of families' (Broadhurst et al. 2007: 454). As many of these Nanny State policies have targeted certain populations, in the main those from minority–ethnic backgrounds, they have been accused of being schemes that re-moralise such communities by moulding the values and behaviours of their individuals (Day-Sclater and Piper 2000; Gillies 2005).

Underpinning this approach is, as Crozier and Davies (2008) argue, 'a form of cultural racism and . . . rejection of what the young people themselves may have to offer' (p. 287). Such a stance illustrates a form of cultural hegemony based on the belief that the host culture is superior in comparison to all others (Said 2003). Norms, values and behaviours, wholly determined by the dominant groups, are deemed to be being promoted via SEL and so, in this way, these initiatives could be viewed as an agent of cultural and ideological hegemony (Apple 1996) that distributes the norms of the dominant culture, creating people with 'appropriate' values and behaviours. Returning to the debate introduced earlier, and in line with research that highlights the reluctance of educational policy makers to embrace cultural pluralism (see Stone 1981; Skinner 1995), the current application of SEL is another example of cultural monism within values education (Gilborn 1995; Skinner and McCollum 2000).

The marginalisation of the values and behaviours regarded by minority ethnic people, by schools, is further evidence of what Apple (2006) terms a 'Westernised attack on cultural pollution' (p. 39). By 'othering' the values of the 'subaltern' (Spivak 1988), some staff members viewed these groups as potential 'pollutants' of the dominant host culture. Staff members also illustrated a 'fear of moral decay and cultural disintegration' (Apple 2006: 17) and felt that SEL could combat such fears, helping to restore the dominant host culture's values. Whilst not explicitly acknowledged by the sample in this study, I contend that schools have interpreted and used SEL to target the practices, norms and values of these subaltern groups to restore 'our' knowledge. This possible application of SEL would, according to Apple (2006), be typical of the West's attack on cultural pollution as, according to him, 'schools and the curricula . . . have become prime areas of attack . . . with the current emphasis on "character education", on patriotism and on restoring "our culture"' (p. 17). As such, it is feasible to allege that SEL schemes are being interpreted by staff as part of the 'revivification of the Western tradition' where the norms, values and behaviours of the Western, middle-class culture are 'not simply taught, but taught as superior to every other . . . culture' (Apple 2006: 39).

Future directions

Calls for schools to recognise the environments in which children live, and for staff to be sensitive to the moral, cultural and social climate in which children grow up (Halsey 1972), are seemingly yet to be heeded. To achieve a more democratic and cooperative approach to schooling, one that recognises 'the point of view of the least advantaged' and not only not 'what is currently authorised' (Connell 1994: 130), I suggest that policy makers, staff, parents and children should work together to tailor education so that the values of the school's constituent communities are embraced. Ultimately there is the requirement of a mutual exchange of knowledge between schools, parents and communities, from a position of openness and willingness to learn, concerning the values, cultural norms and social behaviours regarded within the multiple realities that exist within children's lives. This, I assert, can only be achieved by overcoming what Dale (1996) terms the 'expert and transplant model'. This 'one-way flow of information . . . from "expert" to "novice"' (Warin 2009: 134), or from school to community, illustrates a 'policy blindness to the idea that professional educators can learn from parents' (Wood and Warin 2014: 948). At face value it may appear that there are few opportunities for creating an equal exchange of knowledge between parents and educationalists about children, yet there are numerous examples from practice that typify this principle and which allow the realisation of what Warin (2009) terms 'mutual reach'.

Work on democratic schooling, by Beane and Apple (1999), illustrates that whilst a mutual exchange of knowledge between school and home does not happen by chance, those educational settings who acknowledge and 'reflect difference in age, culture, ethnicity, gender, socio-economic class, aspirations and abilities' (p. 11) are well situated to achieve this. Whalley (2001) offered advice to suggest that such an approach is feasible when describing the regular knowledge exchange meetings between staff and parents within her pre-school setting. Furthermore, a scheme devised by Gonzalez et al. (2005) that encouraged teachers to partake in in-depth interviews with parents as a means of accessing the 'funds of knowledge' of communities allowed staff and schools to learn first-hand about the social behaviours valued within the school's surrounding community. This destabilising of orthodoxy as teacher as expert and parent as novice has also been illustrated in Hughes and Greenhough's (2006) *Home-School Knowledge Exchange Programme*, where strategies such as video viewings and photographic displays of home and school environments were accessed by both parties so that each could learn about the social milieus in which children learn.

There are obvious barriers to the realisation of mutual reach, most notably current educational policy and its narrow emphasis on academic performance that continues to position the educational professional as 'expert', yet what has been described illustrates the potential for a more democratic exchange of knowledge between school and home. Whilst values education has a history of support, values production through SEL is rightly receiving criticism. The reticence of schools to acknowledge the values of the children's communities is producing situations where schools are encouraging behaviours that are discouraged in the home. Such findings highlight the need for improved communication between home and school so that the social behaviours, cultural norms and values apparent within the multiple realities that exist within children's lives are not marginalised.

References

Alexander, R., Armstrong, M., Flutter, J., Hargreaves, L., Harlen, W., Harrison, D., Hartley-Brewer, E., Kershner, R., MacBeath, J., Mayall, B., Northen, S., Pugh, G., Richards, C. and Utting, D. (2009) *Children, their world, their education: final report and recommendations of the Cambridge Primary Review*. London: Routledge.

Allen, G. (2011) *Early intervention: the next steps. An independent report to HM government*. London: Cabinet Office.

Apple, M. W. (1996) *Cultural politics and education*. Buckingham: Open University Press.

Apple, M. W. (2004) *Ideology and the curriculum* (3rd Ed). London: Routledge Falmer.

Apple, M. W. (2006) *Educating the 'right' way: markets, standards, God and inequality* (2nd Ed). London: Routledge.

Ball, S. J. (2006) *Education policy and social class: the selected works of Stephen J. Ball*. London: Routledge.

Ball, S. J. (2008) *The education debate*. Bristol: The Policy Press.

Banerjee, R. (2010) *Social and emotional aspects of learning in schools: contributions to improving attainment, behaviour, and attendance. A report on data from the National Strategies Tracker School Project*. Available from: http://www.nsonline.org.uk/node/486406 (Accessed January 2011).

Beane, J. A. and Apple, M. W. (1999) The case for democratic schools. In M. W. Apple and J. A. Beane (Eds), *Democratic schools: lessons from the chalk face*. Buckingham: Open University Press.

Bottery, M. (2000) Values education. In R. Bailey (Ed), *Teaching values and citizenship across the curriculum*. Derby: Kogan Page.

Bourdieu, P. (1977) Cultural reproduction and social reproduction. In J. Karabel and A. H. Halsey (Eds), *Power and ideology in education*. Oxford: Open University Press.

Bourdieu, P. (1986) The forms of capital. In J. Richardson (Ed.), *Handbook of theory and research for the sociology of education*. New York: Greenwood.

Bourdieu, P. and Passeron, J. C. (1990) *Reproduction in education, society and culture* (2nd Ed). Sage: London.

Bowlby, J. (1969) *Attachment and loss, Vol. 1: attachment*. New York: Basic Books.

Broadhurst, K., Mason, C. and Grover, C. (2007) Sure Start and the 're-authorisation' of Section 47 child protection practices. *Critical Social Policy*, 27 (4), 443–461.

Burman, E. (2009) Beyond 'emotional literacy' in feminist and educational research. *British Educational Research Journal*, 35 (1), 137–155.

Cairns, J. (2000) Morals, ethics and citizenship in contemporary teaching. In R. Gardner, J. Cairns and D. Lawton (Eds), *Education for values: morals, ethics and citizenship in contemporary teaching*. Guildford and Kings Lynn: Kogan Page.

Chang, R. (2001) Value pluralism. In N. J. Smelser and P. B. Baltes (Eds) *International encyclopedia of the social and behavioral sciences*, 16139–45. New York: Elsevier.

Ciarrochi, J. and Mayer, J. D. (2007) *Applying emotional intelligence: a practitioner's guide*. New York: Hove.

Cladis, M. S. (1998) Emile Durkheim and moral education in a pluralistic society. In G. Walford and W. S. F. Pickering (Eds), *Durkheim and modern education*. London: Routledge.

Cohen, J. and Sandy, S. V. (2007) The social emotional and academic education of children: theories, goals, methods and assessments. In R. Baron, R. G. Maree and M. J. Elias (Eds.), Educating people to be emotionally intelligent. Rondebosch: Heinemann Educational Publishers.

Connell, R. W. (1994). Poverty and education. *Harvard Educational Review*, 64 (2), 125–149.

Craig, C. (2007) *The potential dangers of a systematic, explicit approach to teaching social and emotional skills.* Glasgow: Centre for Confidence and Well-Being. Available from: http://www.centreforconfidence. co.uk/docs/SEALsummary.pdf (Accessed July 2008).

Crick Report/QCA (1998) *Education for citizenship and the teaching of democracy in schools*. London: QCA.

Crozier, G. and Davies, J. (2008) 'The trouble is they don't mix': self-segregation or enforced exclusion? *Race, Ethnicity and Education,* 11 (3), 285–301.

Dale, N. (1996) *Working with families of children with special educational needs: partnership and practice.* London: Routledge.

Day-Sclater, S., and Piper, C. (2000) Re-moralising the family? Family policy, family law and youth justice. *Child and Family Law Quarterly*, 12 (2), 135–152.

Department for Education and Skills (2005) *Excellence and enjoyment: social and emotional aspects of learning: guidance*. London: HMSO.

Department for Employment and Education (1998) *Teaching: high status, high standards*. (Circular 4/98) London: DfEE.

Department for Health and Aging (207) *Overview of the initiative: framework, components and implementation details*. Canberra: ACT.

Durkheim, E. (1885) Review of Fouillée, A., *La propriété sociale et la démocratie, Revue Philosophique,* 446–453.

Dworkin, R. (2011) *Justice for hedgehogs*. Cambridge, MA: Harvard University Press.

Ecclestone, K. and Hayes, D. (2008) *The dangerous rise of therapeutic education*. London: Routledge.

Ecclestone, K. and Hayes, D. (2009) Changing the subject: the educational implications of developing emotional well-being. *Oxford Review of Education*, 35 (3), 371–389.

Elias, M. J. (2000) Primary prevention: educational approaches to enhance social and emotional learning. *Journal of School Health*, 70 (5), 186.

Foucault, M. (1991) *Discipline and punish: the birth of the prison*. London: Allen Lane.

Foucault, M. (1979) Governmentality. *Ideology & Consciousness*, 6, 5–21.

Gadre, S. (2004) Effect of school climate on social intelligence. *IFE Psychologia*, 12 (1), 103–111.

Galtung, J. (1990) Cultural violence. *Journal of Peace Research*, 27 (3), 291–305.

Gardner, H. (1983) *Frames of mind: the theory of multiple intelligences*. New York: Basic Books.

Gewirtz, S. (2001) Cloning the Blairs: New Labour's programme for the re-socialisation of working class parents. *Journal of Education Policy*, 16 (4), 365–378.

Gilborn, D. (1995) *Racism in real schools*. Milton Keynes: Open University Press.

Gillies, V. (2005) Meeting parents' needs? Discourses of 'support' and 'inclusion' in family policy. *Critical Social Policy*, 25 (1), 70–90.

Gonzalez, N., Moll, L. and Amanti, C. (2005) *Funds of knowledge: Theorizing practices in households, communities and classrooms*. London and Mahwah, NJ: Lawrence Erlbaum Associates.

Hallam, S., Rhamie, J., and Shaw, J. (2006) *Evaluation of the primary behaviour and attendance pilot: Research Report RR717*. Nottingham: DfES Publications.

Halsey, A. H. (1972) *Educational priority (Vol. 1): EPA problems and policies*. London: HMSO.

Harris, J. R. (1995) Where is the child's environment? A group socialization theory of development. *Psychological Review*, 102, 458–489.

Hartley, D. (2003) The instrumentalisation of the expressive in education. *British Journal of Educational Studies*, 1, 6–19.

Hughes, M. and Greenhough, P. (2006) Boxes, bags and videotape: enhancing home-school communication through knowledge exchange activities. *Educational Review: Special Issue*, 58 (4), 471–487.

Humphrey, N., Kalambouka, A., Bolton, J., Lendrum, A., Wigelsworth, M., Lennie, C. and Farrell, P. (2008) *Primary social and emotional aspects of learning (SEAL): evaluation of small group work*. Nottingham: DfES Publications.

Kroeger, K. A., Schultz, J. R. and Newsom, C. (2007) A comparison of two group-delivered social skills programs for young children with autism. *Journal of Autism & Developmental Disorders*, 37 (5), 808–817.

Maag, J. W. (1992) Integrating consultation into social skills training: implications for practice. *Journal of Educational and Psychological Consultation*, 3, 233–258.

Mistry, M., Burton, N. and Brundett, M. (2004) Managing LSAs: an evaluation of the use of learning support assistants in an urban primary school. *School Leadership and Management*, 24 (2), 125–137.

National Curriculum Council (1993) *Spiritual and Moral Development* (Discussion paper No. 3). London: School Curriculum and Assessment Authority.

Paechter, C. F. (1998) *Educating the other: gender, power and schooling*. London: Routledge Falmer.

Parr, S. (2009) Family intervention projects: a site of social work practice. *British Journal of Social Work*, 39, 1256–1273.

Plaw, A. (2004) Why monist critiques feed value pluralism: Ronald Dworkin's critique of Isaiah Berlin. *Social Theory and Practice*, 30 (1), 105–126.

Robbins, J. (2013) Monism, pluralism, and the structure of value relations: a Dumontian contribution to the contemporary study of value. *Journal of Ethnographic Theory*, 3 (1), 99–115.

Rose. J. (2009) *Independent review of the primary curriculum: final report*. Nottingham: DCSF Publications.

Rousseau, J. J. (1762) *Émile, ou de l'éducation*. Paris: Garnier.

Said, E. (2003) *Orientalism*. London: Penguin Books.

Sigel, R. (1970) *Learning about politics*. New York: Random House.

Skinner, G. D. (1995) *Primary schools with all pupils from Asian backgrounds: research report to the Leverhulme Trust*. Manchester: Centre for Ethnic Studies in Education, University of Manchester.

Skinner, G. D. and McCollum, A. (2000) Values education, citizenship and the challenge of cultural diversity. In R. Bailey (Ed), *Teaching values and citizenship across the curriculum*. Derby: Kogan Page.

Spivak, G. C. (1988) Can the subaltern speak? In C. Nelson and L. Grossberg (Eds) *Marxism and the interpretation of culture*. Urbana, IL: University of Illinois Press.

Stone, M. (1981) *The education of the black child in Britain*. London: Pelican.

Sullivan, A. (2002) Bourdieu and education: how useful is Bourdieu's theory for researchers? *The Netherlands' Journal of Social Sciences*, 38 (2), 144–166.

Warin, J. (2009) Safeguarding children's well-being within educational settings: a critical review of inclusion strategies. In K. Broadhurst, C. Grover and J. Jamieson (Eds), *Critical perspectives of safeguarding children*. Chichester: Wiley-Blackwell.

Weare, K. (2007) Delivering 'Every Child Matters': the central role of social and emotional learning in schools. *Education*, 3–13, 35 (3), 239–248.

Weber, M. (1946) *From Max Weber: essays in sociology*. Translated by H. H. Gerth and C. Wright-Mills. New York: Oxford University Press.

Whalley, M. (2001) *Involving parents in their children's learning*. London: Paul Chapman.

Wilkins, C. (2000) Citizenship education. In R. Bailey (Ed), *Teaching values and citizenship across the curriculum*. Derby: Kogan Page.

Wood. P. and Warin, J. (2014) Social and emotional aspects of learning: complementing, compensating and countering parental practices. *British Educational Research Journal*, 40(6), pp. 937–951.

7 The curriculum

Anyone can teach a dog to whistle

Fiona Shelton

Introduction

You have probably heard this joke before:

> *John:* I taught my dog how to whistle!
> *Kay:* Why isn't he whistling then?
> *John:* I said I'd taught him, I didn't say he'd learned!

I have always thought of this as nothing more than a funny, harmless joke, but if explored more deeply, it has some serious connotations, especially if we think about it in relation to teaching, learning and the curriculum. This is often a starting point for me when thinking about teaching and learning with students. In this joke teaching and learning are quite separate things – in the context of schools they can often be separate too. But for learning to be really effective, teaching and learning have to be intrinsically linked, and the curriculum plays an integral role in this.

In this chapter I will explore teaching, learning and the curriculum from the point at which I entered higher education as an undergraduate student. I have chosen this point in time, 1990, because the national curriculum (introduced into schools in 1989, with implementation continuing into the mid-1990s (Roberts, 2014)) was relatively new; teachers were still learning how to work with its requirements and I was embarking on my degree, to become a primary school teacher. The curriculum, up to that point, was not something with which I had been concerned, and so whilst I might make reference to some historical perspectives in this discussion, my own personal and practical experiences really began at this time. I trained with the national curriculum and have progressed though my career with all its iterations, including working with the Qualifications and Curriculum Authority (QCA) on the Independent Review of the Curriculum, the Rose Review (2008, 2009). I will explore the curriculum to date and consider its content, and ask if it does as Gove (citing Arnold, 1869) proposed: present the best which has been thought and said. I think it is important that attention is given to the freedoms that exist in curriculum design and how teachers can exercise their agency in engaging in curriculum development, particularly as Gove lost his position as the Secretary of State for Education in July 2014.

Johnson (2007) describes how teachers who qualified from 2007 onwards are unlikely to have known a time when the school curriculum was not tightly regulated and centrally imposed. Their own experience, from their schooldays to their first class as a novice professional, would have been in the context of a nationally determined and prescriptive curriculum. So their experience of education and my own experience of education are really quite different. I had a mixture of curriculum experiences, often based on my teachers' own interests, strengths and expertise. Some I remember fondly and others I wish to forget. There was no consistency from school to school, continuity from year to year or documentation imposed from central government. However, there was progression and this was clear in the increasing difficulty and complexity of the conceptual understanding of the material with which we engaged. The curriculum 'diet' was often dependent upon the skills and interest of the teacher. I was delighted to be in a class with a teacher who was a ceramicist; we learned how to glaze and fire pots at 10 years of age. I was less impressed when I was in a class where mathematics was the teacher's area of expertise. But I still had a broad and balanced education, I know the names of the trees, birds and plants common to the United Kingdom and I had a solid understanding of what I would see as some of the fundamental aspects of the subjects we learned.

In my own practice today, I adopt a constructivist approach to teaching and learning. For me, this approach allows for a different interpretation of the curriculum; there is a strong focus on learning and how to ensure concepts and knowledge are understood, their relevance to the world in which we live and how it has been shaped as a result of knowing and understanding. I firmly believe that transmitting knowledge does not lead to understanding, only to the regurgitation of facts and figures, and someone else's thinking. The purpose of education, from my current position, is that education ought to enable individuals to reach their full potential as human beings, both individually and as members of a society. The curriculum, in its widest sense, should allow for children to learn subject-related material but also be able to understand and apply learning in their own context. The national curriculum plays a different role here, as it refers to the statutory requirements in relation to the nature of subjects and the content to be taught and learned. Constructivism as an approach to teaching and learning can be applied to any context if it is properly understood.

From a constructivist perspective (Bruner, 1960; Rogoff and Lave, 1984; Vygotsky, 1978) there is an understanding that children use their own experiences and understanding to construct knowledge so that it makes sense and has meaning; children are the active creators of their own knowledge and the teacher plays an integral role in this process. And that is the key; learning is a process, not a product. Contrary to criticisms by some conservative/traditional educators (such as Glasersfeld, 1979, 1993, 2000), constructivism does not dismiss the active role of the teacher or the value of expert knowledge. According to Rowlands and Carson (2001), constructivism confuses what is being constructed (mental representation) with knowledge itself. There needs to be greater clarity about how constructivism aids teachers when they are helping learners to construct knowledge in such a way that the mental representations and knowledge itself are understood in their own right, so teachers avoid simply reproducing a series of facts that hold no meaning for learners. One of the problems with constructivism is that it can be confused with an approach to learning that is student-led where knowledge itself is not always deemed fundamental in the process (Elkind, 2004).

The further challenge is that without constructivism, knowledge that is learned can lose its meaning and purpose. I can remember learning my times tables at school. I could routinely chant each table, answer the quick-fire question from the teacher: "Fiona, 7 7s?" Me: "49". In reality I knew the answers, the facts, but I did not know what 7×7 meant. I did not understand the concept of multiplication. As a primary school teacher I used practical methods to demonstrate the concept of multiplication so that children could build concrete, physical examples of what 7 7s look like; this would then be transferred to a visual representation until eventually the abstract ideas were understood and embedded and I knew that children understood the concept of multiplication. Of course, some got there more quickly than others, but the key to this learning was not to simply know the answer to 7×7 (the product), but to understand the concept of multiplication and how to arrive at the answer of 7×7 (the process). In mathematics this knowledge would be defined as conceptual knowledge and procedural knowledge; according to Schwartz (2008), conceptual understanding in mathematics, along with procedural skill, is much more powerful than procedural skill alone. In a mathematics class which has a predominantly procedural approach, most of the time is spent practising the procedures so that the student can carry them out faultlessly. In a mathematics class with a conceptual approach, the time is spent helping learners develop insight. Activities and tasks provide learners with experiences that provide opportunities for new understandings. Once they gain understanding, then there is a need for some time to be spent on practice, but less than in the procedurally oriented class. This process of learning means that when conceptual understanding is gained, a person can reconstruct a procedure that may have been forgotten. I have always maintained that if the process is good, the product will inevitably be good too.

Dewey's (1938) philosophy points out that historically a strict authoritarian approach to education overly concerned itself with delivering preordained knowledge, and is therefore not focused enough on the actual learning experiences of students. Dewey sided neither with traditional education nor with progressive education; what he was concerned with was understanding how humans have the experiences they do, and how this understanding is necessary when designing effective education (Moore, 2014). Effective education can be seen as that which strives to provide and maintain academic achievement and progress, allows students sufficient time to learn, practise and demonstrate their mastery and skills of the curriculum, and enables young people to learn and demonstrate ethical and cultural values of long-term benefit to individuals and society as a whole (Barrett et al., 1991). Dewey (1938) was also concerned that experience was not enough, particularly as some experiences are non-educational and may sometimes be a barrier to learning and ineffective in the classroom environment. From the constructivist perspective, these ideas about experience are significant and again highlight the importance of the teacher in planning, teaching and understanding learning experiences.

It is evident now that learning, from a constructivist perspective, is more than knowing facts. For me, this is a problem in the compulsory education system in England, because it seems that young people are tested largely on their ability to restate the facts they have been taught and are less required to consider the implications of the facts learned, or implement them in a meaningful way in an educational context. So there is a tension around learning as process or product. Bruner (1966) makes the case for learning as a knowledge-getting process:

> To instruct someone . . . is not a matter of getting him to commit results to mind. Rather, it is to teach him to participate in the process that makes possible the establishment of knowledge. We teach a subject not to produce little living libraries on that subject, but rather to get a student to think mathematically for himself, to consider matters as an historian does, to take part in the process of knowledge-getting. Knowing is a process not a product.
>
> (Bruner, 1966: 72)

But a curriculum is neither a process nor a product of education. A national curriculum is an imposed set of requirements that children should be taught at each stage of their learning. I say imposed because of the statutory requirements of the national curriculum in England. However, in the current school landscape the national curriculum is not a national curriculum at all, as only local authority-managed schools will be required by law to follow it. It is not an entitlement for all children, as it was first planned. The slimmed-down version concentrates on 'the essential knowledge and skills every child should have' claims Gove, so that teachers 'have the freedom to shape the curriculum to their pupils' needs' (Gove, 2013: online).

This leads to the tricky discussion about what knowledge is, something that philosophers have grappled with for centuries. From a philosophical perspective we can divide knowledge into three types: personal knowledge, which involves coming to know a certain number of propositions *in a particular way*; procedural knowledge, to know how to dance and how to drive, for example; and finally propositional knowledge, the knowledge of facts, knowledge that such and such is the case; in philosophical terms, what we know to be true (Truncellito, 1995). The primary concern of epistemology is propositional knowledge (Truncellito, 1995). This knowledge is the mental grasp of the facts of reality (Landauer and Rowlands, 2001). I contend here that propositional knowledge is not enough to acquire either personal knowledge or procedural knowledge. In education, this is where constructivist approaches recognise that knowing derives from these three different perspectives of knowledge and use all three in building concepts, understanding and facts into the learning process. I endorse that it is from this basis that the foundations of a national curriculum should be built.

In his response to Mary Bousted (General Secretary of the Association of Teachers and Lecturers) in 2013, Gove acknowledged that learning requires both knowledge and skills but that skills cannot be learned in a vacuum. I would argue that just as skills cannot be learned in a vacuum, neither can knowledge. In fact they are intrinsically linked, and as Gove states, the 'knowledge versus skills debate is a false dichotomy' (Gove, 2013: response to ATL). He does, however, go on to say that the new national curriculum sets out the essential knowledge for each subject (Gove, 2013). The problem with essential knowledge is that someone has to decide what that essential knowledge is, and the problem with national curricula is that not all the essential knowledge laid out in statute is necessarily essential knowledge. Alexander (2012) asserts that we should challenge the assumption that it is for 'ministers in a culturally diverse and very plural democracy to determine exactly what knowledge is "essential" and what knowledge is not' (Alexander, 2012: 375). According to Waters (2013), one of the problems with the national curriculum in the UK is that it has become over-complicated. The national curriculum has, over time, had too much added of what children need to learn and therefore we have an uncertain agenda of what children should learn in the twenty-first century (Waters, 2013). The society that children are growing up in is complex and the challenge therefore, according to Waters (2013), is to make children's learning fit for their future. Therefore simply knowing facts and information is not enough; I suggest that the national curriculum needs to promote more opportunities for critical thinking which challenges assumptions and endorses high-level reasoning.

When the new national curriculum (Department for Education, DfE, 2014) is examined in detail, there are examples that can be drawn out and questioned as to whether there is a case for their inclusion; these are explained and discussed in the subsequent discussion. In the English Programme of Study, for example, in Key Stage 1, Year 1: 'Writing – vocabulary, grammar and punctuation' states that:

Pupils should be taught to develop their understanding of the concepts set out in English appendix 2 by . . . leaving spaces between words.

(DfE, National Curriculum, 2014: online)

The curriculum requirements for each aspect of English relate to a series of bullets, of which many refer to the *application* of knowledge as opposed to the learning and development of knowledge. In the English Programme of Study Key Stage 2, Year 3 and 4: 'Writing – vocabulary, grammar and punctuation' it is stated that pupils should be taught to develop their understanding of the concepts set out in English appendix 2, following which is a list referring to extending, using, choosing and so on. I would argue therefore that the statutory elements of the national curriculum in England do not always relate to knowledge in the propositional sense, and do not necessarily introduce pupils 'to the best which has been thought and said' as stated in the aims of the national curriculum (DfE, 2014: 3.1, citing Arnold, 1869).

From a constructivist perspective, to learn, to understand, to really know bestows a freedom of thought, which allows for individuals to express their ideas in an informed and accomplished manner. Anyone can teach a dog to whistle, but it is harder still to know if the dog knew the context in which to whistle and its purpose in different contexts. Or, as Vygotsky (1978: 7) stated:

the animal merely uses external nature, and brings about changes in it simply by his presence; man by his changes makes it serve his ends, masters it.

Learning requires pedagogy where children should be encouraged to think critically to solve problems and understand why what they have learned can have a transformative effect on their outlook on the world. Critical thinking in this context relates to thinking that is self-guided and self-disciplined which attempts to reason at the highest level of quality in a fair-minded way, questioning assumptions and diminishing the power of egocentric and socio-centric tendencies (Paul and Elder, 2008). Many young people who have recently undertaken exams remember little of the subject matter they revised, but can boast high grades in their GCSEs (Anderson, 2000). With this in mind, I concur with Alexander (2010) who states that pupils themselves can and do contribute to a school's curriculum capacity. He suggested that this happens through the knowledge and understanding they bring from outside school to the classroom and the insights that perceptive teachers gain from watching and listening to them at work and play. Effective pedagogy as explained by Alexander (2010) is about unlocking and building upon this prior pupil knowledge.

On reading the current national curriculum for England, it is clear that it stipulates what must be taught, not how to teach it. Yet I believe that this is only partly true. The national curriculum might not tell teachers explicitly how they should teach, but the nature of the curriculum content does, often, imply or promote certain kinds of pedagogy, therefore marginalising others (Moore, 2003). For example, if, as is the case in England, a national curriculum demands a specific list of authors to be studied, along with a high level of specificity as to what aspects of those authors' work must be studied, this might deny teachers their own preferred pedagogies, if they would normally choose their own list of authors for specific pedagogical approaches.

At its inception, the rationale for the national curriculum, developed by the former Department of Education and Science (1989), identified four broad underlying principles and intentions. These were to establish an entitlement to a broad and balanced curriculum; improve school accountability; improve curricular coherence; and aid public understanding of schools. Interestingly, knowledge was not a part of this rationale. This rationale was widely accepted by teachers. Whilst the national curriculum was initially controversial, recent reviews (Alexander, 2010; Rose, 2009) have documented how entitlement and breadth (a wide range of subjects from the ages of 5–16) and balance (knowledge, concepts, skills and attitudes) have been recognised by many as one of the key benefits of having a national curriculum in schools.

The aims of the national curriculum introduced in September 2014 are stated as follows:

> The national curriculum provides pupils with an introduction to the essential knowledge they need to be educated citizens. It introduces pupils to the best that has been thought and said, and helps engender an appreciation of human creativity and achievement.

> The national curriculum is just one element in the education of every child. There is time and space in the school day and in each week, term and year to range beyond the national curriculum specifications. The national curriculum provides an outline of core knowledge around which teachers can develop exciting and stimulating lessons to promote the development of pupils' knowledge, understanding and skills as part of the wider school curriculum.

> (DfE, 2014: 3.1 and 3.2)

I am not convinced that these are aims at all; they are more a rationale and explanation for the curriculum and its use in school.

The national curriculum introduced into schools in September 2014 has been described in the media as archaic, narrow and little more than a list of facts and figures:

> The mountains of detail for English, maths and science leave little space for other learning. Speaking and listening, drama and modern media have almost disappeared from English.

> (Garner, 2013: online)

As is now stated in the national curriculum, the national curriculum is only one part of what children learn; the school curriculum comprises other elements of what is important in children's education, such as the opportunity to play, to make historical visits, to be involved in charity events and community activities. The national curriculum has become so prescribed and overloaded that schools often forget that they have freedoms in their own curriculum design. The existence of a national curriculum should not prevent teaching and learning which extends, enhances and provides something new, something challenging, something exciting, such as trips, speakers, putting on a show, planting seeds and so on. Teachers have the legal right to teach beyond the framework of the national curriculum (Waters, 2013). This is laid out in statute now in the aims of the national curriculum (DfE, 2014: 3.2).

Education, as Bruner (1997) reminds us, is to help learners construct meanings, not simply to manage information. Meaning-making requires an understanding of the ways of one's culture and Bruner emphasises the importance of narrative as an instrument of meaning-making. When I worked at QCA we asked teachers to try out some of the draft materials for the national curriculum as they were being put together. Teachers deviated from their usual timetables to accommodate the tasks. The feedback we received was that the learning that was going on inside those classrooms was deep, engaging and exciting. Children's outcomes were improved and the classroom was a happy place. On further analysis of this, I believe that positive changes noted by these teachers had little to do with the materials and everything to do with the freedom to try out something new and to explore learning in a renewed way.

As a nation we seem to have become obsessed with what is seen as important – gaining high scores in SATs, GCSEs and all the other tests has taken our focus away from the other important things with which education should engage: singing, dancing, painting, playing, acting, growing seeds; the list is endless but these are the things that make us human, these are the things that teach us about our world, our cultures. I am not suggesting that subjects are not important, of course they are, but I do think that we need more balance; we need more knowledge than can be provided by the national curriculum alone. If the government continues to regulate the national curriculum and describe in detail the knowledge that children should acquire and test narrow outcomes, then indeed it is true that anyone can teach that dog to whistle, particularly because education becomes about teaching rather than learning.

We need to reassert the creative design of the school curriculum and exercise the freedoms granted to us so that teacher agency drives the national curriculum, the school curriculum and the classroom curriculum, ensuring that learning is compelling, engaging and meaningful and owned by teachers, schools and children. From a constructivist perspective learning is about more than passing on facts and information; it is about more than transmitting knowledge. Bruner (1996) described the curriculum as an animated conversation 'on a topic that can never be fully defined, although one can set limits upon it' (1996: 115), and so the way we view the curriculum and how we make use of it is key, not the content or structure of the curriculum itself. Learning is an active meaning–making process in which the learning process itself needs to be understood and prioritised. So the shift happens from teaching to learning, and maybe anyone can teach a dog to whistle, but what we should emphasise is the need to think about our own learning and development, as well as that of students, and make constructive connections between the two.

References

Alexander, R. (2012) Neither national nor a curriculum, *Forum*, 54:3, 369–84.

Alexander, R. (ed) (2010) *Children, their world, their education: final report and recommendations of the Cambridge Primary Review*. London: Routledge.

Anderson, J. (2000) *Learning and memory: an integrated approach* (2nd ed.). New York: John Wiley & Sons, Inc.

Arnold, M. (1869) *Culture and anarchy: an essay in political and social criticism*. Oxford: Project Gutenberg.

Barrett, B., Beck, R., Binder, C., Cook, D., Engelmann, S., Greer, R., Kyurklund, S., Johnson, K., Maloney, M., McCorkle, N., Vargas, J. and Watkins, C. (1991) The right to effective education, *The Behavior Analyst*, 1:14, 79–82.

Bruner, J. S. (1960) *The process of education*. Cambridge, MA: Harvard University Press.

Bruner, J. S. (1966) *Toward a theory of instruction*. Cambridge, MA: Belknapp Press.

Bruner, J. S. (1987) Life as narrative, *Social Research*, 54: 11–32.

Bruner, J. S. (1996) *The culture of education*. Cambridge, MA: Harvard University Press.

Bruner, J. S. (1997) Celebrating divergence: Piaget and Vygotsky, *Journal of Human Development*, 40, 63–73.

Department for Education (2013) *The National Curriculum in England: framework for key stages 1 to 4,* available from: https://www.gov.uk/government/publications/national-curriculum-in-england-framework-for-key-stages-1-to-4/the-national-curriculum-in-england-framework-for-key-stages-1-to-4, accessed December 2014.

Department for Education (2014) *The National Curriculum in England: English programmes of study,* available from: https://www.gov.uk/government/publications/national-curriculum-in-england-english-programmes-of-study/national-curriculum-in-england-english-programmes-of-study, accessed September 2014.

Dewey, J. (1938) *Experience and education.* Toronto: Collier-MacMillan Canada.

Elkind, D. (2004) The problem with constructivism, *The Educational Reform,* 68:4, 306–12.

Garner, R. (2013) 'Jingoistic and illegal': what teachers think of Michael Gove's national curriculum reforms, *The Independent,* 3rd June 2013.

Glasersfeld, E. von (1979) Cybernetics, experience, and the concept of self, in M. N. Ozer (ed.), *A cybernetic approach to the assessment of children: toward a more humane use of human beings.* Boulder, CO: Westview Press, 67–113.

Glasersfeld, E. von (1993) Questions and answers about radical constructivism, in K. Tobin (ed.), *The practice of constructivism in science education.* Hillsdale, NJ: Lawrence Erlbaum Associates, 23–38.

Glasersfeld, E. von (2000) Problems of constructivism, in L. P. Steffe and P. W. Thompson (eds.) *Radical constructivism in action: Building on the pioneering work of Ernst von Glasersfeld.* London: Routledge Falmer.

Gove, M (2013) Joint curriculum statement, Letter to Mary Bousted, available from: https://www.atl.org.uk/search/default.asp?searchterms=joint+curriculum+response&searchsub=Go, accessed September 2014.

Johnson, M. (2007) *Subject to change: new thinking on the curriculum.* Eastleigh: Green Tree Press.

Landauer, J. and Rowlands, J. (2001) Epistemology, *The importance of philosophy,* available from: www.importanceofphilosophy.com/Epistemology_Main.html, accessed October 2014.

Moore, A. (2003) *Teaching and learning pedagogy curriculum and culture.* London: Routledge Falmer.

Moore, L. (2014) John Dewey's philosophy of experience and education, *International Centre for Educators' Learning Styles,* available from: http://www.icels-educators-forlearning.ca/index.php?option=com_content&view=article&id=53&Itemid=68, accessed October 2014.

Paul, R. and Elder, L. (2008) *The miniature guide to critical thinking concepts and tools.* Sonoma, CA: Foundation for Critical Thinking Press.

Roberts, N. (2014) *National curriculum review.* London: House of Commons Library.

Rogoff, B. and Lave, J. (Eds) (1984) *Everyday cognition: its development in social context.* Cambridge, MA: Harvard University Press.

Rose, J. (2009) *Independent review of the primary curriculum.* Nottingham: Department for Children, Schools and Families.

Rowlands, S. and Carson, R. (2001) The contradictions in the constructivist discourse, *Philosophy of Mathematics Education Journal* (P. Ernest, Ed.) No. 14.

Schwartz, J. (2008) *Elementary mathematics pedagogical content knowledge: powerful ideas for teachers.* Boston: Pearson.

Truncellito, D. (1995) *Internet encyclopaedia of philosophy,* available from: http://www.iep.utm.edu/epistemo/#H1, accessed October 2014.

Vygotsky, L. (1978) *Mind in society: the development of higher psychological processes.* Cambridge, MA: Harvard University Press.

Waters, M. (2013) *Thinking aloud: on schooling.* Carmarthen: Independent Thinking Press.

8 Monitoring and evaluating learning

Trevor Cotterill

Worthington and Hodgson (2005) argue that academics do not object to being held to account for their performance. What the academics they interviewed did object to was the replacement of traditional self-regulatory forms of professional accountability with a culture of institutionalised distrust. This chapter examines the relationship between learning and assessment, how these are evaluated and how practitioners are held accountable. It begins by discussing how learning and assessment are fundamentally at the heart of this relationship and how these relate to the evaluation of both teaching and learning. The chapter also reflects upon how these principles may alter in the move towards a digital age of teaching and learning.

Monitoring learning and assessment

Trainee teachers are taught that monitoring learning and assessment are linked and that this provides information for both teachers and learners about the validity and reliability of what is being taught. Assessment has been identified as the single most influential factor in student learning with a predominant positivist assumption (Williams, 2014) that it is possible to arrive at a measurement of what is being tested, but which Yorke (2011) refers to as the *measurement fallacy*. Biggs (1996) views assessment as being in constructive alignment with intrinsic value to the learner as well as providing reporting functions for the teacher. This constructivist position is usually referred to as *assessment for learning*, as distinct from the objective *assessment of learning* (Sambell et al., 2013). There are advantages to this method of assessment with its emphasis on outcomes, in that it can be used in accountability measures, such as league tables or the Programme for International Student Assessment (PISA) scores and thus to evaluate education as a *commodity*. Teachers are held accountable for these measures of assessment outcomes, such as exam grades, with success rates being key performance indicators of their practice; this is an assessment of learning model with the emphasis upon summative performance. However, an assessment for learning model could shift its focus to formative assessment and how learners and teachers seek and interpret evidence to decide where the learners are in their learning, where they need to go and how best to get there. Thus accountability for the assessment process could be shared with a move to a more formative assessment of learning performance measures, feeding into large-scale summative assessments by external examinations amongst others.

In an assessment for learning model, a teacher-learner contract is drawn up with an indication of what a learner is expected to know at the end of the course and what the teacher is expected to teach (O'Brien and Brancaleone, 2011). Assessment for learning by outcomes could be said to make education *teacher proof* with an often externally designed curriculum, with the teaching of the content being evaluated by the product of their actions; this accountability measure is often used as an expectation by learners. The 2014 National Curriculum for maintained schools in England reflects the body of essential knowledge all children should learn, in contrast to the wider school curriculum in which individual schools have greater freedom to construct their own programmes of study in subjects outside the national curriculum and develop approaches to learning and study that complement it.

There are, however, numerous disadvantages to an *assessment of learning* approach in education. For example, in the so-called *backwash effect* (Biggs, 1999), the content of what is being assessed influences students to focus only on what will gain them higher grades and what teachers pressurised by performance indicators, such as GCSE *floor results*, could teach to test. Another disadvantage is that it may be better suited to assessing propositional than procedural knowledge (Schön, 1983). Wilson and Bertenthal (2005) describe *learning performances*, whereby vague statements of content standards are turned into something real by specifying what students should be able to do when they have achieved a standard. Learning progressions, on the other hand, tell us where the learning is going, while still recognising that more than one path leads to competence. *Progress variables* combine what is known about learning development with knowledge about how items get more difficult, so we can make the interpretation of assessment results more efficient and useful (Wilson, 2009).

Assessment for learning, on the other hand, views assessment not as summative measurement but as a formative, dialogic process by which the learner constructs knowledge on the basis of evidence from peers and teachers (Biggs and Tang, 2007). Formative assessment practices aligned to this type of assessment include authentic assessment (Torrance, 1995) and mastery learning (Kulik et al., 1990). They also involve learners becoming more active in collaborating and assessing their own practice and often involve evidence contained within portfolios and reflective logs, and are more likely to employ problem solving and enquiry-based learning (Deignan, 2009).

An area of interest for many educationalists is the monitoring and evaluation of learning for learners with special educational needs (SEN), with Meijer (2003) suggesting that what is good for pupils with SEN is also good for all pupils. In recent years, government policy has also promoted the development of assessment for learning approaches within the personalised learning agenda (for example, Pedagogy and Personalisation (DfES, 2007) from the National Strategies). An area of concern relating to this model of assessment and SEN learners could be the notion of the use of feedback loops as a reflective tool, but I believe that although this may not operate in the traditional sense, other communication tools could be developed or adapted for use as a tool for monitoring and evaluating, such as the Picture Communication Exchange System (PECS) (Johnston et al., 2003) commonly used as an augmentative and alternative communication tool for learners on the autistic spectrum. Another tool for assessing SEN learners is that of narrative assessment which moves away from a developmental to a sociocultural perspective. The assessment is premised on the belief that context makes a difference to student learning and assessment results (Cullen et al., 2005) and sees the classroom environment, peers, teachers and parents being integral to the assessment process.

An example of an established model for formative assessment is Recognising and Recording Progress and Achievement (RARPA), a five-stage approach developed to quality-assure provision in the learning and skills sector that focuses on individual learner achievement rather than external accreditation. It is a learner-centred system for recognising and measuring the outcomes of informal learning developed in 2003–04 by the National Learning and Skills Council, NIACE and Learning and Skills Development Agency (LSC, 2005). The process consolidates good teaching and learning practice and is being increasingly adopted as the standard process to be followed for non-accredited learning programmes.

The evaluation process

The Quality Assurance Agency for Higher Education (QAA) (2010: 3) defines quality enhancement as: 'taking deliberate steps to bring about improvement in the effectiveness of the learning experiences of students'. Evaluation involves more than mapping student learning outcomes and collecting evidence of student achievement of those outcomes (French et al., 2014). Increasingly, direct measures of determining student achievements are being used in conjunction with indirect measures such as surveys, exit interviews and employers and other stakeholder queries. An important component of an assurance of learning process is to analyse and use the information gathered for improvement, or closing the loop (Watson, 2003), and should be the raison d'être for assessing student achievement. I assert that it is not sufficient to simply collect data as an audit request, but, for that data to have any validity and authenticity, a quality assurance process should allow reflection on the data which allows improvement in teaching, learning and the curriculum.

Evaluation is complex and problematic. Bamber and Anderson (2012) suggest that there is no easy solution to obtaining good data about learning and teaching. Depending upon the different purposes and uses of evaluation, as well as the different target audience, there is a case for separating out evaluation for assurance and evaluation for enhancement or improvement. Evaluation of learning which is focused on institutional or teacher performativity, such as lesson observation grades, Ofsted inspections or performance tables, may, at best, obtain little more than superficial compliance, or simply be ignored. Evaluation that is rooted in professional practice within the specific discipline may be difficult to quantify, but it is just this type of evaluation which often leads to enhancement. I suggest that teachers walk a narrow path between these two methods of evaluation with respect to their everyday practice. However, evaluation can fulfil a variety of roles in the quality assurance process, including acting as part of the quality assessment process or as a structure for devising quality enhancement plans (Oliver and Conole, 2000).

Evaluation of teaching

I believe that you cannot separate evaluation of learning from the evaluation of teaching, with a key evaluative tool being the use of reflective practice. Both Schön (1991) and Eraut (2000) highlighted the value of developing reflective processes for both organisations and the professionals within them. Most Initial Teacher Education (ITE) courses are now underpinned by concepts of reflective practice (Gibbs and Coffey, 2000; Kahn et al., 2008). According to Carr and Skinner (2009), teachers strive to improve their professional status, and this aspiration has put a focus on the need for teachers to be able to make reflections based on theoretical knowledge and underpinning practice. I agree with Van Manen (1977) and his claim that an absence of theoretical knowledge and interpretative frameworks would leave teachers with a strictly technical application of predefined educational knowledge. However, the practice of teaching is more than just 'hands-on' skills (Hansén et al., 2005). Researchers and advocates of school reform promote critical reflection as an integral part of teacher education (Ward and McCotter, 2004) with the analysis of reflective responses to classroom observation, assignments and professional practice in trainee portfolios providing opportunities for teacher educators to teach reflection on and for action (Etscheidt et al., 2012). However, Etscheidt et al. (2012) argue that consensus about effective strategies for teaching and analysing reflection is lacking. Whilst I acknowledge this, I also believe that teaching is a personal process and that no one teaching strategy or model of reflection would be applicable in every context.

Having said that, whatever model of reflection is used would be beneficial both in terms of pedagogy and professional development. It allows the individual to evaluate their practice and can be useful in a cycle of both quality assurance and quality improvement. Teachers could, for example, employ a cognitive approach to reflection and Rodgers (2002) argues that reflection on and for action is a purposeful activity that is not solely based upon retrospective thought. Trainee teachers could apply Bloom's (1994) taxonomy to evaluation of the planning and delivery of a lesson. Reflection could also be along a continuum, for example Van Manen's (1977) thinking skills, or models related to reflective thinking such as the development from Common Sense Thinkers, through to Alert Novices, and the Pedagogical Thinker (LaBoskey, 1994). Whilst trainee teachers are assessed on their ability to reflect upon their practice and this must be open to objective scrutiny against set criteria, I would suggest that this process becomes more implicit as a teacher develops over time. Much reflection and evaluation of teaching and learning becomes more introspective, but nonetheless thoughtful in what Mezirow (2000) describes as the individual taking charge of their critical reflection and learning from it. Whilst reflection and evaluation of teaching practice is inherent within a teacher training course, I would argue that apart from graded lesson observations, Ofsted inspections or as part of Continuing Professional Development (CPD), evaluation carried out by experienced teachers is often limited to *a car journey thought* on the way home. I do not dismiss the role that evaluation plays in professional development of experienced teachers, but I argue that it is competing for cognitive space alongside curriculum change, behaviour management and other day-to-day activities.

Monitoring and evaluating learning in the digital age

Ideas about knowledge and learning are changing. At the start of the *digital age*, learning in schools appears to be slowly evolving from a focus on what has already been discovered and prescribed as *knowledge* towards a focus on critical thinking skills, knowledge creation and learning through connections (Starkey, 2011). The use of digital technologies within teaching and learning is increasing daily and there have been numerous attempts to evaluate the use of technology. Cassady (2002) summarises ways of evaluating learning in the cognitive domain measured by improved student achievement over his research project and that this type of evaluation differs from one that seeks to evaluate the potential and actual learning in the design of an activity. Cox et al. (2004) concluded that effective learning with technology to enhance opportunities to engage in teaching and learning occurs when a teacher challenges students to think, but I suggest that this may be no different in evaluating other more traditional methods of teaching and learning.

Lowther et al. (2008) gathered student achievement data over two levels of standardised tests and found that the students taking part in the programme which had digital technologies and support performed as well or better than the control students not using these methods in most, but not all, of the tests. In today's classrooms it would be difficult to identify one in which digital technologies are not used. Becta's (2007) review examined how digital technology could be used in collaborative student learning. This included the use of technologies to support learners working together and a model to evaluate the effectiveness of digital technologies. The use of such a collaborative approach to knowledge creation and learning which leads to the co-creation of knowledge through connections is one that is used throughout education. I feel that issues arise when the teacher tries not to assess the end product but rather the contribution made by individuals and the tendency towards *social loafing* (North et al., 2000). The traditional model of the classroom teacher as the *knowledge giver* and the student as the *knowledge receiver* may no longer be a valid one. Even the humanistic role of a facilitator does not account for the fact that students could be connected to a database of knowledge twenty-four hours a day. I believe that the way knowledge is created, monitored, assessed and evaluated by the teacher needs a radical change in how teachers view their role.

Applying traditional measures of monitoring learning to students using digital technologies has been problematic, as often the measures used in these cases were constructed prior to digital technology being available and is emphasised by Loveless (2002) when he argues that evaluating teaching and learning with such measures is unlikely to take account of the way that students learn in a connected world or apply the use of digital technologies to develop their knowledge. Indeed, how knowledge is constructed and transmitted is rapidly changing, with ideas about *knowledge* appearing to be changing from a definition which talks about what is found in the heads of individuals, including teachers, into something that is not fixed and is debatable, accessible through a range of media and created through networks, connections and collaboration (Siemens, 2005). Thus there needs to be a paradigm shift in how knowledge is produced, transmitted and validated which includes collaboration or interaction beyond the classroom and opportunities for students to create and critique knowledge (Starkey, 2011).

Building on this evolving concept of knowledge, Siemens (2005) developed *connectivism* as a learning theory for the digital age. The theory considers how people, organisations and technology can collaboratively construct knowledge. Collaborative learning is based on the view that knowledge is a social construct and an example of this is how universities are using peer review, seminar groups, *flipped classrooms* and other assessment and evaluative tools to support the traditional lecture. With a wireless classroom, students are making notes, watching video clips, reading lecture notes and interacting with both the lecturer and each other. Another example of this is the connectivist massive open online courses *(cMOOCs)*. Siemens (2012) distinguishes between cMOOCs and the MOOCs delivered in world-leading universities as *xMOOCs*, for example Coursera. Bates (2012) argued that the pedagogy in *xMOOCs* is mainly based on behaviourism, not connectivism. Essentially, a *cMOOC* is conceptualised as a huge network of connected people and resources, within which each learner can plot their own course of learning, although according to Armstrong (2012) some authors suggest that these have developed from an economic viewpoint rather than pedagogical process. However the discourse may develop, the personalised learning approach in which anyone can access knowledge at any time and use this to progress their understanding, career path or interest, I would argue, is a paradigm shift in teaching and learning.

Changing the way of monitoring and evaluating learning

Learning using digital technologies has been evaluated by researchers such as Cassady (2002) and Lowther et al. (2008). According to these authors an effective evaluation tool should recognise the range of ways technologies can be used for learning and the importance of critical thinking, creativity (knowledge creation), conceptual understanding and making connections in an information-rich Web 2.0 world.

Existing taxonomies used to monitor and evaluate learning, such as Anderson and Krathwohl (2000), whilst useful and relevant, do not suit the needs of the evaluation tool in the current learning culture surrounding personalised and collaborative learning. The Structure of Observed Learning Outcomes (SOLO) taxonomy provides a simple, reliable and robust model for three levels of understanding – surface, deep and conceptual (Biggs and Collis, 1982), and includes a useful progression for understanding, but it fundamentally focuses on the knowledge within the learner and does not include the learning or knowledge creation that can occur between learners in a connected world such as that described by Siemens (2006). It implies that students are learning what is already known and fails to acknowledge the importance of connections with others in the process of learning. Bloom's (1994) taxonomy, a staple theory for trainee teachers, put knowledge at the lowest level of cognitive processing. A subsequent modification by Anderson and Krathwohl (2000) has 'create' at the highest level in the cognitive domain. The SOLO taxonomy (Biggs and Collis, 1982) has extended abstract at the highest level – noting the link between the learning and other contexts.

In this chapter I have considered the role of assessment, learning and evaluation in education and the relationship between them. Educational practice does not stand still and my thoughts are that in a digital learning world these concepts will become more focused upon the learners as they are exposed to a quasi-marketisation of education. In a knowledge economy, creativity, especially in terms of the creation of knowledge, could be considered as the penultimate learning experience for developing conceptual or procedural understanding. The ultimate goal would be sharing the knowledge that is being created and through this sharing of knowledge critical analysis may occur and the value of the knowledge can be explored. Thus the role of the teacher would radically change from that of the *expert*, or indeed *facilitator* of learning, to a role which involves the individual who validates the co-constructed knowledge created as a shared experience.

References

Anderson, L. W. and Krathwohl, D. R. (2000). *A taxonomy for learning, teaching, and assessing: a revision of Bloom's taxonomy of educational objectives*. New York: Allyn and Bacon.

Armstrong, L. (2012). 'Coursera and MITx: Sustaining or disruptive?' [Web log message 6 August]. Available at: http://www.changinghighereducation.com/2012/08/coursera-.htm (Accessed: 12 December 2014).

Bamber, V. and Anderson, S. (2012). 'Evaluating learning and teaching: institutional needs and individual practices'. *International Journal for Academic Development*, 17 (1), 5–18.

Bates, T. (2012, August 5). What's right and what's wrong about Coursera-style MOOCs? [Web log message 5 August]. Available at: http://www.tonybates.ca/2012/08/05/whats-right-and-whats-wrong-about-coursera-style-moocs/ (Accessed: 12 December 2012).

Becta (2007). *Harnessing technology review 2007: progress and impact of technology in education.* Coventry: Becta.

Biggs, J. (1999). *Teaching for quality learning at university.* Buckingham: SRHE and Open University Press.

Biggs, J. (1996). 'Enhancing teaching through constructive alignment'. *Higher Education*, 32 (3), 347–364.

Biggs, J. and Collis, K. (1982). *Evaluating the quality of learning: the SOLO taxonomy.* New York: Academic Press.

Biggs, J. and Tang C. (2007). *Teaching for quality learning at university: what the student does.* 3rd ed. Buckingham: SRHE and Open University Press.

Bloom, B. S. (1994). 'Reflections on the development and use of the taxonomy'. In Rehage, K. J., Anderson, L. W., and Sosniak, L. A. 'Bloom's taxonomy: a forty-year retrospective'. *Yearbook of the National Society for the Study of Education* (Chicago: National Society for the Study of Education), 93 (2).

Carr, D. and Skinner, D., (2009). 'The cultural roots of professional wisdom: towards a broader view of teacher expertise'. *Educational Philosophy and Theory Special Issue: Philosophy of Teaching*, 41 (2), 141–154.

Cassady, J. C. (2002). 'Learner outcomes in the cognitive domain'. In Johnston, J. and Barker, T. (Eds) *Assessing the impact of technology in teaching and learning* (pp. 9–34). Ann Arbor, MI: Institute for Social Research.

Cox, M., Webb, M., Abbott, C., Blakeley, B., Beauchamp, T. and Rhodes, V. (2004). *ICT and pedagogy: a review of the research literature.* London: Department for Education and Skills.

Cullen, J., Williamson, D. and Lepper, C. (2005). *Exploring narrative assessment to promote empowerment of educators and parents of children with special educational needs.* Paper presented at the Inclusive and Supportive Education Congress, 1–4 August 2005, Glasgow.

Deignan, T. (2009). 'Enquiry-based learning: perspectives on practice'. *Teaching in Higher Education*, 14 (1): 13–28.

Department for Education and Skills (2007). *Pedagogy and personalisation.* Available at: http://www.ttrb3.org.uk/wp-content/uploads/2014/03/Personalisation-and-pedagogy.pdf (Accessed: 4 November 2014).

Eraut, M. (2000). 'Non-formal learning and tacit knowledge in professional work'. *British Journal of Educational Psychology*, 70 (1), 113–136.

Etscheidt, S., Curran, C. M. and Sawyer, C. M. (2012). 'Promoting reflection in teacher preparation programs: a multilevel model'. *Teacher Education and Special Education*, 35 (1), 7–26.

French, E., Kinash, S., Romy Lawson, L., Taylor, T., Herbert, J., Fallshaw, E. and Hall, C. (2014). 'The practice of quality in assuring learning in higher education', *Quality in Higher Education,* 20 (1), 24–43.

Gibbs, G. and Coffey, M. (2000). 'Training to teach in higher education: a research agenda'. *Teacher Development*, 4 (1), 31–44.

Hansén, S. E., Sjöberg, J. and Eklund-Myrskog, G. (2005). 'Must know, good to know, nice to know'. *Kärnstoffsanalys i lärarutbildningar. Nordisk Pedagogik*, 4, 400–412.

Johnston, S., Nelson, C., Evans, J. and Palazolo, K. (2003). 'The use of visual supports in teaching young children with autism spectrum disorder to initiate interactions'. *Augmentative and Alternative Communication*, 19 (2), 86–103. Newark, DE: Pyramid Educational Products, Inc.

Kahn, P., Young, R., Grace, S., Pilkington, R., Rush, L., Tomkinson, B. and Willis, I. (2008). 'Theory and legitimacy in professional education: a practitioner review of reflective processes within programmes for new academic staff'. *International Journal for Academic Development*, 13 (3), 161–173.

Kulik, C. L. C., Kulik, J. and Bangert-Drowns, R. (1990). 'Effectiveness of mastery learning programs: a meta-analysis'. *Review of Educational Research*, 60 (2), 65–299.

LaBoskey, V. (1994). *Development of reflective practice.* New York: Teachers College.

Loveless, A. (2002). *Literature review in creativity, new technologies and learning. Report 4: A report for NESTA Futurelab*. Available at: http://www.nestafuturelab.org/research/reviews/cr01.htm (Accessed: 9 November 20014).

Lowther, D. L., Inan, F. A., Strahl, J. D. and Ross, S. M. (2008). 'Does technology integration work when key barriers are removed?'. *Educational Media International*, 45, 195–213.

LSC (2005). *Recognising and recording progress and achievement in non accredited learning*. Learning and Skills Council, July 2005. Available at: http://niace.rcthosting.com/en/newsdetail.asp?Section=4&Ref=810 (Accessed: 5 July 2005).

Meijer, C. J. W. (2003). *Inclusive education and classroom practices*. Middelfart: European Agency for Development in Special Needs Education.

Mezirow, J. (2000). 'Learning to think like an adult: core concepts of transformation theory'. In Mezirow, J. (Ed.), *Learning as transformation* (pp. 3–34). San Francisco, Jossey-Bass.

North, A. C., Linleya, P. A. and Hargreaves, D. J. (2000) 'Social loafing in a co-operative classroom task'. *Educational Psychology: An International Journal of Experimental Educational Psychology*, 20 (4), 389–392.

O'Brien, S. and Brancaleone, D. (2011). 'Evaluating learning outcomes: in search of lost knowledge'. *Irish Educational Studies*, 30 (1), 5–21.

Oliver, M. and Conole, G. (2000). Assessing and enhancing quality using toolkits. *Journal of Quality Assurance in Education*, 8 (1), 32–37.

Quality Assurance Agency (2011). *Evaluating learning and teaching: institutional needs and individual practices*. Available at: http://eresearch.qmu.ac.uk/2431/1/2431.PDF (Accessed: 11 November 2014).

Rodgers, C. (2002). 'Defining reflection: another look at John Dewey and reflective thinking'. *Teachers College Record*, 104 (4), 842–866.

Sambell, K., McDowell, L. and Montgomery, C. (2013). *Assessment for learning in higher education*. Abingdon: Routledge.

Schön, D. (1983). *The reflective practitioner: how professionals think in action*. New York: Basic Books.

Siemens, G. (2005). *Connectivism: a learning theory for the digital age*. Available at: http://www.itdl.org/Journal/Jan_05/article01.htm (Accessed: 10 December 2014).

Siemens, G. (2006). *Knowing knowledge*. Available at: http://ltc.umanitoba.ca/KnowingKnowledge/index.php/Main_Page (Accessed: 1 April 2010).

Siemens, G. (2012). *MOOCs are really a platform*. Available at: http://www.elearnspace.org/blog/2012/07/25/moocs-are-really-a-platform (Accessed: 9 November 2014).

Starkey, L. (2011). 'Evaluating learning in the 21st century: a digital age learning matrix'. *Technology, Pedagogy and Education*, 20 (1), 19–39.

Torrance, H. (1995). *Evaluating authentic assessment: problems and possibilities in new approaches to assessment*. Buckingham: Open University Press.

Van Manen, M. (1977). 'Linking ways of knowing with ways of being practical'. *Curriculum Inquiry*, 6 (3), 205–228.

Ward, J. and McCotter, S. (2004). 'Reflection as a visible outcome for preservice teachers'. *Teaching and Teacher Education*, 20, 243–257.

Watson, S. (2003). 'Closing the feedback loop: ensuring effective action from student feedback '. *Tertiary Education and Management*, 9 (2), 145–157.

Williams, P. (2014). 'Squaring the circle: a new alternative to alternative assessment'. *Teaching in Higher Education*, 19 (5), 565–577.

Wilson, M. (2009). 'Measuring progressions: assessment structures underlying a learning progression'. *Journal for Research in Science Teaching*, 46 (6), 716–730.

Wilson, M. and Bertenthal, M. (Eds) (2005). *Systems for state science assessment*. Washington, DC: National Academies Press.

Worthington, F. and Hodgson, J. (2005). 'Academic labour and the politics of quality in higher education: a critical evaluation of the conditions of possibility of resistance'. *Critical Quarterly*, 47 (12), 97–110.

Yorke, M. (2011). 'Summative assessment: dealing with the 'measurement fallacy'. *Studies in Higher Education*, 36 (3), 251–273.

Part II
Policy

9   Policy research

In defence of *ad hocery*?

Nic Lightfoot

In this chapter I argue in support of policy research, which acknowledges the complexity and contestability of policy creation and application, or, as some would call it, *implementation*. I defend the idea that the outcomes of policy cannot be simply identified with the implementation of the policy but rather they need to be considered from the perspective of the numerous interventions and interpretations of that policy. Other advocates of this approach include Jenny Ozga and Stephen Ball. As Ozga (1987) suggests:

> practice and the effects of policy cannot be simply read off from texts and are the outcome of conflict and struggle between interest in context.
>
> (Ozga 1987: 21)

Ball (1993), however, departs from Ozga (1987) in the scope and range of any policy investigation. Ball argues that complexity at both macro and micro level, what he describes as ad hocery, informs social action and thus policy, and cannot be ignored 'because they [macro and micro complexities] seem awkward or theoretically challenging' (Ball 1993: 10). He argues therefore for a wider view of the influences of policy and of practice.

Ozga alternatively argues against ad hocery, focusing on:

> [bringing] together structural, macro level analysis of education systems and education policies and micro level investigation, especially that which takes account of people's perception and experience.
>
> (Ozga 1987: 359)

Both authors are opposed to policy research which has a curtailed or confined outlook, the auditing of outcomes or the evaluation of effects; in other words, the notion of a policy science.

My support for this research approach, seeing policy as a process rather than an outcome, arose out of my doctoral studies, which focused on the interpretation and practice of widening participation within a higher education institution (Lightfoot 2007). The research design identified an organisational staff structure for widening participation within a faculty of higher education. I proceeded to interview each of the staff, focusing on their understanding of what was meant by widening participation and how they implemented widening participation policy. The multiplicity of responses and rationales for the approach taken to widening participation and my own naivety in undertaking the research made me begin to explore policy research and form my own view of how it should be undertaken. This chapter focuses on undertaking policy research which acknowledges the multidimensional influences on policy, and is in defence of ad hocery.

What is policy?

To understand what is meant by policy research there is a need to conceptualise what is meant by policy. Ball (1993) has defined policy in two ways: policy as text and policy as discourse; neither, he argues, operate in isolation of the other. Through the application of these definitions, policy cannot be perceived as an object to be implemented, but rather as a process. Policy as text refers to 'policies as representations which are encoded in complex ways' (Ball 1993: 44). He argues for a view of policy as never being completed or fully written, but rather as texts to be read and interpreted by others. Consequently he asserts that policy is subject to compromise and contest and must take account of the changing power relationships within and outside of the institution.

The notion of policy as discourse draws upon the work of Foucault (1974) in recognising how collections of related policies exercise their own power through their production of 'truth' and 'knowledge'. A policy and its makers create regimes of truth within which a policy operates. These regimes lead to a need to understand the wider policy context and systems and how these are informed by and confined by regimes of truth, for example:

> In Foucault's terms we would see policy ensembles that include for example the market, management, appraisal and performativity as 'regimes of truth' through which people govern themselves and others.
>
> (Ball 2005: 49)

The result of these regimes of truth is to confine and distribute voice to those deemed to be legitimate within the regime. Ball would argue those who articulate policy within the dominant regime of truth, for example the market as producer and distributor of educational services, are empowered and privileged.

I argue if policy is conceptualised in this manner it is clear that the activity of policy research needs to look outside of the policy itself to the macro environment, political, economic, cultural and social, in which the policy operates.

Ball (2005) uses the notion of regimes of truth to critique the evolution of policy research and the movement towards a science of policy research. The dominance of neoliberalistic regimes of truth in education, for example the market, performativity and managerialism, he asserts, have led to a particular emphasis on 'effectiveness research':

> policy is both de-politicised and thoroughly technicised; the purview of the policy scientist is limited to and by the agenda of social and political problems defined elsewhere and by solutions already embedded in scientific practice.
>
> (Ball 2005: 56)

Policy research which is undertaken in a neoliberalistic framework, for example an evaluation of the impact of the pupil premium on educational achievement, agrees that outcomes can be measured. In addition it supports the idea that the language of policy emphasises effectiveness and efficiency and, perhaps crucially, that these concepts are agreed and understood. Using this model, certain voices are privileged and others are not, for example researchers and organisations that provide quantitative analysis of the impact of policy tend to be heard, i.e. OECD PISA scores, UNISTATS and KIS data. Arguably, this is also reflected in the nature and distribution of research grants. Whitty (2006), in his presidential speech to BERA, discusses the implication of government's stated aim to have evidence-based policy on the nature of education(al) research. He outlines the pressure for 'what works' research, based on a medical science model:

> Under this commitment, and as the main funder of research and initiatives, the Government has been increasingly explicit about the type of research that it sees as best fulfilling its aims.

> (Whitty 2006: 164)

Funded research of this ilk includes investigations on the impact of class size (e.g. Blatchford et al. 2004) and more controversially that based on academies (e.g. Smithers et al. 2005). Whitty, like Ball, argues for 'blue skies' research where the impact on policy may be considered accidental but no less important.

The conclusion to be drawn here is that policy is given to educational practitioners who implement it. The two acts, of policy creation and implementation, are separate and thus linear in nature. Ball argues that there is a need to be outward looking from the policy, to consider the wider context and other voices. He argues against a linear model of policy creation and practice in terms of the distribution of power, that policy is created elsewhere and given to organisations. He also suggests that there are slippages of ad hocery, which means that policy is influenced and melded by its practice.

My doctoral research exposed a variety of slippages, for example a defining of widening participation students and activities that enabled access to funding but did not interrupt previous understanding of the university student or academic identity within the institution. The institution that the research was undertaken in was a post-1992 university which recruited rather than selected students. Whilst prioritising third-stream income, its major source of funds was, at this time, HEFCE and thus the number of undergraduate students it could recruit. As a result, its engagement with widening participation policy was to access funding, and its activities were created solely to access that funding with the least impact on current practice. There were retrospective claims for funds for activities which had already taken place and the inclusion of international students in definitions of widening participation students. Through the external pressures of funding and status, the latter driving the University to recruit high-calibre students who were willing and able to benefit from higher education and would support the University's attempts to move up the league tables, the policy was refashioned at an institutional level. In addition, academics vying for their own identity and status, through prioritising research and subject knowledge before teaching and learning, interpreted widening participation policy to fit rather than be transformative of what took place in academia:

> the failure of government policy to take into account the culture of higher education has meant that widening participation can be seen as an option and also be addressed using the means of least resistance within that culture.

> (Lightfoot 2007: 168)

The policy cycle

Bowe and Ball (1992) introduced the contexts of policy making, which they argue make up a policy cycle. The argument for the cycle is that policy creation and practice do not occur in isolation of each other, but rather that they operate in contexts which influence and are influenced by them. Thus each area of activity within the cycle is made up of a number of public and private interests, and the power or position of these interests changes within and over time.

The *context of policy influence* area is where public policy originates. Those actors within the legislative sphere are at play here, both those directly associated with party politics and government and those who are deemed to be legitimate lobbyists, who operate within the regime of truth. In this context key concepts are developed which sit within the wider power context, for example markets, accountability and managerialism. The *context of policy influence* has become increasingly centralised. Central government has increasingly become involved in defining the practices of the classroom, originating in the 1988 Education Reform Act; for example, the introduction to the National Curriculum and continuing up to the present day with discussions concerning the nature of appropriate assessment and assessment patterns. Interestingly this is within a regime of truth which privileges the marketplace as the producer and distributor of educational services.

The area of *context of text production* mediates how policy is represented. This representation is not necessarily identical to the policy text but rather made more palatable and possibly ambiguous, highlighting the key messages to be taken from the policy text. It is this context that often creates the first iteration with which educational practitioners engage. The assumption of the *context of text production* is that policy cannot be written in a universal and sustainable manner, able to provide for all circumstances, which occur now and in the future; thus it has a tendency to be represented in a generalised and idealised manner.

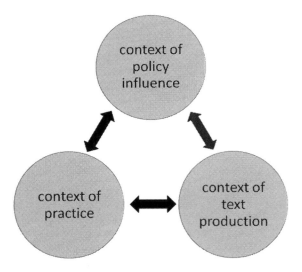

Figure 9.1 Adapted from policy cycle (Bowe and Ball 1992: 19)

Policy is not finished at the legislative moment, it evolves in and through the texts that represent it, texts have to be read in relation to the time and particular site of their production.

(Bowe and Ball 1992: 21)

Ball refers to the need to read policies with and against one another, described as intertextuality (Rizvi and Lingard 2009). Finally, the representation of the meaning of policy is a competitive process in relation to who controls the text production.

The final context is that of *practice*. Policy interventions carry with them consequences for practitioners. The implementors of education policy are not passive or neutral; rather, they come to the policy with their own biographies. Policy is subject to interpretation and recreation as a result of practitioners' experiences and positionality. This denies the policy creator the ability to control the meaning of their text. In this context the text can be edited, interpreted, rejected, reformulated and deliberately manipulated. Again this process is a competitive one with different stakeholders becoming more or less legitimated to speak over time.

The implications for policy research of the policy cycle are an awakening to the complexity of policy formation and practice. Policy cannot be considered as a linear, sanitised activity where the policy creator passes policy to the practitioner to implement and thus judgments can be made in relation to these limited variables. Rather policy is contested at all levels, and to understand policy, a wider lens needs to be used which introduces a range of 'variables' or contexts.

In Ball's (2007, 2008) later work he has updated his theory to include two further contexts, those of globalisation and the private sector. The impact of globalisation on policy is to set the agenda or rules of the game – the use of the OECD's PISA scores as an evaluation of a country's education system appears to have real 'value' for governments. Both the OECD and the World Bank are willing and able to construct both the agenda and frameworks of best practice for education on a global footing. As with the other contexts, the power of different interest groups in influencing policy change over time. International perspectives on education are seen by Ball (2008) to be important in setting the agenda and also the 'market' in which educational provision now takes place. Increasingly education systems cannot be conceived of as being purely national; increasingly they are open, to a greater or lesser extent, to the influence of globalisation. It is perhaps more understandable to insert Westernised views and values where globalisation is writ, as these large global organisations can be seen to be dominated by Western countries, their principles and finance.

The final context is the private sector in education, and it is bound up with the globalised context as many of these large private corporations are multi-nationals, for example Pearson:

In the domain of testing, Pearson is working together with the OECD, having been commissioned to help develop PISA. Pearson's philanthropic arm is also involved in producing materials with the OECD about the lessons that can be learnt from international comparative performance on PISA.

(Lingard and Sellar 2013: 273)

Conclusions

I have argued for a complex and problematic view of policy research, using Ball's work in the main to support my approach. This type of approach is not reductive or simplistic; it endeavours to capture the reality of policy practice at all levels. For example, it would not agree or admit to the effectiveness of widening participation policy being measured or evaluated through participation numbers by socio-economic group; rather, it would explore and discuss the qualitatively different experiences of widening participation students both in conceptualisations of choice and experiences (Reay et al. 2001). In a similar manner this research approach would not naively place the 'fault' for failed or inequitable policy purely at the 'feet' of government policy, but rather look for and at other agents who have co-constructed the interpretation and practice of policy, for example academics in the defining of widening participation.

Criticisms of this approach centre on the failure to construct actions as a result of research, to discuss 'what works'. However, as Whitty (2006) suggests, research that focuses on policy effectiveness and best practice is both constrained and convergent in its thinking. It is also to place the future of education research into the hands of government as the major grant provider.

Rather this type of research, this ad hocery, moves beyond practical solutions, redefining the ability to act as the ability to contest accepted values. It does not prohibit action; this research approach argues for a wider critique of policy and more creative solutions. As Foucault states:

> The real political task in a society such as ours is to criticize the working of institutions which appear to be both neutral and independent; violence which has always exercised itself obscurely through them will be unmasked, so that we can fight fear.
>
> (Foucault 1974: 171)

This chapter has argued in defence of ad hocery, the notion of complexity in policy research, and in support of a more creative and divergent approach to policy research which begins by critiquing the structures and frameworks rather than accepting them as a given.

References

Ball, S.J. (1993) What is policy? Texts, trajectories and toolboxes. *Discourse* 13(2) 10–17.

Ball, S.J. (2005) *Education policy and social class: the selected works of Stephen Ball.* Hoboken, NJ: Taylor & Francis.

Ball, S.J. (2007) *Education PLC: understanding private sector participation in public sector education.* London: Routledge

Ball, S.J. (2008) *The education debate.* Bristol: Policy Press.

Blatchford, P., Bassett, P., Brown, P., Martin, C. and Russell, A. (2004) *The effects of class size on attainment and classroom processes in English primary schools (Years 4 to 6) 2000–2003.* Research Brief, Department for Education and Skills, December.

Bowe, R. and Ball, S.J. (1992) *Reforming education & changing schools. Case studies in policy sociology.* London: Routledge.

Foucault, M. (1974) *The archaeology of knowledge.* London: Tavistock.

Lightfoot, N.J. (2007) *Interpretations and practices of widening participation within an institution of higher education.* EdD, Sheffield Hallam University.

Lingard, B. and Sellar, S. (2013) Globalization, edu-business and network governance: the policy sociology of Stephen J. Ball and rethinking education policy analysis. *London Review of Education* 11(3) 265–280.

Ozga, J. (1987) Studying education policy through the lives of policy makers, in Walker, S. and Barton, L. (eds) *Changing policies. Changing teachers.* Milton Keynes: OUP.

Reay, D., Ball, S.J., David, M. and Davies, J. (2001) Choices of degree or degrees of choice? Social class, race and the higher education choice process. *Sociology* 35(4) 855–874.

Rizvi, F. and Lingard, B. (2009) *Globalizing education policy.* London and New York: Routledge.

Smithers, R., Curtis, P. and Taylor, M. (2005) Academies claim boosts for GCSEs, *Guardian*, 26 August.

Whitty, G. (2006) Educational(al) research and education policy making: is conflict inevitable? *British Educational Research Journal* 32(2) 159–176.

10 Education and social class

Examining the fuzziness of choice and belonging

Tina Byrom

Introduction

Successive governments have placed an emphasis on education as being a route out of poverty (Blyth 2001; DfES 2003), conducive to economic growth and instrumental in processes of social mobility (HM Government 2012). Whilst such ideas pave the way for the construction of an equitable education system, a significant body of research identifies a problematic relationship with education for individuals from disadvantaged backgrounds (for example, Rose 1989; Holloway 1997; Parr 1997; Reynolds 2001; Skeggs 1997; Reay 2001). In relation to higher education participation, the term 'disadvantaged' has become synonymous with young people identified as, for example, 'first in the family', 'non-traditional', 'first generation' and 'widening participation students'. Identifying young people in this way immediately places them as 'other' and raises questions in relation to their social class positioning. In addition, such descriptors frame their higher education experiences as different from those who are perceived to naturally 'fit' into the system. In understanding the complexities of this relationship, this chapter builds from an ESRC-funded doctoral study, in which 16 students from disadvantaged backgrounds participated in an intervention programme that sought to increase participation of such students in HE.

Problems with class categorisation

Categorisation of individuals into a social class group is inherently problematic, with various explanations of what constitutes social class position. For example, most government policy initiatives are based upon data produced by the Office for National Statistics (ONS), which categorises individuals based on employment: occupation type and employment status. From 2001, the newly introduced National Statistics Socio-economic Classification (NS-SEC) intended to cover the entire adult population as illustrated in Table 10.1 (previous schemes did not include the unemployed or those who had never worked).

The participation of disadvantaged groups in higher education is instrumental in supporting movement from one class position to another or, in other words, critical to social mobility. Approaches that focus on income as a classification measure ignore the social and cultural differences that can exist both between and within social class groups and the concomitant class divisions (Savage 2000; Savage et al. 2013). There is therefore an inherent difficulty associated with classification systems – social groups are not wholly homogenous in nature and yet classification by its very nature seeks to homogenise (Sørensen 2000) and predict or explain patterns of behaviour according to such classifications.

Table 10.1 Socio-economic classification analytic classes

The National Statistics Socio-economic Classification analytic classes	
1	Higher managerial and professional occupations
	1.1 Large employers and higher managerial occupations
	1.2 Higher professional occupations
2	Lower managerial and professional occupations
3	Intermediate occupations
4	Small employers and own account workers
5	Lower supervisory and technical occupations
6	Semi-routine occupations
7	Routine occupations
8	Never worked and long-term unemployed

Alternative ideas on class categorisation posit class fractions as a possible way to understand differences within social class groups (Ball and Vincent 2005; Bourdieu 1986). Bourdieu approaches this idea through the use of correspondence analysis in which he draws parallels between occupational status, access to the various forms of capitals (economic, social and cultural) and consumption patterns (Bourdieu 1986). Importantly, for Bourdieu,

> the dominant class constitutes a relatively autonomous space whose structure is defined by the distribution of economic and cultural capital among its members, each class fraction being characterized by a certain configuration of this distribution to which there corresponds a certain life-style, through the mediation of the habitus.
>
> (Bourdieu 1986: 260)

For Bourdieu, habitus is key to understanding social positions and positioning: it serves as an explanatory tool for class-based action and/or inaction. In particular, Bourdieu reflects on the predictability of habitus and its disposition to 'protect itself from crises and critical challenges by providing itself with a milieu to which it is as pre-adapted as possible' (Bourdieu 1990a: 61). This paves the way to a deterministic interpretation of habitus, particularly as

> [e]arly experiences have particular weight because the *habitus* tends to secure its own consistency and its defence against change through the selection it makes within new information by rejecting information capable of calling into question its accumulated information, if exposed to it accidentally or by force, and especially by avoiding exposure to such information.
>
> (Bourdieu 1990a: 60–61)

According to this explanation of habitus, where movement between differing class position does occur, a dissonance between the individual and the new contexts within which they find themselves is possible. In relation to working class students' higher education participation, such dissonance is illustrated in a significant body of literature which describes the experienced lack of fit: both social and academic depending on the institution attended and the theoretical distance travelled (see, for example, McGivney

1990; Reay 1997; Lawler 1999; Archer and Hutchings 2000; Wentworth and Peterson 2001; Bowl 2003; Walkerdine et al. 2003; McNicol 2004).

There is a sense in the argument of 'fit' that some students belong in HE and others do not – that the class-based habituses of some young people are pre-destined to feel comfortable in educational settings. As dominant members of society, or being 'born into a position that is distinguished positively' (Bourdieu 1990: 11), a high percentage of students who go to Oxford University, for example, are 'immediately adjusted to the immanent demands of the game' (Bourdieu 1990: 11). They do not need to transform themselves as they already hold the appropriate levels of cultural capital to establish an immediate fit. They merely need to

> be what they are in order to be what they have to be, that is, naturally distinguished from those who are obliged to strive for distinction.
>
> (Bourdieu 1990: 11)

Students who 'strive for distinction' are invariably categorised as working class – or in HE participation terms, 'first in the family', 'non-traditional', 'first generation' or 'widening participation students'. Such 'othering' establishes difference based on a perception that education is for some young people and not for others, resulting in what Bourdieu and Passeron (1977) refer to as a natural process of elimination.

The process of elimination and the ability of young people to get involved in the 'game' of education are dependent on class background. Social class background equips young people to know how to act in what Ball calls 'defining moments' (Ball 2003), with one such defining moment being university choice. Although progression through the field of education is relatively unproblematic for middle-class young people, deciding to pursue HE is an unfamiliar experience for many working-class young people. To reach the point at which progressing onto university is an inevitable outcome, working-class young people have to adapt to the rules of the education game and become conversant with its particular doxa. In a Bourdieuian analysis, such an outcome requires habitus transformation or the acceptance that people from the same class background may have 'more than one identifiable habitus' (Nash 1999: 178).

Whilst the clash between the habitus of working-class individuals and education is homogenised in much of the literature (see, for example, Bourdieu 1990; Lawler 1999; Archer 2003), the perspective that there is more than one identifiable habitus within a class connects more closely with individual action than it does with general collective practice. Nash's notion of a *general* habitus, with its close links to statistical modes of reproduction, infers that working-class academic success is a matter of chance (Nash 1999). The notion of a *specific* habitus in transforming the discordant relationship into a harmonious one is important in understanding the HE participation of identified disadvantaged groups. The 'specific' habitus, although loosely based on class connections, facilitates understanding of class relationships with education that do not appear to correlate with traditional understandings of the term.

Despite the limitations of class categorisation and the deterministic emphasis connected with habitus, there are two possible explanations that enable successful class transition to be examined and explained. First, Bourdieu refers to habitus as being an 'embodied history' (Bourdieu 1990a: 56) which is 'variable from place to place and time to time' (Bourdieu 1990b: 9), highlighting the possible influence complex interactions between an individual and the various contexts they inhabit may have on their social positioning. Second, Bourdieu suggests the notion of a *habitus clivé* (Bourdieu 2004: 130, cited in Reed-Danahay 2005: 3); a split habitus which provides a possible explanation for those who, through participation in education, do successfully move between social groups.

However, given the attention paid to the emotional difficulties attached to this process within a wide body of literature, the students' perspectives presented here are illustrative of the ways in which their decisions about higher education were framed within particular institutional habituses.

The importance of the university of . . .

The long-standing problem connecting working-class students with academic failure is evidenced in government statistics and much academic literature (DfE 2014; Power et al. 2003; Savage 2000; Wedge and Prosser 1973). From a Bourdieuian perspective, there is a clear relationship between levels of cultural capital and academic attainment where 'differences of aptitude' are 'inseparable from social differences according to inherited [cultural] capital' (Bourdieu 1998: 20). Effectively this results in differentiated educational experiences across differing social class groups. Middle-class children have their 'inherited capital' validated through the structures of schooling due to their close alignment with the values and principles evident in education. Education can therefore be understood as a site primarily concerned with social reproduction.

Mechanisms through which working-class children deviate from this primary function involve dynamic and complex interactions within the field where their successful participation in the game results in 'the feeling of *being torn* that comes from experiencing success as failure or, better still, as transgression' (Bourdieu 1999: 510). It is evident from the students' narratives that much emotional work went into their respective school choices, particularly for those who ended up in a school that was far removed from the context within which their home location was situated (as established through the Indices of Multiple Deprivation (IMD) associated with the postcode for each location).

Sayda had travelled the furthest given that 'spatial distances on paper are equivalent to social distances' (Bourdieu 1998: 6) with her home IMD score being significantly lower than that of the school her parents sent her to. Reay et al. (2005) argue that institutional habitus is key in framing students' educational experiences. This was evident in Sayda's story as she recounted the ways in which her school appeared to be structuring her higher education choices. Sayda states:

> *I know I should apply for a good university – everyone says that I should, including my teachers. I really really want to do nursing but my dad and my friends tell me I'm better than that. But universities like Manchester and Nottingham offer nursing and they're good universities aren't they?*
>
> *(Sayda: Interview)*

Not only is Sayda confirming her limited knowledge of the field in questioning whether Nottingham and Manchester Universities are 'good', she is also illuminating the conflict evident with her family as a result of her chosen career aspiration. On further exploration, Sayda explained that she had obtained a place in the school through parental appeal. She further explained that her father in particular had been impressed with the high numbers of students from the school who had gone on to universities placed high in league tables. In this context and given the level of emotional investment in her education, her father considered her career choice as 'beneath her'. Sayda found herself in the middle of competing habituses – as reflected in the differing views her parents had on her decision:

> *My dad, who I don't live with, and my friend can't understand why I want to become a nurse; all of them are saying that I am better than that, that I could do better. My dad wishes that I would think about medical school. My mum, though supportive of my choice of career, really would like me to find another way of entering it – a way other than uni.*
>
> *(Sayda: Interview)*

Sayda was not the only student to be pre-occupied with the perceived status of universities. Sally, for example, was reliant on those around her when considering whether her choices were valid:

> *One girl said that she was applying to Durham and I looked around and saw that everyone was nodding . . . I think someone said something like 'that's good, isn't that a really good university?' and everyone agreeing that it was. It made me remember what my teacher had said about the 'university of . . .' stuff and it was then that I knew, I just knew that I should apply to universities with good reputations . . . I would have felt stupid applying to newer universities.*
>
> *(Sally: Interview)*

Sally's ideas about what constitutes a good university are revealing. For her, it matters which university she goes to as it has implications for what she believes about herself – if she went to a post-1992 institution, she would have felt 'stupid'. The perceived HE hierarchy was also emphasised by her 6th form tutor who told her that she should only consider universities that began with 'The University of . . .'.

This acceptance of an HE hierarchy was reflected across the sample. Ollie also became caught up in the doxa (Bourdieu 1977) presented through school, which led him to describe post-1992 institutions as 'little crummy universities' (Ollie: Focus Group). Although all the other students in the focus group held as part of the research had laughed at this, they all agreed that the information they had been given emphasised traditional universities during sessions on application processes.

The idea of a perceived hierarchy in higher education has been critiqued and explicated in a wide body of research (for example, Shattock 1996; Archer 2003; Power et al. 2003). Published league tables and more recently the inclusion of Key Performance Indicators (KPIs) are indicative of an education marketplace in which students are expected to make decisions about their future education trajectories.

The reputations of post-1992 institutions have improved since their formation although they have failed to acquire the same perceived status as traditional universities (Archer 2003; Leathwood 2006; McNay 2006): a message that seemed to be re-enforced through the students' schools. Particular HE institutions were 'favoured' in some schools and 6th form colleges as illustrated in the above student quotes. Young people become caught up in a 'school system [that] is most successful in imposing recognition of the value of itself and its classifications', particularly 'when its action is applied to social classes or class fractions who are unable to counterpose to it any rival principle of hierarchy'

(Bourdieu and Passeron 1977: 147). This is particularly the case where the habitus of the individual is incongruent with the habitus of the institution – without access to 'hot knowledge' (Ball and Vincent 1998), working-class individuals are not only unable to counterpose any 'rival principle of hierarchy' but are also unfamiliar with the inherent logic that is being presented to them.

The logic of education

Bourdieu and Passeron (1977) claim that education has a particular logic: one that seeks to secure middle-class advantages. This view appears to be supported by data that illuminates academic attainment (see DfE 2014) and higher education participation (HESA 2014) by social class. This inherent logic is further emphasised by Ball who states

> in developed societies around the world, education policies are primarily aimed at satisfying the concerns and interests of the middle class.
>
> (Ball 2003: 25)

There is a significant body of literature to support Ball's view and it is evident that within this 'logic', working-class identities become eroded as students from such class-based backgrounds seek to acquire a 'practical sense' for 'adjustment to the demands of the field' (Bourdieu 1990a: 66). They must embrace the values inherent within the field to occupy their space with any degree of certainty. Being able to choose a university is an act of consumption, but in the game of education, it is important to choose the right institution as exemplified above.

University choice is a complex process in which there is much at stake. Going to university involves much more of an emotional and psychological shift for working-class students. Although students are perceived as active consumers within a higher education market (Naidoo and Jamieson 2005), the process of choice is not equal across social groups. In effect, 'classed capitals and dispositions engage with classed policy regimes' (Ball 2003: 4) with inequitable results. Post-1992 universities, for example, attract students with lower A Level grades than traditional universities. They have, as a consequence, become associated with working-class individuals and therefore contribute to perceptions that consider traditional universities as the 'preserve of the elite' (Bowl 2003: 145). Whilst working-class students report a lack of academic fit within such institutions, a lack of social fit has also been identified (Wilcox et al. 2005). Students establish a sense of 'otherness' in which they determine their own position in social space in relation to others (Bourdieu 1998). The social *space* or distance between individuals represents, in Bourdieuian terms, levels of capital (Bourdieu 1998) and along with habitus are the fundamental tools for existing and participating in the 'game'.

Students involved in this study illustrated the extent to which they had been structured into specific higher education students through particular discourses presented to them by their teachers. Going against the 'logic' within the field, they recounted their first term at university and how they had felt at home in their new environments. This feeling affirmed the preparation they had received through school had been successful: they had been ready for the move. However, they found it difficult to deconstruct and make meaning out of their sense of comfort in their new environment. When asked to explain how they experienced a sense of being at home, they commented on the way in which they had settled, how they were coping with academic life, and importantly how they had felt dislocated from their previous homes. This was particularly the case for Zara who had felt out of place when she had visited home – it seemed familiar, but she did not feel that she belonged there. Theoretically this shift can be explained as part of the development of a secondary habitus – one which was being inculcated into middle-class values and dispositions evident within the elite institution Zara attended.

The ability to choose high-status institutions reflects much more than previous educational experiences: it is indicative of wider social and structural inequalities and class-based practices. The act of consumption, closely linked to a strategy of distinction, has a particular logic that is class-related (Bourdieu 1986). Determined by the habitus, university choice 'brings about a unique integration, dominated by the earliest experiences, of the experiences statistically common to members of the same class' (Bourdieu 1990a: 60).

Bourdieu recognises that in practising distinction, a 'social hierarchy of the consumers' is produced which 'predisposes tastes to function as markers of "class"' (Bourdieu 1986: 1). The practice of consumption brings with it a code to be deciphered. Anyone who 'lacks the specific code feels lost in a chaos of sounds and rhythms, colours and lines, without rhyme or reason' (Bourdieu 1986: 2). In relation to the middle class, working classes are 'discursively constituted as an unknowing, uncritical, tasteless mass from which the middle classes draw their distinctions' (Reay 2001: 335). There is no place for working-class consumption patterns to be considered legitimate. Instead, consumption patterns of the dominant classes are normalised and as such legitimated through their capacity to secure dominant positions in the field.

Sophie was the only student to comment explicitly on social differences – she had befriended a student who was extremely wealthy which had served as a reminder of her own limited resources and possibly a background which could not be exposed in this context. Walkerdine (2003) refers to feelings of discomfort during the process of social mobility and it could be that Sophie

> was very caught up with an understanding of the issue of upward mobility and the terrifying invitation to belong in a new place, which was simultaneously an invitation to feel shame about what one had before.
>
> (Walkerdine 2003: 238)

The manifestation of social difference was experienced through economic capital. Sophie stated that she had been shocked by how much money was at the disposal of some students and their capacity to spend large amounts of money. It seemed to expose the very real distance between her social background and what she perceived to be theirs. Sophie was straddling two social worlds and did not feel entirely comfortable in either. This gets to the heart of what Bourdieu describes when he talks of success as 'transgression' (Bourdieu 1999: 510) and is indicative of habitus transformation where context influences the malleability of the primary habitus.

University choice therefore becomes much more than a place of study – participation for working-class students represents a space within which individual identities come under scrutiny.

Ball et al. (2002) believe that 'university choice is a choice of lifestyle and a matter of taste' (53) with middle-class students being discerning choosers. However, with the massification of UK higher education, and the increase in the number of universities and courses, the once completely elitist system is in danger of losing its previously held status – a point emphasised by Bourdieu:

> It follows from what has been said that a simple upward displacement of the structure of the class distribution of an asset or practice (i.e., a virtually identical increase in the proportion of possessors in each class) has the effect of diminishing its rarity and distinctive value and threatening the distinction of the older possessors.
>
> (Bourdieu 1986: 229)

Working-class success goes against regularities within the field or the logic that acts as a social filter to maintain the field's structure and structuring possibilities. However, not all working-class young people take up their rightful position within the field. A small minority do succeed within education and apply to elite institutions. However, such movement cannot be without its costs – educational success 'is not about the valorization of working classness but its erasure' (Reay 2001: 334). That is, within the field of education, success is dependent on close alignment to its embedded practices, values and principles where the development of a secondary habitus is essential for working-class young people to no longer feel like 'fish out of water' (Reay et al. 2009: 1106) within an inherently inequitable system.

Conclusion

Class categorization based on occupation is inadequate in illuminating the subtle nuances associated with class practices. Whilst education has been identified as bringing positive outcomes for those who are closely aligned to its cultures and practices, there is consistent evidence that illustrates the limited choices and opportunities for those whose primary habitus does not closely align. Bourdieu offers a theoretical lens through which the reproduction of inequality in education can be examined. Whilst the field of education becomes increasingly more complex, the history of education as being about social class (Ball 2013) is not without foundation. However, it is important to consider the ways in which institutional habituses can be mobilised to support the educational progression of students from disadvantaged backgrounds and as such support processes of social mobility.

References

Archer, L. (2003). The 'value' of higher education. *Higher education and social class: issues of exclusion and inclusion.* London: RoutledgeFalmer, 119–136.

Archer, L. and Hutchings, M. (2000). 'Bettering yourself?' Discourses of risk, cost and benefit in ethnically diverse, young working-class, non-participants' constructions of higher education. *British Journal of the Sociology of Education* 21(4): 555–574.

Ball, S. (2003). *Class strategies and the education market: the middle classes and social advantage.* London: RoutledgeFalmer.

Ball, S. (2013). *Education, justice and democracy: the struggle over ignorance and opportunity.* London: The Centre for Labour and Social Studies.

Ball, S., Davies, J., David, M., Reay, D. and Davies, J. (2002). 'Classification' and 'judgement': social class and the 'cognitive structures' of choice of higher education. *British Journal of the Sociology of Education* 23(1): 51–72.

Ball, S. and Vincent, C. (1998). 'I heard it on the grapevine': 'hot' knowledge and school choice. *British Journal of Sociology of Education* 19(3): 377–400.

Ball, S. and Vincent, C. (2005). The 'childcare champion'? New Labour, social justice and the childcare market. *British Educational Research Journal* 31(5): 557–570.

Blyth, E. (2001). The impact of the first term of the new labour government on social work in Britain: the interface between education policy and social work. *British Journal of Social Work* 31(3): 563–577.

Bourdieu, P. (1977). *Outline of a theory of practice*. Cambridge: Cambridge University Press.

Bourdieu, P. (1986). *Distinction: a social critique of the judgement of taste*. London: Routledge and Kegan Paul.

Bourdieu, P. (1990). *The logic of practice*. Cambridge: Polity Press.

Bourdieu, P. (1998). *Practical reason*. Cambridge: Polity Press.

Bourdieu, P. (1999). The contradictions of inheritance. *The weight of the world: social suffering in contemporary society*. P. Bourdieu, A. Accardo, G. Balazs et al. Cambridge: Polity Press, 507–513.

Bourdieu, P. and Passeron, J. (1977). *Reproduction in education, society and culture*. London: Sage.

Bowl, M. (2003). *Non-traditional entrants to higher education: 'They talk about people like me'*. Stoke on Trent: Trentham Books.

DfE (2011). *Youth cohort study and longitudinal study of young people in England: the activities and experiences of 19 year olds: England 2010*. Sheffield: DfE.

DfE (2014). *Measuring disadvantaged pupils' attainment gaps over time*. London: DfE.

DfES (2003). *The future of higher education*. London: The Stationery Office.

Higher Education Statistics Agency (2014). *UKPIs: widening participation of under-represented groups (tables T1, T2)*. Cheltenham: HESA.

HM Government (2012). *Social Justice: transforming lives*. London: The Stationery Office.

Holloway, G. (1997). Finding a voice: on becoming a working-class feminist academic. *Class Matters: 'Working-Class' Women's Perspectives on Social Class*. P. Mahony and C. Zmroczek. London: Taylor and Francis.

Lawler, S. (1999). 'Getting out and getting away': women's narratives of class mobility. *Feminist Review* 63: 3–24.

Leathwood, C. (2006). Accessing higher education: policy, practice and equity in widening participation in England. *Beyond mass higher education: building on experience*. I. McNay. Maidenhead: The Society for Research into Higher Education and Open University Press.

McGivney, V. (1990). *Education's for other people: access to education for non-participant adults*. Leicester: National Institute of Adult Continuing Education.

McNay, I. (2006). Delivering mass higher education – the reality of policy in practice. *Beyond mass higher education: building on experience*. I. McNay. Maidenhead: Open University Press.

McNicol, S. (2004). Access to higher education among lower socio-economic groups: a historical perspective. *Journal of Access Policy and Practice* 1(2): 162–170.

Naidoo, R. and Jamieson, I. (2005). Empowering participants or corroding learning? Towards a research agenda on the impact of student consumerism in higher education. *Journal of Education Policy* 20(3): 267–281.

Nash, R. (1999). Bourdieu, 'habitus', and educational research: is it all worth the candle? *British Journal of Sociology of Education* 20(2): 175–187.

Parr, J. (1997). Women, education and class: the relationship between class background and research. *Class matters: 'working-class' women's perspectives on social class*. P. Mahony and C. Zmroczek. London: Taylor and Francis.

Power, S., Edwards, T. and Wigfall, V. (2003). *Education and the middle class*. Buckingham: Open University Press.

Reay, D. (1997). The double-bind of the 'working-class' feminist academic: the success of failure or the failure of success? *Class matters: 'working-class' women's perspectives on social Class*. P. Mahony and C. Zmroczek. London: Taylor and Francis.

Reay, D. (2001). Finding or losing yourself? Working-class relationships to education. *Journal of Education Policy* 16(4): 333–346.

Reay, D., Crozier, G. and Clayton, J. (2009). 'Fitting in' or 'standing out': working-class students in UK higher education. *British Educational Research Journal* 32(1): 1–18.

Reay, D., David, M. E. and Ball, S. J. (2005). *Degrees of choice: social class, race and gender in higher education.* Stoke on Trent: Trentham Books.

Reed-Danahay, D. (2005). *Locating Bourdieu.* Bloomington, IN: Indiana University Press.

Reynolds, A. J., Temple, J. A., Roberson, D. L. and Mann, E. A. (2001). Long-term effects of an early childhood intervention on educational achievement and juvenile arrest: a 15-year follow-up of low-income children in public schools. *Journal of the American Medical Association* 285(18): 2339–2346.

Rose, M. (1989). *Lives on the boundary: a moving account of the struggles and achievements of America's educational underclass.* New York: Penguin Books.

Savage, M. (2000). *Class analysis and social transformation.* Buckingham: Open University Press.

Savage, M., Devine, F., Cunningham, N., Taylor, M., Li, Y., Hjellbrekke, J., Le Roux, B., Friedman, S., and Miles, A. (2013). A new model of social class? Findings from the BBC's Great British Class Survey Experiment. *Sociology* 47(2): 219–250.

Shattock, M. (1996). The creation of the British university system. *The creation of a university system.* M. Shattock. Oxford: Blackwell, 1–27.

Skeggs, B. (1997). Classifying practices: representations, capitals and recognitions. *Class matters: 'working-class' women's perspectives on social class.* P. Mahony and C. Zmroczek. London: Taylor and Francis.

Sørensen, A. (2000). Employment relations and class structure. *Renewing class analysis.* R. Crompton, F. Devine, M. Savage and J. Scott. Oxford: Blackwell.

Walkerdine, V. (2003). Reclassifying upward mobility: femininity and the neo-liberal subject. *Gender and Education* 15(3): 237–248.

Walkerdine, V., Melody, J. and Lucey, H. (2003). Uneasy hybrids: psychosocial aspects of becoming educationally successful for working-class young women. *Gender and Education* 15(3): 285–299.

Wedge, P. and Prosser, H. (1973). *Born to fail?* London: Arrow Books.

Wentworth, P. and Peterson, B. (2001). Crossing the line: case studies of identity development in first-generation college women. *Journal of Adult Development* 8(1): 9–21.

Wilcox, P., Winn, S. and Fyvie-Gauld, M. (2005). 'It was nothing to do with the university, it was just the people': the role of social support in the first-year experience of higher education. *Studies in Higher Education* 30(6): 707–722.

11 A snapshot of contemporary education discourse

The Pupil Premium policy

Claire Pass and Deborah Outhwaite

Introduction

The Pupil Premium policy is additional funding that is provided to schools to allow targeted support to be provided to pupils from lower socio-economic backgrounds. These pupils are identified through their eligibility for Free School Meals (FSMs). The limitation of this is that not all pupils from deprived backgrounds will apply for FSMs, although if they apply once, they will be eligible for Pupil Premium funding for the next six years of their education. In this chapter we explore, consider, and analyse the concept of the Pupil Premium policy, as found in the 2010 manifestos for both of the Coalition partners, the Lib Dems (p. 35) and the Conservatives (p. 53), as one of the most significant contemporary education policies to have been put forward. We consider that it is both challenging and controversial. Here we analyse the issues with the Pupil Premium policy: how it leaves some schools awash with money, but often unsure about the criteria that Ofsted now has to assess them to use the premium for its intended purpose. DfE have done significant work here, publishing extended guidance and launching an award to engender enthusiasm and share good practice (DfE, 2014), and the Education Endowment Fund have published research to help guide schools to use the capital more effectively. Proponents, such as Gove and his successor Morgan, argue that individualised solutions to educational inequality are the answer. The policy itself provides an individual sum of money: currently £935 per secondary pupil and £1300 per primary 'disadvantaged' pupil (DfE, 2014), to be ring-fenced for these children, arguably to improve their educational attainment.

Wider societal factors are wholly disregarded by this recourse to individualised policies. Structural issues such as wealth inequalities and other inequities are pushed to one side, with a positive refrain that something is now being done to help teachers stretch and support FSM children who have, for too long, underachieved, as the data shows below. But what this individualised approach does is to take the macro policy emphasis down to a micro level: so individual schools or chains of schools have to deal with areas of disadvantage, therefore removing responsibility from finding regional or national political solutions. Our chapter seeks to outline the potential difficulties with this approach, and highlights how much greater the challenge is for these children than such a targeted policy acknowledges.

A context of inequality

The Pupil Premium is funding paid into schools to close the attainment gap between affluent students and students from poorer backgrounds (Cabinet Office, 2011). Only

20 per cent of pupils from the poorest backgrounds attain 5 A★–C grades at GCSE (Cabinet Office, 2011). If these pupils made up the entirety of the school population, that school would be closed as a failing school. Pupil Premium funding is intended to address this challenge by enabling schools to offer additional resources to these lower socio-economic group students, who do not enter education on an equal footing to pupils from higher socio-economic backgrounds.

At age 5, there is already a significant difference between the cognitive development of children from lower socio-economic backgrounds and those from higher ones (Joseph Rowntree Foundation, 2010). However, Demos suggested that in 2013 the attainment gap (where students from higher social groups routinely achieve significantly better results than their peers from lower groups) actually widened, as 43 per cent of local authorities reported having a wider attainment gap now than they did prior to the introduction of the Pupil Premium policy (Demos, 2014). Although this policy has only been in place a few years, it does suggest that a policy of securing equity of attainment for students from lower socio-economic groups may involve more than simply providing financial capital.

The funding was introduced in 2011 as a result of one of the 88 recommendations made by a report to the then Labour government (Cabinet Office, 2009). Despite a change in administration and widespread cuts to the public sector, Pupil Premium payments have not only continued, but have more than doubled since the last academic year (DfE, 2014). How the ring-fenced money is spent depends on the school leadership, as once the money is paid into schools – either by the Local Authority or, in the case of academies and free schools, directly – the leadership of the school is responsible for allocating the money as they see fit (DfE, 2014). In the context of spending cuts, the increase in Pupil Premium funding brings with it an ever-increasing sense of accountability for school leaders.

The 2009 Cabinet Office report, which recommended the Pupil Premium, was titled 'Unleashing Aspiration', suggesting that aspiration was not lacking in students from lower socio-economic groups but that they were being hindered by a lack of genuine equality of opportunity. Mongon and Chapman (2011) echoed this idea, stating that aspiration and expectation are distinct phenomena, and whilst pupils can be aspirational – or hopeful – about future prospects, 'low expectation, arguably with good reason, begins to dominate' (2011: 16). If we consider what is meant by 'with good reason', it becomes necessary to consider the deep-rooted inequalities embedded within society.

'Unleashing Aspiration' (Cabinet Office, 2009) refutes the idea that poor parents are less aspirational for their children and cites instead a lack of 'good schools' as the reason for lack of attainment (Cabinet Office, 2009: 68). The implication of this is that if we increase the number of good schools, we will automatically achieve a more equitable society, as long as pupils are prepared to work hard and possess the necessary attributes (Cabinet Office, 2011). Working-class underachievement therefore becomes part of a deficit model (Brown, 2013) where the 'solutions to low social mobility are seen to be greater working-class industry and better teaching' (Reay, 2013: 667). Brown argues that 'social justice is often reduced to fair access' (2013: 690) to good schools and consequently upward social mobility. It is therefore argued here that the wider context of societal inequality is being brushed aside, and education has become the single political focus for providing social justice.

The reference to a limited supply of good schools (schools which achieve highly across their intake) also implies that competition for places is intense. Bourdieu references the nature of 'games' in society, which have '"rules" only for those who are excluded'

(1992: 304) from them. This suggests that inequalities are heightened by the competitive 'game' of applying for limited places in good schools and that by failing to engage with the system – or 'play the game' – parents from lower socio-economic groups have not taken available opportunities to secure the best education for their child, precisely because they don't know the 'rules of the game'.

A deficit model, therefore, implies that working-class parents are to be blamed for their children's lack of achievement (Reay and Ball, 1997). In his criticism of the injustice of market competition within education, Brown (2013) states that 'policy measures may legitimately be aimed at those who have failed to make the most of market "opportunities"' (2013: 687). If we see the Pupil Premium as one of the policy measures described by Brown, this too becomes part of the deficit model. In their description of Pupil Premium funding, DfE (2014) calls it funding to 'raise the attainment of disadvantaged pupils and close the gap between them and their peers' (DfE, 2014). The word 'peers' implies 'everyone else', making the middle-class experience of education normative and marking out working-class pupils as 'other'. In light of this, it is difficult to reconcile Pupil Premium funding, intended to provide equality of opportunity, with genuine equality and true social justice.

Reay and Ball assert that essentially, education is about 'working-class failure, middle-class success' (1997: 92): in other words, academic success means upward social mobility. If the qualitative data collected by Reay and Ball is accepted, success in education for a child from a lower socio-economic group background is about more than academic ability: it is about challenging deeply rooted values passed from parents to children, and about the nature of how cultural capital is transmitted in wider society. In addition to seeing their own children as not academic, 'Working-class parents also tended to regard differences and individual qualities as fixed within the child and not susceptible to school effects' (Reay and Ball, 1997: 91). We argue, here, that this pervasive value is one that needs to be identified and challenged, among both parents and educators alike.

Cultural capital and social mobility

The Cabinet Office report (2011) states that 'high levels of absolute social mobility can go hand in hand with a society in which background has an unfair influence on life chance"' (p. 15), implying that relative mobility will highlight inequalities in society. The current economic climate (2008–2015) has meant a shift from absolute mobility to relative mobility. The solution offered to the economic downturn has been to ensure a focus on both academic achievement and the development of cultural capital (Cabinet Office, 2009; Cabinet Office, 2011; Ofsted, 2013) as: 'Unlike absolute mobility, "relative" mobility is based on a positional competition' (Brown, 2013: 682), which means that the development of 'soft skills' – or cultural capital – becomes crucial (Cabinet Office, 2011; Ofsted, 2013). Directing Pupil Premium funding toward a cultural type of intervention, rather than focusing on raising the academic achievements by which schools are judged, relies on moral leadership. At a time when league tables and a competitive market-environment are at work, this means that 'efficiency and justice are pulling in opposite directions' (Brown, 2013: 693).

Held up as an example of how cultural capital can be developed through the use of Pupil Premium funding is a faith school in an ethnically diverse area of London, where a large number of pupils were eligible for the Pupil Premium (Ofsted, 2013). One pupil had achieved exceptionally well academically, and so the school used Pupil Premium funding 'to help her to raise her aspirations, know what might be possible and challenge her further. She had visited universities and attended courses, plays and concerts' (Ofsted, 2013: 21). Whilst seemingly offering equality of opportunity, this particular intervention was offered because the pupil in question was already achieving academically. Most pupils from lower socio-economic backgrounds are unlikely to be offered such opportunities as the priority – dictated by both league tables and accountability to Ofsted – is academic achievement. The fact that developing this cultural capital is seen as necessary to ensure upward social mobility also serves to highlight and reinforce the inequalities present in society, where the dominant culture – the middle classes – set the agenda.

Bourdieu and Passeron (1990), when describing students from lower social class backgrounds in higher education, stated that students would give vague, non-committal responses to mask any perceived lack of understanding of the discourse of education – in other words, a lack of knowledge of the 'game' (Bourdieu, 1992). If we extend this argument to school pupils, it could be suggested that strategies identified by the Education Endowment Fund toolkit (2014) as having a positive impact on learning do so as a result of breaking down the barriers to learning created by the 'game'. For example, feedback, reported to add significant learning gains (Hattie, 2009; Education Endowment Fund, 2014), can be seen as a two-way dialogue, with the student also giving feedback to the teacher about what they know, and more importantly, what they do not know. It is feedback to the teacher, rather than from the teacher, which is most powerful (Hattie, 2009). Interestingly, aspiration interventions such as those outlined by Ofsted (2013) have been found to have no learning gains (Education Endowment Fund, 2014).

Reay (2013) argues that in times of little social mobility, policy makers make social mobility their main focus. Social mobility has therefore been reduced to a rhetorical device used by policy makers and politicians:

> Social mobility, rather than the ailments it is supposed to cure, has become the main focus of attention, a politically driven distraction that diverts our attention from the real problems.
>
> (Reay, 2013: 663)

This suggests that inequality is never genuinely addressed; the focus has instead become equity in academic achievement as a means to social mobility. The Cabinet Office states that whilst 'not everyone can be a doctor or a lawyer', those who are able should be given the opportunity to 'realise their aspirations' (2009: 7). The focus here is on raising aspiration: raising hope rather than realistic expectation (Mongon and Chapman, 2011), which supports Reay's implication that these aspirations take on a fairy-tale-like quality (2013). Of course, if social mobility is just a myth or a fairy-tale, there cannot be true social justice. This is only true, however, if we accept the discourse that assumes social justice and social mobility to be one and the same. Instead, we argue that social justice should be about equality, not mobility; the fact that without mobility you cannot have equality speaks of the inequality at the heart of our society (Reay, 2013).

Brown suggests that focusing on social mobility as a means to equality is 'a "fallacy of fairness" as policies to increase educational standards, including the student premium' (2013: 682), will not impact on relative mobility (the chances of pupils from poorer backgrounds moving into the same income group as their more affluent peers). We argue here that focusing on education to provide social mobility and presenting this as equality is erroneous and perhaps indicates a need to challenge 'the taken-for-granted, implicit assumptions that it is an ideal all the working classes should be striving for' (Reay and Ball, 1997: 99). Such an assumption suggests that to achieve 'equality', pupils from lower socio-economic groups need to become a part of the normative middle class, which in turn indicates the inequality at the heart of society. Sahlberg (2014) states that the greater the income inequalities in a particular society, the greater the gap in educational achievements between different social groups. Although causal conclusions cannot be drawn, this suggests that rather than being a means to equality in society, equity of achievement stems from this more equal society, whereas the UK currently has one of the most unequal societies in the world (Pickett and Wilkinson, 2009).

The fact that schools are held accountable for the performance of different social groups (Ofsted, 2014) indicates that the 'ideology of meritocracy' (Brown, 2013: 686) is still at work in schools. Bourdieu and Passerson (1990) discussed the methods by which the education system achieved apparent neutrality; meritocracy promoted as the route to equality (Cabinet Office, 2009) could actually strengthen inequalities in society by implying that working-class disadvantage is acceptable if they do not have the 'skills and talents' required to be upwardly socially mobile (Cabinet Office, 2011: 5). Any working-class success serves to reinforce the image of apparent neutrality by giving credibility to the idea of meritocracy when in fact the 'merits of a few are celebrated at the expense of the majority' (Brown, 2013: 685), resulting in what Reay refers to as a 'pale, insipid version of social justice' (2013: 663). We feel that this version of social justice compromises the aims and intentions of the Pupil Premium policy.

Implications for leadership

In a review of how Pupil Premium money was being spent, Ofsted visited 68 schools (Ofsted, 2013). When outlining why some schools were not using Pupil Premium funding effectively, the report stated that schools focused on the minimum nationally expected requirements rather than the ability of individual pupils, which meant that 'more able eligible pupils underachieved' (Ofsted, 2013: 3). This lack of expectation for pupils reflects the pervasive values highlighted by Reay and Ball (1997) and perhaps indicates a focus by school leaders on what, until recently, were the headline figures by which schools were judged. Hopkins calls the link between social class and achievement 'an important myth to explode for both social justice and strategic reasons' (2013: 307) and calls attention to schools who are successful in closing the gap, echoing Ofsted who reported on schools which 'defy the association of poverty with outcomes' (Ofsted, 2012: 5).

If we consider school leadership as an 'essentially moral activity' (West-Burnham, 2013), it becomes the role of school leaders to both challenge the assumption that poverty is inextricably linked to poor achievement and to use effective strategies to break this association, as 'closing the gaps is both a moral and a pragmatic matter' (Mongon and Chapman, 2011: 3). If we accept this argument, it suggests that it is the role of education to provide equity of attainment for pupils from lower socio-economic groups and that failure to do this is a failure of educational leadership.

There is an emphasis on leaders to engage in moral leadership to equalise the life chances of young people: good leaders take responsibility for the outcomes of their students (Mongon and Chapman, 2011). Hopkins (2013) states that 'the elimination of poverty as a determinant is not the result of aspiration, as important as that is, rather it is the consequence of deliberate actions' (p. 307) taken by teachers and leaders. This contradicts the assertions made in the 2009 Cabinet Office report that raising aspiration is the key factor in narrowing inequalities. Instead, it echoes West–Burnham's (online, 2013) statement that it is the 'quality of leadership and the effectiveness of teaching and learning strategies' that are the crucial factors in raising attainment. School leaders are 'enabled' to 'drive improvements in their own schools' (Cabinet Office, 2011: 36), making them accountable to the Department for Education for their allocation of Pupil Premium funding.

Two years on from the introduction of the Pupil Premium, Ofsted (2013) reported that pupils from disadvantaged backgrounds were still attaining at a lower level than their peers. The data from Demos (2014) indicates a widening of the gap in attainment between rich and poor. This suggests that funding alone is not enough to close the gap and that the education system is currently providing neither equity in terms of academic results nor the wider social equality suggested by Gove (2014). Gunter (2012) argues that the language of social justice has been used by New Labour – and continues to be used by the Coalition government – to link educational policy with educational standards: 'The problem of standards as measured by student outcomes was directly linked to the quality of the headteacher as leader' (Gunter, 2012: loc 595). She suggests that this has been done to justify reforms to the education system. We argue here, therefore, that the power of school leaders to provide equality for young people is an illusion, as leadership itself is simply an example of political rhetoric – a solution to the problem of standards introduced by New Labour (Gunter, 2012). Providing funding for pupils from lower socio-economic backgrounds therefore gives the appearance of a simple solution to the complex issue of inequality. In actuality, it is difficult for education to provide true equality in an unequal society (Brown, 2013).

Accountability of school leaders

As an accountability measure schools are now expected to work collaboratively with a system leader – these are professionals who work outside their own schools to develop other leaders and raise standards for pupils, to close the attainment gaps (when there are concerns about the attainment of pupils eligible for the Pupil Premium) or if a school's leadership is rated as 'requires improvement' (RI) by Ofsted (2014). Rea et al. (2013) state that system leaders play a vital role in improving both educational standards and equity of attainment. West–Burnham argues that '"closing the gap" is more achievable through collaboration and the "deprivatisation" of successful practice' (online, 2013). This is echoed by Sahlberg (2014), who stresses the need to aim for collaborative leadership, rather than competition, if we are to raise standards and have a more equitable education system. However, Sahlberg (2014) states that the current culture of competition and accountability is hindering the drive to raise educational standards. We argue that a truly collaborative culture is impossible in a system where competitive market forces are at work and schools are ranked against one another in league tables.

There is an assertion that the 'effects of high quality teaching are especially large for pupils from disadvantaged backgrounds' (Sutton Trust, 2011: 5). If true, this assertion means that how we deploy teachers in schools is equally as important as the teaching strategies used in the quest for equity of achievement (West–Burnham, 2013). This echoes Hopkins' argument that it is 'strategic whole school planning' (2013: 307) that makes the difference to the attainment of all pupils, because it enables the organisation to focus on narrowing (and subsequently closing) the gap. The importance of the strategic deployment of teachers to ensure equity of pupil attainment may explain why Ofsted commented that in successful schools

> Inspection and research have both shown that the quality of leadership is second only to the quality of teaching in terms of the school's impact on students' achievements.
>
> (Ofsted, 2012: 20)

The research referred to by Ofsted was the study by Leithwood et al. (2006), which was published by the National College and criticised by Gunter (2012) as reinforcing ideas that support the National College's agenda for leadership. The follow-up report by Day et al. (2009) had a particular focus on how 'successful heads improve pupil outcomes' (p. 2). The implication that the head–teacher was the source of all effective practice in a school was strongly criticised by Gunter as beginning with a 'functionalist assumption' (Gunter, 2012: loc 932) and confirming the notion that a 'single person as leader' (loc 881) is an acceptable norm.

Ofsted reported that system leaders, as head–teachers of outstanding schools, saw working with other schools as a 'moral purpose' but also 'a strategy for developing staff and bringing new knowledge and ideas into the school' (Ofsted, 2012: 50), emphasising that a culture of collaboration is key to raising levels of both attainment and equity in schools (West-Burnham, 2011–2013; Rea et al., 2013; Sahlberg, 2014). However, Gunter (2012) argues that far from system leadership encouraging collaboration, it is part of the competitive marketplace of education which Sahlberg (2014) believed to be a flawed method of achieving quality and equality. Gunter (2012) also argues that whilst appearing to foster distributed leadership, this type of system leadership is actually part of a centralisation of pedagogy. We believe that this level of control reinforces the implicit values that have contributed to social inequality. It also reinforces the notion of a "single person as leader" (Gunter, 2012: loc 881) which in turn reinforces the hierarchical nature of an unequal society.

When focusing on schools that have successfully narrowed or closed the attainment gap between middle and working classes, Ofsted (2012) noted a common thread: 'All the head–teachers place a strong emphasis on creating effective leadership at all levels through their schools' (p. 20). The collecting of effective characteristics to provide a homogenised view of one 'correct' style of leadership is criticised by Gunter (2012) as reinforcing a hierarchical system of leadership. This results in prescriptive methods of how to deliver 'predetermined outcomes' (Gunter, 2012: loc 193); for example, through lists such as the one provided by Leithwood et al. (2006) and Day et al. (2009). We argue that the functionalist assumptions outlined above, reinforced by research by the National College (Gunter, 2012), result in educational leadership maintaining a status quo and as such it will never be able to offer true equality to pupils from lower socio-economic backgrounds.

Conclusions

This chapter has discussed the introduction of the Pupil Premium policy. During his speech to the London Academy of Excellence, Gove said that this policy is to provide the means to 'ensure that our society becomes fairer, more progressive, more socially just'

(2014). We must bear in mind the distinction between equality and equity of attainment. Gove uses the rhetoric of social justice to imply that education can cure the social ills brought about by inequalities which stem from the unequal distribution of resources in our society. In isolation, we argue, it cannot.

It is debatable whether it is possible for schools to provide equity in terms of attainment, although raising levels of educational standards and levels of equity in terms of achievement we believe are not compatible with a competitive system (Sahlberg, 2014). Pupil Premium funding currently requires further research as it does not appear to be achieving equity of attainment for pupils from lower socio-economic backgrounds, therefore it becomes necessary to examine how education currently operates through the filter of the middle-class norm (Reay, 2013). Strategies which break through the language and rituals of the middle-class 'game' (Bourdieu, 1992) have been shown to have the greatest impact on attainment. Achieving equity in terms of results is not, however, the same as achieving equality. We have contended here that education cannot compensate for wider social injustices and therefore the only way to provide true equality is to challenge the functionalist ideas on which the education system operates, thereby changing the status quo in society.

References

Blair, T. (2001), *Full text of Tony Blair's speech on education* [online]. Available at: http://www.theguardian.com/politics/2001/may/23/labour.tonyblair [accessed 21 April 2014].

Bourdieu, P. and Passerson, J.C. (1990), *Reproduction in education, society and culture*, 2nd Edition, London: Sage.

Bourdieu, P. (1992), *The Logic of Practice*, Cambridge: Polity Press.

Brown, P. (2013), Education, opportunity and the prospects for social mobility, *British Journal of Sociology of Education*, 39:6, 811–827.

Cabinet Office (2009), *Unleashing aspiration: the final report of the panel on fair access to the professions* [pdf] London: Cabinet Office. Available at: http://www.agcas.org.uk/assets/download?file=1208&parent=465 [accessed 27 March 2014].

Cabinet Office (2011), *Opening doors, breaking barriers: a strategy for social mobility* [online] London: Cabinet Office. Available at: https://www.gov.uk/government/uploads/system/uploads/attachment_data/file/61964/opening-doors-breaking-barriers.pdf [accessed 10 April 2014].

Conservative Party 2010 Manifesto, available at: https://www.conservatives.com/~/media/files/activist%20centre/press%20and%20policy/manifestos/manifesto2010 [accessed 23 October 2014].

Day et al. (2009), *10 strong claims about successful school leadership* [pdf] Nottingham: National College for Leadership of Schools and Children's Services. Available at: http://www.almaharris.co.uk/files/10strongclaims.pdf [accessed 21 April 2014].

Demos (2014), *A tale of two classrooms: London results skew national picture as educational inequality on the rise* [online], Demos. Available at: http://www.demos.co.uk/press_releases/ataleoftwoclassroomslondonresultsskewnationalpictureaseducationalinequalityontherise [accessed 21 April 2014]

DfE (2014), *Pupil premium: funding for schools and alternative provision* [online]. Available at: https://www.gov.uk/pupil-premium-information-for-schools-and-alternative-provision-settings [accessed 10 April 2014].

Education Endowment Fund (2014), *Toolkit* [online]. Available at: http://educationendowmentfoundation.org.uk/toolkit/ [accessed 10 April 2014].

Gove, M. (2014), *Michael Gove, Secretary of State for Education, speaks at the London Academy of Excellence about securing our children's future* [online], London: DfE. Available at: https://www.gov.uk/government/speeches/michael-gove-speaks-about-securing-our-childrens-future [accessed on 21 April 2014].

Gunter, H. (2012), *Leadership and the reform of education*, Kindle Edition, Bristol: Polity Press.

Hattie, J. (2009), *Visible learning: a synthesis of over 800 meta-analyses relating to achievement*, Oxford: Routledge.

Hopkins, D. (2013), Exploding the myths of school reform, *School Leadership and Management: Formerly School Organisation,* 33:4, 304–321.

Joseph Rowntree Foundation (2010), *Poorer children's educational attainment: how important are attitudes and behaviour?* [pdf] York: Joseph Rowntree Foundation. Available at: http://www.jrf.org.uk/system/files/poorer-children-education-full.pdf [accessed on 21 April 2014].

Leithwood, K. et al. (2006), *7 strong claims about successful school leadership* [pdf] Nottingham: National College for Leadership of Schools and Children's Services. Available at: http://dera.ioe.ac.uk/6967/1/download%3Fid%3D17387%26filename%3Dseven-claims-about-successful-school-leadership.pdf [accessed 10 April 2014].

Liberal Democrat Party 2010 Manifesto, available at: http://www.politicsresources.net/area/uk/ge10/man/parties/libdem_manifesto_2010.pdf [accessed 23 October 2014].

Mongon, D. and Chapman, C. (2011), *Leadership for closing the gap and reducing variations in outcomes: developing a framework for action* [pdf] Nottingham: National College for Leadership of Schools and Children's Services. Available at: http://learn2.winchester.ac.uk/pluginfile.php/228255/mod_folder/content/0/L3%20Leading%20Change%20for%20Improvement%20(Elective)/cm-ctg-framework-for-action.pdf [accessed 10 April 2014].

Ofsted (2012), *Twelve outstanding secondary schools excelling against the odds* [pdf] London: Ofsted. Available at: http://www.ofsted.gov.uk/resources/twelve-outstanding-secondary-schools-excelling-against-odds [accessed 10 April 2014].

Ofsted (2013), *The Pupil Premium: how schools are spending the funding successfully to maximise achievement* [pdf] London: Ofsted. Available at: http://www.ofsted.gov.uk/resources/pupil-premium-how-schools-are-spending-funding-successfully-maximise-achievement [accessed on 10 April 2014].

Ofsted (2014), *The framework for school inspection* [pdf] London: Ofsted. Available at: http://www.ofsted.gov.uk/resources/framework-for-school-inspection-january-2012 [accessed on 10 April 2014].

Pickett, K. and Wilkinson, R. (2009), *The spirit level: why equality is better for everyone,* London: Penguin.

Rea, S., Hill, R. and Dunford, J. (2013), *Closing the gap: how system leaders and schools can work together* [pdf] Nottingham: National College for Teaching and Leadership. Available at: http://www.nationalcollege.org.uk/docinfo?id=303288&filename=ctg-how-system-leaders-and-schools-can-work-together-full-report.pdf [accessed 10 April 2014].

Reay, D. (2013), Social mobility, a panacea for austere times: a tale of emperors, frogs and tadpoles, *British Journal of Sociology of Education*, 34:5–6, 660–677.

Reay, D. and Ball, S.J. (1997), Spoilt for choice: the working classes and educational markets, *Oxford Review of Education*, 23:1, 89–101.

Sahlberg, P. (2014), *Educational inequality in England* [video online]. Available at: https://www.youtube.com/watch?v=Dck990d6Wac&feature=youtu.be [accessed on 23 April 2014].

Sutton Trust (2011), *Improving the impact of teachers on pupil achievement in the UK – interim findings* [pdf] The Sutton Trust. Available at: www.suttontrust.com/public/documents/1teachers-impact-report-final.pdf [accessed 10 April 2014].

West-Burnham, J. (2013), Reframing school leadership, *Educational Leadership Development* [online]. Available at: http://www.johnwestburnham.co.uk/index.php/reframing-school-leadership?showall=1&limitstart= [accessed 27 March 2014].

12 Meeting the needs of ESOL and EAL learners

A critical discussion of policy

Jennifer Marshall

Introduction

Over the past decade, the media has spread fear into the British public about migration in the United Kingdom. Some recent news articles with headlines such as 'Number of Romanian and Bulgarian workers in Britain hits new high' (Barrett, 2014) and 'Net migration into UK up by more than 38% to 243,000' (Casciani, 2014) claim that the UK is being overrun by immigrants and that the number of people moving to the UK is at an all-time high. Many of these news reports fail to tell the whole story or provide the bigger picture. In this chapter, I argue that, historically, government policy has never really adequately addressed immigrants' English language learning needs.

Migration to the UK is nothing new. Throughout history, the UK has always been subject to influxes of people from various tribes and societies across Europe. In ancient times, some of the earliest settlers were the Celts and Picts, then the medieval period saw an influx of Angles, Saxons and Jutes followed by the Normans in 1066. However, it was not until around the Second World War that immigration became a significant feature in British society with the need for labour being the driving force (Migration Watch UK, 2014). In the mid-1950s, the majority of immigrants came from the West Indies in the Caribbean, India, Bangladesh and Pakistan (The Bullock Report, 1975). The 1970s saw nearly 30,000 Ugandans enter the UK as a result of being expelled by President Idi Amin (Endo et al., 2011). Large numbers of people came from Australia, New Zealand and South Africa in the 1980s, while in the following decade thousands sought asylum in the UK as a result of ethnic conflict in the Balkans (HPA, 2006). Finally, since 2000, the easing of restrictions in the European Union has led many from Eastern Europe to come to the UK for work-related reasons (ONS, 2014).

Recent reports that state immigration is at an all-time high are unfounded. In fact, recent figures continue to be much lower than in previous years. Home Office estimates that net intake from January 1955 to June 1962 was 472,000 (Migration Watch UK, 2014). The Office for National Statistics (ONS) publishes a quarterly report on migration statistics in the UK. In 2014, they reported that the number of migrants moving to the UK in the year ending March 2014 was 560,000 and the number of people leaving was 316,000 (ONS, 2014). They report that net migration was at 243,000 over this period which is much lower than 2005 when net migration peaked at 320,000. The point is that immigration has been and will always be very much a part of the fabric of British society. Behind the statistics are people – individuals, families and communities, many trying to make better lives for themselves and their loved ones. I argue that immigration adds richness and diversity to life in the UK and should be celebrated, not feared. Immigrants should have the opportunity to successfully participate in all aspects of British society and having English language skills is an important part of this success.

The importance of the English language

Some immigrants are proficient in English while others will struggle to read and write in their native language, let alone communicate in English. I believe language is intrinsically linked to identity, citizenship, social and economic integration, inclusion and cohesion. Acquisition of the English language is ultimately the key in their transition to life in the UK and is a matter of social justice. In my view, Ward (2008: 3) quite rightly states that

> Refugees and asylum seekers, migrant workers, family migrants and members of settled communities want to learn English.

While many of these groups will have different motivations and circumstances for learning English, they are united by the fact that they need access to good-quality provision to meet their learning needs. In this chapter, I will examine government policy directly pertaining to English for Speakers of Other Languages (ESOL) and English as an Additional Language (EAL) in the context of immigration and equality; I ask whether the current needs of those who want to learn English are being met and if government policy is a source of marginalisation for certain groups in the UK. I further argue that financial support and government funding is vitally important for the future prospects of individuals who need ESOL for full participation in UK society. It is also noteworthy that while ESOL is an umbrella term that includes many forms of English language learning, in the UK, EAL is used primarily for younger learners in compulsory education while ESOL is mainly associated with adult and community learning.

EAL policy overview

Historically, the UK government has acknowledged the importance of learning English for immigrant communities through various policy initiatives, but I purport that these policies have failed to fully address their English language needs. Under section 11 of the 1966 Local Government Act, funding was made available for the first time for

> immigrants from the Commonwealth whose language or customs differ from those of the community.
>
> (HMSO, 1966: 12)

A substantial percentage of this money was spent on English language provision for both children and adult immigrants (Hamilton and Hillier, 2009). In 1975, the government set up a committee, chaired by Alan Bullock, to look into the teaching of language in the UK. The resulting report (Bullock, 1975: 291) called for greater attention to be paid to immigrant children's English language needs, stating

> We would strongly urge the appointment of advisers with special responsibility for the language development of immigrant children, able to provide suitable and sustained in-service training and to support groups of teachers in their response to local problems.

Ten years later, the Swann Report (1985) repeated this demand. The Swann Report (1985: 407) identified

> the key to equality of opportunity, to academic success and, more broadly, to participation on equal terms as a full member of society, is good command of English and the emphasis must therefore we feel be on the learning of English.

One of the main conclusions of the report (p. 426) was

> The needs of English as a second language learners should be met by provision within the mainstream school as part of a comprehensive programme of language education for all children.

Finally, a key recommendation was that

> All teachers in schools with substantial numbers of pupils for whom English is not their first language have a responsibility to cater for the linguistic needs of these pupils and should be given appropriate support and training to discharge it.
>
> (p. 427)

My experience suggests that despite this recommendation, teachers do not have adequate support and training to meet EAL pupils' needs and schools often do not understand what those needs are. The National Association for Language Development in the Curriculum (NALDIC) has been campaigning since 1992 to improve the teaching and learning of bilingual pupils in UK schools. NALDIC (2011a) maintains that teachers who specialise in EAL play a key role in meeting those needs. However, most initial teacher education courses (ITE) contain very little content on EAL. Furthermore, anecdotal evidence suggests that teaching assistants with no specialist training in EAL are often tasked with supporting learners in the classroom.

As mentioned previously, communities throughout the UK are becoming much more diverse. According to the annual school census (DfE, 2014), the number of children in English primary schools whose first language is not English is 654,405 or 18.7 per cent of the total pupil population and in secondary schools there were 455,205 pupils or 14.3 per cent of the overall student population. This brings the total number of pupils in compulsory education that have English language learning needs to over a million. This is double the number of learners from 1997 (NALDIC, 2011b). In other words, a significant proportion of the schooling population have EAL needs. For the reasons mentioned previously, I contend that current policy and practices will most likely fail a large percentage of these learners.

EAL funding

In addition to the challenge of increased student numbers, recent changes in funding add additional complexity to EAL provision. As previously mentioned, the first funding for EAL pupils came from section 11 of the 1966 Local Government Act. In 1999, section 11 funding was replaced by the Ethnic Minority Achievement Grant (EMAG) which, according to the Department for Education (DfE, 2012a), 'was set up to narrow achievement gaps for pupils from those minority ethnic groups who are at risk of underachieving and to help meet the particular needs of bilingual pupils'. In a critical analysis of EMAG, Tikly et al. (2005) found that since the introduction of the 'Grant' there have been some improvements in minority ethnic achievement but these have been largely limited to groups receiving EAL support. This shows just how effective English language support can be; however, they also highlighted that Pakistani and Bangladeshi pupils continue to underachieve. Policy has still failed these two groups of young people, potentially leaving them marginalised as a result.

Despite there being some improvements, EMAG was incorporated into the Schools Direct Grant (SDG) in 2011 giving schools total control over its spending. In the *School Funding Reform: Arrangements for 2013–2014*, EAL is an option for Local Authorities to consider in their formulae for allocating funding to schools. Students with EAL needs can only receive funding for additional support for three years from the point at which they start compulsory schooling (DfE, 2012b). NALDIC (2011c) deems that:

> Under this new system, there is no accountability mechanism regarding schools' use of this funding. This contrasts with the requirement on schools to account for their use of pupil premium funding annually.

Others such as the National Association of Schoolmasters Union of Women Teachers (NASUWT) (2012) believe that the move has decreased the level of funding available for ethnic minorities and EAL provision and as a result has led to negative consequences for learners.

ESOL policy overview

Adults learning ESOL in the post-compulsory sector were largely left in the hands of local authorities until 2001 when it became part of the government's nationwide *Skills for Life* strategy (DfES, 2001). This was created in response to the Moser Report (1999) which found that one in five adults in the UK were functionally illiterate. *Skills for Life* set out to improve the basic literacy, language (ESOL) and numeracy skills of the nation and initially had a target of improving the skills of 750,000 young people and adults by 2004 (DfES, 2004). However, the specific needs of ESOL students were not addressed in the Moser Report and ESOL was not originally planned to be incorporated as a 'skill for life' (Roberts et al., 2007). It was not until a working group on ESOL set up by the government published a report titled *Breaking the Language Barriers* (DfEE, 2000) that ESOL became a part of the *Skills for Life* agenda.

The Leitch Review (2006) which reflected the Labour government's commitment to becoming a world-class leader in skills by 2020 set an objective that 95 per cent of working adults should achieve the basic skills of functional literacy and numeracy as well as more than 90 per cent of adults obtaining GCSEs or vocational equivalents and more than 40 per cent of adults with degree or higher-level qualifications by 2020. The report mentions that

> The English for Speakers of Other Languages (ESOL) programme will also be important for helping those coming to the UK succeed.

(p. 63)

Lack of basic language, literacy and numeracy is a prime source of marginalisation for certain groups within the UK population. In the 2012 round of the International Survey of Adult Skills which compares literacy, numeracy and problem-solving skills in England, it was found that compared with adults who had English as a first language, adults with English as an additional language were more likely to have low numeracy proficiency (DBIS, 2013). Moreover, adults who were both of mixed ethnicity and had English as an additional language were much more likely to have low numeracy proficiency than white adults who had English as a first language. The UK is moving towards a knowledge-based economy where creativity, innovation and technical expertise creates wealth. It is evident, therefore, that the need for a highly skilled workforce where numeracy is vital has become ever more important. If steps are not taken to increase individuals' language proficiency and numeracy skills, many adults face being even further marginalised both socially and economically.

I argue that there is much rhetoric in government policy and it takes some understanding to disentangle it from the reality. If the government were really interested in increasing adult skills, ESOL would feature more prominently in policy. Take the example above regarding the Leitch Review (2006); ESOL was only mentioned once in the entire 148-page-long report. This is not the first time ESOL has been marginalised in national policy making. Hamilton and Hillier (2009) point out that ESOL was for many years excluded from representation at national policy level. It was not part of the 1975 *Right to Read* literacy campaign which was highly important in laying the foundations for a publicly funded adult basic education (ABE) service (Hamilton and Merrifield, 2007). The *Right to Read* campaign began with volunteers who were motivated by social justice (Hillier, 2009). Their goals, although formed at the grassroots level, were to raise public awareness and increase involvement in the teaching and learning of adult literacy at the national level. Literacy for ESOL learners should have been recognised in this important step in providing basic adult literacy provision in the UK.

ESOL funding

As previously mentioned, the *Skills for Life* strategy (DfES, 2001) placed ESOL firmly at the centre of public policy for the very first time. According to the Department of Innovation, University and Skills (DIUS) (2009), over 2 million people had engaged with ESOL provision since its inception and improvements in quality had equally been made (Ofsted, 2008). However, since their 2008 report, Ofsted have not conducted any further evaluation of ESOL in the post-compulsory learning and skills sector. The Department for Education tripled its expenditure on ESOL between 2001 and 2004 and it reached around £300 million in 2006–2007 (NAO, 2008). In 2007, despite investing millions of pounds into the sector, the Labour government announced that it would no longer support automatic fee remission and new eligibility requirements were introduced for those wishing to study. Prior to this, ESOL provision was provided for free to the learner and the changes meant that only certain categories of students would be entitled to free ESOL classes. This included those on income-based Jobseeker's Allowance (JSA), council tax benefit, housing benefit, income support, working tax credit and pension credit (Hubble and Kennedy, 2011).

In 2010, the government significantly cut funding again for ESOL provision (DBIS, 2010). The Coalition government's *Skills for Sustainable Growth Strategy* (2010) outlined a number of changes that have profoundly affected ESOL provision in England. Before considering the exact nature of those changes, it is important to understand the context of the report. The overarching goal of the strategy was to increase the country's skills base to maintain a global competitive advantage in terms of the economy. The strategy also recognised the importance that skills play in helping individuals transform their lives, thereby increasing chances for social mobility, social inclusion and social cohesion. It was underpinned by the Coalition government's principles of fairness, responsibility and freedom.

The strategy outlined a move from government to individuals and employers paying for certain post-compulsory education provision. The strategy states

> English for Speakers of Other Languages (ESOL) provision is important to help those who do not speak English to gain employment and to contribute to society. However, we believe that those who come from other countries to work in England, or their employers, should meet the cost of their English language courses. Therefore we will not fund ESOL training in the workplace. This will enable us to focus publicly-funded provision on people whose lack of English is preventing them from finding work. Full funding will only be available for those actively seeking work on Jobseekers Allowance and Employment Support Allowance (work related activity group) benefits. For others ESOL will be co-funded.
>
> (DBIS, 2010: 32)

The DBIS (2011) conducted an equality impact assessment on the potential effects of the 2010 strategy on adult learning provision. In consultation with stakeholders it concluded that the strategy had a potential negative impact on spouses and women, asylum seekers, the low paid, and young people. The report was published in July 2011 and in August 2011 the government altered their position on funding, allowing those on inactive benefits to receive funding. The Skills Funding Agency (SFA, 2011: 21) announced

> The Agency recognises that there are unemployed individuals who are in receipt of a state benefit (other than JSA or ESA (WRAG)), who want to enter employment and need skills training to do so. For 2011/12, at the discretion of the provider, they will be eligible for full funding for units and other learning aims that will help them enter employment.

This has since been extended to 2014 but funding issues continue to have a major effect on who can access ESOL provision, and many on low wages such as women and refugees are being particularly disadvantaged (Exley, 2011). Lack of funding excludes and marginalises these individuals which in turn negatively affects society as a whole.

The overall impact of government policy is clear to see when looking at the recent release by the SFA of statistics on participation rates (see Figure 12.1). Participation rates for funded adult learners in ESOL (19+) have steadily decreased from 2008–09 to the first three quarters of 2013–14 with provisional data identifying that there were 127,200 participants in ESOL courses (2013–14) in England compared to 188,700 in 2008–09, 178,600 in 2009–10, 163,600 in 2010–11, 139,400 in 2011–12 and 146,200 in 2012–13 (SFA, 2014).

As organisations receive less money for ESOL provision, the number of classes offered decreases. This has resulted in long waiting lists for those wishing to study ESOL in some cases as demand for courses surpasses supply (BEGIN, 2013). The National Association for Teaching English and Community Languages to Adults (NATECLA) conducted a survey in 2014 of 212 colleges and adult education centres in the UK and found that over 80 per cent of providers have significant waiting lists of up to 1,000 students for ESOL courses, with 60 per cent of those providers stating a lack of government funding being the main reason for the lists (NATECLA, 2014).

Figure 12.1 Participation rates for funded adult learners in ESOL. Adapted from SFA (2014)

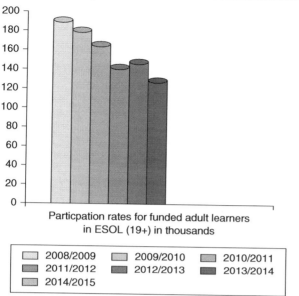

Particpation rates for funded adult learners
in ESOL (19+) in thousands

- 2008/2009
- 2009/2010
- 2010/2011
- 2011/2012
- 2012/2013
- 2013/2014
- 2014/2015

Conclusion

Immigration to the UK has taken place for centuries. For immigrants, both settled and new, asylum seekers, refugees, migrant workers and their families to successfully integrate (both socially and economically), there needs to be a fundamental shift in the way ESOL and EAL provision is viewed and funded by the government and indeed wider society. Constant changes in government policy and subsequent funding make ESOL and EAL learners vulnerable in an ever-changing political landscape. The English language is vital for an individual's own personal development and future prospects, enabling them to fully participate in society. Learning the English language can empower people through better communication skills. These skills make it possible for them to have a real voice and say in what happens in their lives. A grasp of English can help individuals with their employability so they benefit economically while helping them to integrate socially. Until financial barriers are removed from the provision of ESOL courses and EAL in schools, ESOL and EAL learners will continue to face marginalisation through policy. The future of both ESOL and EAL depends on a strong commitment from the government to ensure learners' needs are met through consistent, equitable and socially just policies which guarantee they have access to quality provision throughout the UK.

References

Barrett, D. (2014) *Number of Romanian and Bulgarian workers in Britain hits new high*, Available at: http://www.telegraph.co.uk/news/uknews/immigration/11030392/Number-of-Romanian-and-Bulgarian-workers-in-Britain-hits-new-high.html, Accessed January 2015.

Basic Educational Guidance in Nottinghamshire (BEGIN) (2013) ESOL data, Available at: http://www.begin.org.uk/esol-data, Accessed July 2014.

Bullock Report (1975) *A language for life*, London: HMSO, Available at: http://www.educationengland.org.uk/documents/bullock/bullock1975.html, Accessed July 2014.

Casciani, D. (2014) *Net migration into UK up by more than 38% to 243,000*, Available at: http://www. bbc.co.uk/news/uk-28964323, Accessed January 2015.

Department for Business, Innovation and Skills (DBIS) (2010) *Skills for Sustainable Growth Strategy*, Available at: https://www.gov.uk/government/uploads/system/uploads/attachment_data/file/32368/ 10-1274-skills-for-sustainable-growth-strategy.pdf, Accessed June 2014.

DBIS (2011) *English for Speakers of Other Languages (ESOL) Equality Impact Assessment*, Available at: https://www.gov.uk/government/uploads/system/uploads/attachment_data/file/32297/11- 1045-english-for-speakers-of-other-languages-equality-impact.pdf, Accessed July 2014.

DBIS (2013) *The International Survey of Adult Skills 2012: adult literacy, numeracy and problem solving skills in England*, Available at: https://www.gov.uk/government/publications/international-survey-of- adult-skills-2012, Accessed July 2014.

Department for Education (DfE) (2012a) Ethnic *minority achievement grant*, Available at: http:// webarchive.nationalarchives.gov.uk/20130903145512/http://www.education.gov.uk/schools/ pupilsupport/inclusionandlearnersupport/mea/a0076833/ethnic-minority-achievement-grant, Accessed April 2015.

DfE (2012b) School funding reform: arrangements for 2013–14, Available at: https://www.gov.uk/ government/uploads/system/uploads/attachment_data/file/244364/school_funding_reform_-_ final_2013-14_arrangements.pdf, Accessed July 2014.

DfE (2014) *Statistical first release: schools, pupils and their characteristics: January 2014*, Available at: https:// www.gov.uk/government/uploads/system/uploads/attachment_data/file/319028/SFR15_2014_ main_text_v2.pdf, Accessed July 2014.

Department for Education and Employment (DfEE) (2000) Breaking the language barriers: the report of the working group on English for speakers of other languages (ESOL), London: Basic Skills Agency.

Department for Education and Skills (DfES) (2001) Skills for Life: the national strategy for improving literacy and numeracy skills, Available at: http://webarchive.nationalarchives.gov.uk/20100210151716/ dcsf.gov.uk/readwriteplus/skills_for_life_policy_documents, Accessed October 2014.

DfES (2004) Skills for Life: the national strategy for improving adult literacy and numeracy skills: deliv- ering the vision 2001–2004, Available at: http://rwp.excellencegateway.org.uk/resource/Skills+for +Life%3A+the+national+strategy+for+improving+adult+literacy+and+numeracy+skills%3A+deli vering+the+vision+2001-2004/pdf, Accessed July 2014.

Department for Innovation, Universities and Skills (DIUS) (2009) *A new approach to English for Speakers of Other Languages (ESOL)*, Available at: http://www.adapttech.it/old/files/document/866ENGLISH_ LEARNING.pdf, Accessed July 2014.

Endo, I., Namaaji, J. and Kulathunga, A. (2011) *Uganda's remittance corridors from United Kingdom, United States and South Africa: challenges to link*, Washington, D.C.: IBRD/World Bank.

Exley, S. (2011) *Esol cuts 'not thought through', claims Niace*, Available at: http://www.tes.co.uk/article. aspx?storycode=6070629, Accessed July 2014.

Hamilton, M. and Hillier, Y. (2009) ESOL policy and change, in *Language Issues*, 20(1), 4–8.

Hamilton, M. and Merrifield, J. (2007) *Adult learning and literacy in the United Kingdom*, 1(7), Available at: http://www.ncsall.net/index.html@id=520.html. Accessed July 2014.

Health Protection Agency (HPA) (2006) *Migrant health: infectious diseases in non-UK born populations in England, Wales and Northern Ireland. A baseline report*, Available at: http://www.hpa.org.uk/webc/ HPAwebFile/HPAweb_C/1201767922096, Accessed July 2014.

HMSO (1966) *Local Government Act 1966*, Available at: http://www.legislation.gov.uk/ukpga/1966/42/ pdfs/ukpga_19660042_en.pdf, Accessed July 2014.

Hubble, S. and Kennedy, S. (2011) *Changes to funding for English for Speakers of Other Languages (ESOL) courses*, Available at: http://www.parliament.uk/business/publications/research/briefing-papers/ SN05946/changes-to-funding-for-english-for-speakers-of-other-languages-esol-courses, Accessed July 2014.

Learning and Skills Improvement Service (LSIS) (2013) *Qualifications for teachers, trainers and those supporting learning in the FE sector in England*, Available at: http://www.excellencegateway.org.uk/node/64, Accessed August 2014.

Leitch Report (2006) *Prosperity for all in the global economy – world class skills*, Available at: http://www. delni.gov.uk/leitch_finalreport051206[1]-2.pdf, Accessed July 2014.

Migration Watch UK (2014) *A summary history of immigration to Britain*, Available at: http://www. migrationwatchuk.com/Briefingpaper/document/48, Accessed June 2014.

Moore, K. (2011) *Women affected most by English language funding cuts*, Available at: http://www.bbc. co.uk/news/uk-england-london-13412811, Accessed July 2014.

Moser Report (1999) *A fresh start: improving literacy and numeracy*, Available at: http://www.lifelonglearning. co.uk/mosergroup/index.htm, Accessed July 2014.

National Association for Language Development in the Curriculum (NALDIC) (2011a) *How do I become an EAL teacher?* Available at: http://www.naldic.org.uk/eal-teaching-and-learning/faqs/how-do-I-become-an-eal-teacher, Accessed July 2014.

NALDIC (2011b) *EAL pupils in schools: the latest statistics about EAL learners in our schools*, Available at: http://www.naldic.org.uk/research-and-information/eal-statistics/eal-pupils, Accessed July 2014.

NALDIC (2011c) *How the EAL needs of bilingual learners in schools are funded*, Available at: http://www. naldic.org.uk/research-and-information/eal-funding, Accessed July 2014.

National Association of Schoolmasters Union of Women Teachers (NASUWT) (2012) *Ethnic minority achievement*, Available at: http://www.nasuwt.org.uk/consum/groups/public/@education/documents/ nas_download/nasuwt_009956.pdf, Accessed April 2015.

National Association for Teaching English and other Community Languages to Adults (NATECLA) (2014) *Migrants on huge waiting lists for English courses as government funding is cut again*, Available at: http://www.natecla.org.uk/news/779/ESOL-waiting-lists, Accessed July 2014.

National Audit Office (NAO) (2008) *Skills for life: progress in improving adult literacy and numeracy*, Available at: http://www.nao.org.uk/wp-content/uploads/2008/06/0708482.pdf, Accessed July 2014.

National Institute of Adult Continuing Education (NIACE) (2011) *Policy update: the impact on English for Speakers of Other Languages (ESOL) learners of the funding and eligibility changes*, Available at: http://www.niace.org.uk/sites/default/files/ESOL%20policy%20update%208%20Sep_0.pdf, Accessed June 2014.

Office of National Statistics (ONS) (2014) *Migration statistics quarterly report August 2014*, Available at: http://www.ons.gov.uk/ons/dcp171778_375307.pdf, Accessed August 2014.

Ofsted (2008) *ESOL in the post-compulsory learning and skills sector: an evaluation*, Available at: http:// www.ofsted.gov.uk/sites/default/files/documents/surveys-and-good-practice/e/ESOL%20in%20 the%20post-compulsory%20learning%20and%20skills%20sector%20an%20evaluation.pdf, Accessed July 2014.

Roberts, C., Cooke, M., Baynham, M. and Simpson, J. (2007) Adult ESOL in the United Kingdom: policy and research, in *Prospects*, 22(3), 18–31.

Skills Funding Agency (SFA) (2011) *2011/12 Learner eligibility and contribution rules: version 2.1*, Available at: http://readingroom.lsc.gov.uk/SFA/LearnerEligibilityandContributionRules_2011_12_12 Aug2011__June_revision_V2.1.pdf, Accessed July 2014.

SFA (2014) *Statistical first release: further education & skills: learner participation, outcomes and level of highest qualification held*, Available at: https://www.gov.uk/government/publications/learner-participation-outcomes-and-level-of-highest-qualification-held, Accessed July 2014.

Swann Report (1985) *Education for all*, London: HMSO, Available at: http://www.educationengland. org.uk/documents/swann/swann18.html, Accessed July 2014.

Tikly, L. Osler, A. and Hill, J. (2005) The ethnic minority achievement grant: a critical analysis, in *Journal of Education Policy*, 20(3), 283–312.

Ward, J. (2008) *ESOL: the context and issues*, Available at: http://www.niace.org.uk/lifelonglearninginquiry/ docs/Jane-Ward-migration-evidence.pdf, Accessed July 2014.

13 Where care and education meet?

Social pedagogy in England and the policy of integration

Nicole Chavaudra

Social pedagogy is described as education in its broadest sense, and bringing up children in a way that addresses the whole child (Petrie, 2006). It is concerned with the educational dimensions of social issues, and the social dimensions of educational issues (Schugurensky and Silver, 2013). It is not a model, or intervention, nor is it a toolbox of pedagogical methods; rather it is a way of thinking in which social and educational considerations are united (Hämäläinen, 2012).

Although social pedagogy first emerged as a distinct field of thought in Germany in 1904 through the writings of Paul Natorp (1854–1924), the notion of looking at the child as a whole person, and unifying the social and educational aspects of life, was not unique to social pedagogy. Natorp asserted that all pedagogy should be social, with the aim of closing the gap between rich and poor – and such themes are common in the works of many earlier educational thinkers. Looking at the child as a whole person, or child–centredness, was an educational aspiration for Jean–Jacques Rousseau (1712–1778). For Rousseau (1762), education must be individualised and carried out in harmony with a child's natural development and capabilities, inducting them to the social world. Rousseau's view was in contrast to the prevailing authoritative view of education, with teachers delivering learning according to a fixed curriculum. The drive of creating a new system of education was also an inspiration of Pestalozzi (1827), one of Natorp's greatest influences. Education for Pestalozzi emphasised the importance of focusing on the nature of the child, and nurturing to support the formation of character and the possibility of social mobility.

Such social pedagogical themes are also evident in the educational thought of John Dewey, in particular his work *Democracy and Education* (1916). For Dewey (1916), 'Education is a process of rearing or bringing up' (p. 7), just as for Cameron and Moss (2011), writing a century later, social pedagogues are described as *upbringers on behalf of society*. Social pedagogy theories such as the *common third* (Hatton, 2013) are also evident in Dewey's writings. The *common third* is understood as a shared project or activity in which both parts of the relation (the practitioner and the child or young person) can connect on equal terms (Hatton, 2013). Dewey describes 'when the parent or teacher has provided the conditions which stimulate thinking and has taken a sympathetic attitude toward the activities of the learner by entering into a common or conjoint experience, all has been done which a second party can do to instigate' (1916: 79). Dewey also described what in social pedagogy is described as the *bildung* – the actualisation of human potential, or how we form ourselves and are formed by others, eventually to become mature individuals within in a never-ending process of maturation

(Smith, 2013). Dewey (1916) also defined education as growth and the proper end of education as being the promotion of the best possible realisation of humanity as humanity (p. 41). The commonalities between the writings of John Dewey and social pedagogy also continue through themes such as child-centredness, the importance of relationships and values, and the drive for social equality.

Within social pedagogy, and much of the educational thought that informs it, integration is a key theme. An emphasis is placed on the integration of care and education, of theory and practice, and of mind, body, feelings and spirit in relationships. The integration of disadvantaged children into society, and the integration of concepts and language across government services and professional fields, are also explored within the social pedagogy literature. The particular focus of this chapter is on the latter of these in England – a country without a social pedagogy tradition. Interest in social pedagogy in England has grown since the Social Education Trust's social pedagogy conferences in 2001. The report which emerged (Social Education Trust, 2001) concluded that there may be scope to establish a new approach in children's services based on the model of social pedagogy. Rather than reacting to scandals and countering abuse, such an approach would aim to positively meet children's needs, to foster skills and values to create a confident and competent workforce. The Social Education Trust report proposed that social pedagogy would not offer a solution, but could offer a holistic view of children's needs and holistic approaches, and develop skills, professionalism and helpful debate. As such, it is unsurprising that insights and experience of social pedagogy began to be sought from European countries where an established social pedagogy tradition exists. From such countries we learn that social pedagogy has developed uniquely in each country's own context. As Lorenz (2008) argues, social pedagogy emerges as a construction of the socioeconomic and political context in which it has been applied.

The socio-political context in which social pedagogy found itself emerging in England in the early 2000s was one of poorer educational and life outcomes for many vulnerable and disadvantaged young people than in other European countries. Cameron et al. (2007) identified that young people in care in England, compared to Germany and Denmark – countries with a social pedagogy heritage – were more likely to be out of education and/ or employment, and at greater risk of teenage pregnancy and/or engagement in criminal activity. Cameron and colleagues (2007) identified that better outcomes were associated with a more stable and professionalised workforce using child-centred approaches, but that in England this is frequently hampered by procedural and policy pressure and limited by an underdeveloped workforce.

To varying degrees since the early 2000s, policy has set expectations of a more holistic view of the child through greater integration across care and education. This was in part influenced by the findings of Lord Laming (2003) in his inquiry report into the death of Victoria Climbié in 2000. In his report Lord Laming asserted that, 'I am in no doubt that effective support for children and families cannot be achieved by a single agency acting alone. It depends on a number of agencies working well together' (2003: 5). Amongst Lord Laming's recommendations was the need for coordination of children and family services, and for a common language across all agencies. The publication of *Every Child Matters* (DCSF, 2003) sought to address much of the inquiry's recommendations by producing an integrated language with five shared outcomes across services for children. A future was envisioned where through a collaborative effort across all services for children, all children would be healthy, safe, experience both enjoyment and achievement, enjoy economic well-being and make a positive contribution to society. Soon after the publication of *Every Child Matters*, the Children Act (2004) directed a greater level of structural integration of services for children and families. The Act included the requirement to integrate education and children's social services within local authorities, to establish multi-agency Children's Trust Boards, and to apply integrated assessment tools to be used by schools, social care workers and health staff.

The concept of social education in the context of formal education also experienced increased profile and focus, with the addition of personal, social and health education (PSHE) to the curriculum from 2000. PSHE offered a planned programme of learning as part of a whole-school approach, to enable children and young people to gain the qualities needed to thrive as individuals, family members and members of society. The development of SEAL (social and emotional aspects of learning) also required that schools engage well with other schools, the local community, wider services and local agencies (Humphrey et al., 2010). It seemed promising at the time that both the services for children, and the structures in which they were delivered, would move increasingly towards the point where viewing the child as a whole person might be possible, and where the walls between the educational and the social would be removed.

Every Child Matters had introduced a child-focused policy approach that integrated educational and social services across a common language. In doing so, it perhaps had the potential to produce a system of values that resonated with those of social pedagogy. Eichsteller and Holtoff (2011), for example, assert that social pedagogy has four core aims that are closely linked – well-being and happiness, holistic learning, relationship, and empowerment – aims that found a comfortable fit with the five *Every Child Matters* outcomes. However, a change of government in 2010 was shortly followed by the abolition of *Every Child Matters* and its creator, the Department for Children, Schools and Families. This was replaced by the new Department for Education, and a new approach to educational policy planning aiming to develop skills for life and work and to create a more responsible, engaged and cohesive society (Cabinet Office and Department for Education, 2014). The language of enjoyment, positive contribution and well-being was replaced with a new focus on schools, curriculum, attainment and improving the quality of state-funded schools and teaching – a move which Fielding (2011) describes as a focus on education in its narrowest sense. PSHE also remained a non-statutory subject for schools, leading to its marginalisation in the curriculum. This increased 'schoolification' of education policy certainly presented new challenges for proponents of social pedagogy as an agent for change.

As Fielding (2011) argues, social pedagogy reminds us of the distinction between education and schooling. Social pedagogy emphasises the view that the growth and bringing-up of children is a responsibility that should be shared across agents of the state and wider community, in the pursuit of equality and the fulfilment of human potential. Rather than this vision of social pedagogy, the policy of schoolification risks the production, or perhaps exacerbation, of a series of multiple and detached services occupied with their particular accountabilities and interests. Such an approach prevents the child from being viewed or supported as a whole person, with schools focused on curriculum and attainment, and child and family support services focusing on deficits in the social aspects of a child's life. A critical challenge for social pedagogy and the journey to integration in England is whether professionals in the world of children's services will ever, as practitioners in public services, be able to practise social pedagogy within the policy and legislative framework in which they operate. As Coussée et al. (2010) argue, 'both policy makers and researchers criticize the fact that high walls are put up between care, education, health and justice and that the distinct sectors each further develop within their own logic' (p. 791). Social pedagogy could provide a common conceptual framework to underpin the approaches used by services and agencies observing and acting through distinct lenses, based on their own policy and inspection interests, and their diverse theoretical traditions. If social pedagogy's integrated approach across disciplines is embraced then education in its fullest sense can be achieved (Stephens, 2009). A children's workforce of social educators, underpinned by the values and concepts of social pedagogy, would be an approach worthy of consideration if greater integration is to be enabled.

Yet despite a plethora of evidence regarding the influence of the social aspects of a child's life on educational outcomes (Paget et al., 2007; Raffo et al., 2007; Ladd, 2011), and even with 'pedagogy' in its title, social pedagogy is often unobservable in English schools. Perhaps with the exception of pastoral care provision, which Stephens (2013) describes as 'the elusive realm of hidden curriculum' (p. 34), educational policy often makes it difficult for teachers to provide an education that explicitly promotes social learning, with the social only aligned to pastoral aspects of schooling if it exists at all. This point is also argued by Kyriacou (2009) who notes that the discourse of educational policy and teacher standards has led to the marginalisation of the caring role in teaching in the UK. The *Every Child Matters* agenda provoked a new thinking about the role of teachers in the social as well as the educational sector, but the focus on a differing and more academically focused curriculum that followed halted much of the progress being made to enable a social pedagogically oriented policy framework for achieving positive change for children.

Nevertheless, as Cameron (2007) notes, trusting relationships have been found to support educational aims that are a priority for formal education in England, such as attendance and achievement. As such, perhaps social pedagogy is of interest to those in the school sector. For many children and young people, their upbringing and growth requires little input from state organisations, other than their formal schooling. With reduced budgets for children and family support services, the role for schools in social development may be necessarily greater in future. This presents an opportunity for social pedagogy to provide the conceptual framework to underpin a developing role in schools. As Rosendal Jensen (2013) suggests, 'upbringing and socialisation practices can only be understood with knowledge of the educational function of the family, the child care institutions, and the school' (p. 4). Therefore integration across care and education is vital if improved outcomes for children and families are to be enabled.

Further to the challenge of integrating values and approaches across services, the policy culture in England could present a further barrier to social pedagogy's potential as an agent for social change. As Lorenz (2008) notes, central to all traditions of social pedagogy is the conceptualisation of the relationship between individual and society. Lorenz also argues that, 'the social professions are particularly susceptible to social policy influences, which, while not determining the shape and direction of training, create a context that is often regarded as constraining but that, in reality, represents an inalienable part of the identity shaping and purpose-defining process of this profession' (p. 626). This is perhaps a critical challenge for social pedagogy in England, in the context of social and educational policy for children, which could be considered as risk oriented at its worst and child–centred at its best. Social pedagogy, by contrast, emphasises the 'twin directions' – the aim to simultaneously be more child–centred, whilst also supporting the child to integrate more deeply into society. The cultural restrictions to transferring models or methods from one country to another are likely to stifle social pedagogy's potential in England. An emergent English social pedagogy would need to adapt to its unique context, or shift the policy context in its favour – or both.

What social pedagogy provokes in England regarding the purpose of education, and the role of those supporting the growth and development of children, is not new or radical. It reminds us of the fact that each child is unique, and requires support to mobilise their individual capabilities in the context of their complete existence, including the family, social and other relational supports in their life. Children do not fit neatly into the fragmented services that the policy, structure and ideology of children's services have evolved to deliver. Unless there is a profound policy and culture shift towards child and community centredness, so those who support children who are skilled and insightful social educators, it is unlikely that the English system will enable the actualisation of its young people's potential. Given the challenge of such a policy shift, I argue that social pedagogy as a way of thinking underpinned by values and beliefs could affect the culture of children's services from within. With its theoretical positioning at the interface of education, social care and community development, social pedagogy has an emphasis on the rights of children as part of society. From this ethical standpoint, the conditions for dialogue and reflection are created where the nature of social pedagogy and social change can be explored. If sufficient enthusiasm and commitment for its values and approaches were gained, a critical mass of social pedagogy activators could begin to create the conditions for social change from within children's services organisations.

There is evidence that social pedagogy supports this type of integration. The shared language of social pedagogy means that multi-professional discussions could occur on a more equitable footing – a footing that values all participants' expertise (Cameron, 2012). And furthermore, an underpinning conceptual framework based on the principles of social pedagogy could shift the culture of education in England from one focused on formal schooling to one focused on the individual child and their growth within the society in which they live. It is only by changing the culture and values of services and practitioners that support the most vulnerable children and young people that such social integration can be tackled. And such values must unite services and practitioners, rather than fuel fragmentation of cultures. As Coussée and colleagues (2010) argue, 'social pedagogy can contribute to the achievement of a set of shared values and skills across the various child-oriented sectors' (p. 794).

Achieving improved outcomes for children does not require the creation necessarily of a new role of social pedagogue within English children's services, as the essence of social pedagogy is the combination of a social objective and educational means. Rather, as Paget et al. (2007) suggest, all roles should develop a pedagogical perspective. Achieving such a workforce of social educators requires leadership – the language and intent of policy that can shape this. It may be impossible to achieve such ambitions for social change through social pedagogy without a policy framework that reflects its values and expectations for the workforce. As Úcar (2013) argues, 'social pedagogy cannot alone improve their standard of living through pedagogical actions . . . policies should provide the means and scenarios to do so. Social pedagogy can be one of those means' (p. 5).

Without a policy framework that assists with the critical establishment of a shared framework of values, child-centred and ethical approaches to leadership and delivery of services for children and families may be unachievable. Social pedagogy may provide an opportunity to embed those values from within, and should this be the case, perhaps a time may come when policy moves from controlling the system to enhancing and enabling the professionals within it, and with growing interest and increased deployment in services for children, its story will be told over the years to come.

References

Cabinet Office and Department for Education (2014) *Increasing opportunities for young people and helping them to achieve their potential.* London: Cabinet Office.

Cameron, C. (2007) Social pedagogy and the children's workforce. *Community Care.* 1685: 24–25.

Cameron, C., McQuail, S. and Petrie, P. (2007) *Implementing the social pedagogic approach for workforce training and education in England.* London: Thomas Coram Research Unit, Institute of Education, University of London.

Cameron, C. and Moss, P. (2011) Social pedagogy: current understandings, in Cameron, C. and Moss, P. (eds) *Social pedagogy and working with children and young people: where care and education meet.* London: Jessica Kingsley Publishers.

Cameron, C. (2012) Social pedagogy in the UK: time to reflect. *Community Care,* 2 March, available at: http://www.communitycare.co.uk/Articles/02/03/2012/118035/Social-pedagogy-in-the-UK-time-to-reflect.htm.

Coussée, F., Bradt, L., Roose, R. and Bie, M. B. (2010) The emerging social pedagogical paradigm in the UK child and youth care: deux ex machina or walking the beaten path? *British Journal of Social Work.* 40:3, 789–805.

Department for Children, Schools and Families (2003) *Every child matters.* London: Department for Children, Schools and Families.

Dewey, J. (1916) *Democracy and education.* New York: Macmillan.

Dewey, J. (1977) The relation of theory to practice in education, in Boyston, J. A. (ed.) *John Dewey: the middle works, 1899–1924.* Carbondale, IL: Southern Illinois University Press, pp. 249–272.

Eichsteller, G. and Holtoff, S. (2011) Conceptual foundations of social pedagogy: a transnational perspective from Germany, in Cameron, C. and Moss, P. (eds) *Social pedagogy and working with children and young people: where care and education meet.* London: Jessica Kingsley.

Fielding, M. (2011) Radical democratic education and emancipatory social pedagogy: prolegomena to a dialogue, in Cameron, C. and Moss, P. (eds) *Social pedagogy and working with children and young people: where care and education meet.* London: Jessica Kingsley.

Hämäläinen, J. (2012) Social pedagogical eyes in the midst of diverse understandings, conceptualisations and activities. *International Journal of Social Pedagogy.* 1:1, 3–16.

Hatton, K. (2013) *Social pedagogy in the UK: theory and practice.* Lyme Regis: Russell House.

Humphrey, N., Lendrum, A. and Wigelsworth, M. (2010) *Social and emotional aspects of learning (SEAL) programme in secondary schools: national evaluation.* London: Department for Education.

Kyriacou, C. (2009) The five dimensions of social pedagogy in schools. *Pastoral Care in Education: An International Journal of Personal, Social and Emotional Development.* 27:2, 101–108.

Ladd, H. (2011) *Education and poverty: confronting the evidence.* Sanford School of Public Policy, Duke University: Presidential Address to the Association of Public Policy Analysis and Management in Washington, D.C.

Laming, L. (2003) *The Victoria Climbié Inquiry: report.* London: UK Government.

Lorenz, W. (2008) Paradigms and politics: understanding methods paradigms in a historical context: the case of social pedagogy. *British Journal of Social Work.* 38:4, 625–644.

Page, B. (2007) Creating a high aspiration culture for young people in the UK. Findings of a report published by Ipsos Mori, available at: http://www.suttontrust.com/our-work/research/item/creating-a-high-aspiration-culture-for-young-people-in-the-uk.

Paget, B., Eagle, G. and Citarella, V. (2007). *Social pedagogy and the young people's workforce*. Liverpool: CPEA.

Pestalozzi, J. (1827) *Letters on early education*. Accessed at INSERT OAIster, EBSCO*host*, viewed 27 October 2013.

Petrie, P. (2006) Extended 'pedagogy'. *Journal of Education for Teaching: International Research and Pedagogy*. 31:4, 293–296.

Raffo, C., Dyson, A., Gunter, H., Hall, H., Jones, D. and Kalambouka, A. (2007) *Reviews of research on the links between education and poverty*. Joseph Rowntree Foundation. Available at: http://www.jrf.org.uk/publications/review-research-links-between-education-and-poverty.

Rosendal Jensen, N. (2013) Social pedagogy in modern times. *Education Policy Analysis Archives*. 21:43, 1–11.

Rousseau, J.-J. (1762) *Émile*, London: Dent (1911 edn.).

Schugurensky, D. and Silver, M. (2013) Social pedagogy historical traditions and transnational connections. *Education Policy Analysis Archives*. 2135: 1–16.

Smith, M. (2013) Forgotten connections: reviving the concept of upbringing in Scottish child welfare. *Scottish Journal of Residential Child Care*. 12:2, 13–29.

Social Education Trust (2001) *Social pedagogy and social education*. Formerly known as the Radisson Report. A report of two workshops held on 11–12 July 2000 and 14–15 January 2001 at the Radisson Hotel, Manchester Airport.

Stephens, P. (2009) The nature of social pedagogy: an excursion in Norwegian Territory. *Child and Family Social Work*. 14:3, 343–351.

Úcar, X. (2013). Exploring different perspectives of social pedagogy: towards a complex and integrated approach. *Education Policy Analysis Archives*. 21:36, 1–16.

UK Parliament (2004) *The Children Act*. London: UK Parliament.

14 Early years workforce development

Jon White and Joanne Byrd

Historical background and government reforms in the early years

Childcare, childhood and education are social constructs and to understand where England is with regards to its current early years childcare/education provision for under 5s, one has to examine the historical, cultural, social and political background that has underpinned our understanding of what it means to be a child and to have high-quality care/education.

From 2000 a clearer direction and emphasis on childcare for under 5s in England began to take shape (see Baldock et al., 2013) for policies and dates during the subsequent 10 years). Education at this time took the place of health as the department in charge of early years and here we can see the shift in emphasis away from early child*care* towards early child *education*. The notion of an integrated approach to working with children grew and so children's centres were developed where professionals from different disciplines could work together to best serve the needs of the child and her/his family. These strategies led to a much more integrated system of care and duty for under 5s. Tougher regulation was demanded under the Office for Standards in Education, Children's Services and Skills (Ofsted) and the early years received a much greater profile than previously. A curriculum was designed that focused on birth to 5 years of age (DfES, 2007).

The Coalition Government (2010 to present) has made many changes in the area of the early years; many of the programmes developed under the Labour Government have been dismantled (Baldock et al., 2013). The priority is now with children and families who are struggling to support their children (Tickell, 2011). Resources have been targeted at providing free nursery places for 2-year-olds for families on a low income. The implication is that the children will be better educated at a setting than at home and that they will be more 'school ready'. There is also the economic consideration of the parents; they will be able to work as their childcare is paid for.

Characteristics of the early years workforce

From 2000 there has been much criticism directed towards the early years workforce (Ofsted, 2014). According to the Tickell Review (2011), many young children are not entering school ready and poor-quality early years settings play a part in this. The language of current government policy is that of reform – improving the qualifications and professionalism of the workforce – which suggests that what was done before was not good enough. To be in a low-paid, low-valued job and then to be continually hearing a message that what you are doing is not enough must be very demoralising.

McGillivray (2008) highlights the many terms used for the early years workforce, from child-minders to nannies to nursery workers/practitioners, early years practitioners, etc., and how this creates confusion about identity. Fairclough (2003) argues that the language and discourse around early years and the workforce and the construction of identity as a caring maternal type have allowed for gender imbalance within the workforce and also created a role that has traditionally been undervalued in much the same way as motherhood and early childhood have in general. Singer (1993) uses the term 'attachment pedagogy' to describe how children in settings need a relationship that acts as a substitute for their mother–child relationship, and this has been the dominant view of early years settings – as substitute home environments. As childcare now distinctly falls under the remit of education, Cameron et al. (2002) argue it is time to reconceptualise childcare and to no longer view it as a substitute for mothering. With this re-conceptualisation it is hoped that the image of early years staff and settings can be moved away from the undervalued, traditionally female 'motherly' type to a situation where they are valued for the positive and rich contribution they can make to a young child's life.

High-quality settings

The Effective Provision of Pre-School Education (EPPE) study (Sylva et al., 2004) states that pre-school has an impact on all children who attend and that the higher the quality of the setting, the better the impact. High quality has been defined as being where care and education are integrated. Settings with the highest-quality scores were settings which had a strong ethos of early years education and employed higher-qualified staff who had a deeper understanding of pedagogy and child development.

The authors of the research go on to state:

> whilst not eliminating disadvantage, pre-school can help to ameliorate the effects of social disadvantage and can provide children with a better start to school. Therefore, investing in good quality pre-school provision can be seen as an effective means of achieving targets concerning social exclusion and breaking cycles of disadvantage.
>
> (Sylva et al., 2004: iii)

It is not difficult to see how the EPPE study has had a major impact on local and national policy regarding pre-schooling. Both the previous Labour Government and the current Coalition Government have advocated for a better-qualified, more professional workforce. (See, for example, Choice for Parents, HMT, 2004; Children's Workforce Development Council, 2010.) An expectation that settings would have a graduate-led leader was developed. These graduates became known as Early Years Practitioners (EYPs) and it was hoped that EYPs would raise the standards in the settings and lead with good practice as they would be educated to degree level in child development and pedagogy from birth to age 5. The inference by Government was that previously the workforce was deficient by not being qualified enough and by not driving standards up.

The Childcare and Early Years Providers Survey (DfE, 2011) found that there were a number of clear trends emerging with regards to the qualifications of the workforce. The clearest of these is that there are now far more members of the workforce with a degree-level qualification, usually in a specialist early years subject (e.g. B.A. (Hons) Early Childhood Studies). The Early Years Foundation Stage Framework (2008) allowed

Ofsted to create a yardstick by which their understanding of quality could be measured. This led to seeing the early years institution as the manufacturer of a product, with echoes of the tools used to measure performance in schools being applied to settings for younger children. As Singer (1993) commented, in relation to the impact of measuring performance, researchers often identify quality with characteristics of care facilities that correlate well with favourable scores on developmental tests. For this reason, it is safe to assume that, while having standards may be desirable, any attempt to use them as a simple tool for measuring the quality of provision is likely to be a naïve oversimplification.

Mathers et al. (2011) explored the role of graduate leaders and found that leadership within a setting was often more effective with a practitioner with EYP status. This status was launched in 2005 to enable the quality of leadership to be enhanced through a validated award. Mathers et al. (2011) found that settings with an EYP in place tended to be more effective, to be further reiterated (Teather and DfE, 2013) in a study of over 6000 professionals with EYP status across the country.

The Nutbrown Review (2012) further reiterated the need for a highly qualified and skilled workforce. Nutbrown (2012) recommended that early years graduates should be given equal parity with teachers and should be called teachers and be awarded qualified teacher status (QTS). She firmly stated that the sector demands to be valued. We also argue this. As a society we must value the early years and move away from the notion of substitute mothering which suggests that only low-qualified and low-paid 'kind' females are needed to care for our children. Nutbrown (2012) observed many EYPs were dissatisfied with the status awarded to them and the correlating low pay offered after graduating. This has also been echoed by many others (Cameron et al., 2002; Miller, 2008). We will return to this later in the chapter.

Aside from raising the status of the EYP, Nutbrown (2012) has recommended raising expectations of the standards of qualifications and training for the entire workforce. She proposed that a Level 3 requirement should be a minimum for all staff, which is currently (2014) a requirement for a leading practitioner. Nutbrown (2012) recommends clear career progression with many opportunities for professional development. She also criticises the proliferation of accreditation awarded to the workforce as this has made it difficult for potential students, parents and employers to identify the 'best' course with the most credence. Whilst acknowledging a single qualification model could be too restrictive, she does recommend the design of some standards for EYPs in a similar style to teacher standards.

Top-down regulations

The consistently referred to notion of the workforce needing to become more professional has been discussed by many. Osgood (2006: 2) refers to the 'disempowering regulatory gaze' that the early years sector is faced with. The dominant discourse of professionalism and the top-down regulations that have been placed upon the sector with little or no opportunity for consultations and opportunities to reflect, critique and deconstruct the status quo have been criticised. This reflects post-structuralism theory in which Foucault (1983) suggests that discourse can become truth and can be used by those in power to dominate and control. In this case, the workforce is set against standards that have been imposed upon them and against which they are then viewed as not good enough, or not professional enough. Osgood (2004) reports that the (almost entirely) female sample of professionals in her two studies were opposed to the perceived top-down 'masculinised' and 'new managerialised' policies introduced under the Labour Government as being non-conducive to the community-oriented and collaborative nature of the sector.

The paradoxical notion of professionalism is discussed by Moyles (2010): the work-force is being criticised for not being professional and doing what is required of it, and yet professionalism actually means to challenge the status quo. Challenging top-down authority, however, requires high levels of knowledge and self-confidence:

> Partly because of insecurity about professional status—after all, everyone has been a young child and therefore knows about young children!—many practitioners have learned to feel that others' visions and experiences are somehow better than their own, mindful responses.

> (Moyles, 2010: 87)

Miller (2008: 260), however, argues that the early years workforce can be active and negotiate 'where they are "positioned and defined" and thus take on the role of autono-mous professionals'. She has argued that both trainee providers and the workforce are not merely passive recipients but can act as agents of change and have some say in what becomes of them and how they are perceived by themselves and others. Moyles (2010) discusses one project where the 'shift of awe' moved from the academics and the 'profes-sionals' to the practitioners. The research shows that given space and time practitioners can become very reflective and can change their practice, acting as agents of change. She argued that EYPs will be central to instigating change; however, the reality is that EYPs have had a mixed experience. Whilst some have reported being treated with respect and have been listened to and actively promoted change, many have not been given the professional credence they thought they would have. Sometimes this has been due to working alongside teachers who have not respected the EYP because of a lack of parity in roles (Simpson 2010).

We believe, alongside Simpson (2010), that EYPs have not had the transformatory potential it was hoped they would have. In some settings EYPs have facilitated change, but these individuals have often left the sector because their status and pay have remained so low. Often these individuals will go back to university to study for a PGCE and then become a school-teacher, where the status, pay and career progression routes are incomparable.

Unfortunately, things have not improved since 2010. The current government has rejected probably the most important recommendation from the Nutbrown Review (2012): to make a new early years specialist QTS route for practitioners working with children from birth to 7. This would be acceptable if it was because it was considering an alternative approach to early years education and care (similar to the Swedish model, for example) but it is not. Although the government has coined the new title of Early Years Teacher to replace Early Years Practitioner, in practice nothing will change. The Early Years Teacher will not have QTS and so will not be equal to teachers and will therefore not be given the same pay, career progression and status.

A further alternative route available to EYPs, other than leaving a well-loved profes-sion, could be to engage in a role as an action researcher. Whalley (2011), however, admits that EYPs are not as comfortable with the notion of engaging in action research as their European counterparts. A social pedagogue engages with action research as part of the role without seeing it as special or difficult. A natural part of doing a job well for a social pedagogue is to be reflective and to improve one's own practice for the sake of the children. It is not done because someone has imposed this as part of a new checklist for them to work through.

A theoretical framework for workforce development

Workforce development takes place in a specific context, and needs to be understood in a social and cultural framework, with an appreciation of the power dynamics at play between the stakeholders in the setting. There is interplay between children and adults, just as there is interplay between adults as they develop their skills and understanding of their job role and the extent to which they can impose meanings on others (Giddens, 1998). The EYP is working within a number of narratives, with each having an influence on their practice e.g. the expectations of children, communities and the government. Add to these the influences of parents and quality assurance brokers (e.g. Ofsted) and there are a considerable number of views regarding what learning is and how to construct a high-quality environment in which it can take place. Each practitioner will need to resolve conflicts emerging from these multiple narratives and yet maintain their professional integrity in spite of the contested demands placed on them every day (Dahlberg et al., 2007).

The EYP therefore needs to learn how to manage these demands. Jenks (2004) considers learning as a dynamic process, with interactions between the learners and those leading the learning as the participants construct their understanding. There needs to be a consideration of what learners need and the power dynamic between those involved. One tool for conceptualising this process can be adapted from MacNaughton (2005), who considers this as a technique to try to understand the meanings behind the play of children through rhizoanalysis, developing a complex network of observations, documents and relationship development in an attempt to create meaning on which there can be reflection. In the context of trying to understand practice, this technique can also be applied to adult interactions and the frameworks within which practitioners are operating. This section of this chapter considers the approach that can be taken to staff training and development, whether an early childhood setting is able to operate as an example of a Learning Organisation (LO), and how doing so would contribute to the development of the early years workforce. The next section explores how a theoretical framework is one way through which this cultural structure (e.g. an early years environment) is maintained.

The concept of a LO was proposed by Peter Senge in the 1990s. It considers that the role of any organisation is to invest in how its members can be encouraged to develop their knowledge, skills and attitudes within the organisation. To reflect on the extent to which an early years setting can be a LO is the subject of the next section.

Farago and Skyrme (1995) suggested that LOs have two important features. First, they will be open to unexpected changes, not seeing change as a curse, but as an opportunity to develop in new directions. Second, they will able to respond to change by encouraging innovation in the workforce. An illustration of how this might lead to a change in practice is seen in the research of Clark et al. (2005) in their exploration of listening to children, and trying to unpick what the pre-schoolers liked best in the new nursery being planned. This naturally leads to staff being able to focus on customer needs, taking a commercial phrase, and recognising that the practitioners are often working in a commercial context – where there is a need to listen to the children and respond to their preferences.

The proposition under discussion has therefore become re-focused on what the early years workforce can do for itself. The increasing requirement for early years practitioners to have achieved professional status demands a move towards working environments where there are continuous learning opportunities, with dialogue and enquiry being the daily norm. There needs to be time for leaders in the setting to capture and share the learning of the children and colleagues as well, thereby supporting the development of a collective vision. In this way, settings may understand that they are not operating in isolation, but are a network of practitioners, able to support each other, as they flourish within an ethos of generative learning.

An alternative approach: the social pedagogue

I am suggesting that a full review of the qualifications framework for EYPs to support the development of the right skills and values desired in the workforce is worth considering by government. If one looks at how some European countries have developed their early years workforce (Brown and White, 2014), one can see that a somewhat different strategy is being employed. Lancaster (2006) recognises that there is a basic requirement for those who work with children to listen and engage with them, as well as to provide them with opportunities to be active participants in the decisions affecting them, as specified in the UN Convention on the Rights of the Child (UNCRC). A higher level of involvement with the children and their families allows the creation of an environment where children can feel confident to explore. This may be seen to contrast with the current expectations in England, where children are subjected to regular testing and assessment from an early age.

A European practitioner may have a wholly different concept of what is meant by high-quality provision. Whether it is the direct implementation of the UNCRC or simply a reforming of *Every Child Matters*, the new generation of practitioners we would like to see in England would be less regarded as Early Years Teachers and more as Social Pedagogues.

To contrast a social pedagogue and an EYP is a useful exercise. The social pedagogue is a role less familiar within a UK context and combines a number of areas of expertise. Primarily, they are knowledgeable in all aspects of child development. They will have expertise in dealing with emotional and social areas of childhood, and understanding the needs of children. They will be willing to consider the wider social context in which the child is found, which might include family matters and aspects of economics, culture and history. However, the most significant feature of the social pedagogue role is the requirement for them to be led by the children with whom they are working. The skill is to be supportive when needed and to be able to step back when required to give the children space to learn for themselves. In this way the opportunity to try and then fail, and therefore develop resilience, is seen as a crucial part of their learning. It would be anathema for many social pedagogues to work to targets and learning goals and the concept of an externally imposed 'curriculum' is also alien; social pedagogues are concerned with supporting creativity and developing the imagination. Obenheumer (2012) observes that Rinaldi (2006) encourages the social pedagogue to work with the child, enjoys spending time with children and considers the care and education of each child in equal measure. Children are considered as citizens of their community, respected and valued.

Of course, teachers, EYPs and early years teachers will demonstrate aspects of these in their daily work. However, the social pedagogue will be more driven by the child, and this brings with it an alternative mind set. The extent to which early years teachers (or qualified teachers) can maintain this focus remains an open question.

Conclusion: drawing on the past to inform the future?

In this chapter, we have considered the development of the early years workforce, in particular how practitioners are prepared for the demands of working with children. We have considered this as an evolving role, having begun with an emphasis on simple care, but now requiring a high degree of knowledge and understanding of both children and childhood.

A review of recent government strategy relating to early years has been presented, together with a consideration of a theoretical model to support the development of the early years workforce in practice. We recognise the importance of dialogue between the government, training organisations and higher education to plan and provide meaningful career progression for the early years workforce. Finally, we have reviewed the European model of the social pedagogue, in which practitioners are encouraged to work with children as they explore their world.

But what kind of world are they going to find? It is to this question that we turn in Chapter 18.

References

Baldock, P., Fitzgerald, D. and Kay, J. (2013) *Understanding early years policy*. London: Sage.

Brown, M. and White, J. (2014) *Exploring childhood in a comparative context*. London: Routledge.

Cameron, C., Mooney A. and Moss P. (2002) The child care workforce: current conditions and future directions, *Critical Social Policy* 22: 572.

Children's Workforce Development Council (2010) The common core of skills and knowledge. Available at http://webarchive.nationalarchives.gov.uk/20120119192332/http:/cwdcouncil.org.uk/common-core, accessed 14 April 2015.

Clark, A., Kjorholt, A.T. and Moss, P. (2005) *Beyond listening: children's perspectives on early childhood services*. Bristol: Policy Press.

Dahlberg, G., Moss, P. and Pence, A. (2007) *Beyond quality in early childhood education and care: languages of evaluation*. Abingdon: Routledge.

DfE (2011) *The Tickell Review: the Early Years Foundation Stage (EYFS) Review: report on the evidence*. London: DfE.

DfES (2003) *Every child matters* (Green Paper). London: HMSO.

DfES (2006) *Children's workforce strategy: the government's response to the consultation*. Nottingham: DfES.

DfES (2007) *The Early Years Foundation Stage: setting the standard for learning, development and care for children from birth to five*. London: DfES.

Fairclough, N. (2003) *Analysing discourse*. Abingdon: Routledge.

Farago, J. and Skyrme D. (1995) *Insight 3: the learning organisation*. KMKnowledge.com, accessed 1 November 2014.

Foucault, M. (1983) The subject and power: afterword to H. Dreyfus and P. Rainbow (Eds) *Michel Foucault: beyond structuralism and hermeneutics*, pp. 208–264. Chicago: Chicago University Press.

Giddens, A. (1998) *The third way: the renewal of social democracy*. Cambridge: Polity Press.

Her Majesty's Treasury (2004) *Choice for parents: the best start for children: a ten year strategy for childcare*. London: Her Majesty's Treasury.

Jenks, C. (2004) *Constructing childhood sociologically* in M. Kehily (Ed.) *An introduction to childhood studies*. Maidenhead: Open University Press.

Lancaster, Y.P. (2006) *RAMPS: a framework for listening to children*. London: Daycare Trust.

Lorenz, W. (2008) Paradigms and politics: understanding methods paradigms in an historical context: the case of social pedagogy, *British Journal of Social Work* 38, 625–644.

MacNaughton, G. (2005) *Doing Foucault in early childhood studies*. Abingdon: Routledge.

Mathers, S., Ranns, H., Karemaker, A., Moody, A., Sylva, K., Graham, J. and Siraj-Blatchford, I. (2011) *Evaluation of the graduate leader fund: final report*. London: DfE.

McGillivray, G. (2008) Nannies, nursery nurses and early years professionals: constructions of professional identity in the early years workforce in England, *Critical Social Policy*, http://csp.sagepub.com/content/22/4/572, accessed 14 April 2015.

Miller L. (2008) Developing professionalism within a regulatory framework in England: challenges and possibilities, *European Early Childhood Education Research Journal* 16:2, 255–268. https://www.gov.uk/governmenstem/uploads/attachment_data/file/175.

Moyles J. (2010) Passion, paradox and professionalism in early years education, *Early Years: An International Research Journal*, 1 July, http://www.tandfonline.com/loi/ceye20, accessed 14 April 2015.

Noddings, N. (1994) An ethic of caring and its implications for instructional arrangements, in Stone, L. (Ed.) *The education feminism reader*. New York: Routledge.

Nutbrown, C. (2012) *Foundations for quality: the independent review of early education and childcare qualifications: final report* (Nutbrown Review). London: Department for Education.

Nutbrown, C. (2013) Shaking the foundations of quality? Why 'childcare' policy must not lead to poor-quality early education and care. Available at: http://www.shef.ac.uk/polopoly_fs/1.263201!/file/Shakingthefoundationsofquality.pdf, accessed 11 November 2014.

Obenheumer, J. (2012) *Who is an early years professional: reflections in policy diversity in Europe*, in Miller, L. and Cable, C. (Eds) *Professionalism in the early years* Abingdon: Hodder Education.

Ofsted (2014) *Are you ready? Good practice in school readiness*. Available at: www.ofsted.gov.uk/resources/140074, accessed 14 April 2015.

Osgood, J. (2004) Time to get down to business? The responses of early years practitioners to entrepreneurial approaches to professionalism, *Journal of Early Childhood Research* 2(1), 5–14.

Osgood J. (2006) Rethinking 'professionalism' in the early years: perspectives from the United Kingdom, *Contemporary Issues in Early Childhood* 7(1), doi: 10.2304/ciec.2006.7.1.1.

Petrie, P., Body, J., Cameron, C., Hepinstall, E., McQuail, S., Simon, A. and Wigfall, V. (2005) *Pedagogy: a holistic, personal approach to working with children and young people – European models for practice, training, education and qualification*. Briefing Paper, Thomas Coram Research Unit, Institute of Education, University of London.

Rich, D. (2006) Does birth to three matter? *Practical Professional Childcare*, November: 10.

Rinaldi, C. (2006) *In dialogue with Reggio Emilia: listening, researching and learning*. Abingdon: Routledge.

Senge, P. (1990) *The fifth discipline: the art and practice of the learning organisation*. New York: Doubleday.

Simpson, D. (2010) Becoming professional: exploring early years professional status and its implications for workforce reform in England, *Journal of Early Childhood Research* 8(3): 269–281.

Singer, E. (1993) Shared care for children, *Theory and Psychology* 3(4): 429–448.

Sylva K., Melhuish, E., Sammons, P., Siraj-Blatchford, I. and Taggart, B. (2004) *The effective provision of pre-school education [EPPE] project*. Nottingham: DfES.

Teather, S. and DfE (2013) *Improving the quality and range of education and childcare from birth to 5 years*. London: HMSO.

Tickell, C. (2011) *The early years: foundations for life, health and learning – an independent review on the early years foundation stage to Her Majesty's Government*. London: Department for Education.

Whalley, M. (2011) *Leading practice in early years settings*. Exeter: Learning Matters.

15 Why bother with masterliness?

Andrew Clapham

Introduction

Schools in England are held accountable, through inspections by the Office for Standards in Education (OfSTED), for outcomes which range from test and examination results to punctuality and exclusions. Through acknowledging such an inspection-facing climate, I explore masterliness against a backdrop of performativity in English schools (Lyotard, 1977; Ball, 2003; Perryman, 2009; Clapham, 2014a, 2014b). For La Velle (2012: 7), masterliness is a 'state of advanced professional critical thinking linked to action and informed by research and evidence'. Whilst not uncontested, for the purpose of this chapter I use La Velle's definition to describe the key informants' engagement with master's professional development (PD) whilst working at challenging inner-city English secondary schools as well as highlighting the broader discussion regarding PD and education professionals.

Using the data generated as part of a small-scale research project, I explore master's-level study and with it masterliness in the professional lives of 10 teachers working in 5 English secondary schools. The contexts of the 5 schools used as the settings for the project are important to map out at the beginning of this chapter. All 5 schools are located in areas of socio-economic deprivation in English cities. At the time of writing all 5 schools had recently been inspected by OfSTED, with 3 being highlighted as requiring improvement and 2 ranked as inadequate and placed in the serious weaknesses category. Even for those not familiar with the English education systems, these categories spell out that these schools are facing challenging circumstances and, in some cases, are fighting for survival.[1]

In this chapter, I present an overview of how the key informants felt about masterliness and why some did, and others did not, 'bother' with master's PD. To do so, I examine some of the macro-level structures, such as neo-liberalism and performativity, which appear to impinge on teachers' engagement with masterliness and which shape the methodological and philosophical choices made by those who do decide that master's study is for them.

Masterliness and the performative school

To understand masterliness, it is necessary to consider the performative environment in which the teachers in this study worked.[2] Performativity engenders a universal production of designated outcomes concerned with productivity and effectiveness, imposed from within and outside organisations, which frame the activities of that organisation and beyond (Lyotard, 1979). Performativity has been described as the prominent policy technology mediating changes to the English education system and the conditions in which teachers work, giving rise to what Ball (2003) calls post-professionalism. For Ball, teachers have to demonstrate 'success' by conforming to the ways in which others – inspectors, governors, government and the market – define their work.

Central to performativity is the 'legitimation of knowledge' (Lyotard, 1979: 27) and the 'transmission of learning' (48). For Lyotard, performativity mediates what constitutes knowledge, what knowledge is of worth and whose knowledge has legitimacy. Similarly, the decisions regarding how, and what, knowledge is 'transmitted' are also mediated through performative parameters. Lyotard claims that 'scientific knowledge' (25) – attained through the production, storage and analysis of easily quantifiable forms of data – is replacing 'narrative knowledge' (27). In doing so, knowledge is increasingly made legitimate through the epistemological boundaries of science and technology with the result that non-scientific narrative knowledge, based on experiences, values and beliefs, is increasingly marginalised. For Lyotard (46–47), the upshot of the legitimation of scientific knowledge is the commodification of knowledge and with it a 'context of control'.

Performativity is not separate from social contexts and is the 'policy technology' which mediates neo-liberal education systems (Ball, 2007). In England, performative conditions in education emerged from the neo-liberal policies of successive UK governments (Parsons and Welsh, 2006). Neo-liberalism encompasses varying degrees of conservative political ideologies and marries these with traditional liberal principles of right-of-centre economics (see Apple, 2006). Neo-liberalism has situated schools and education firmly within the competitive market through conservative modernisation (Apple, 2006). Neo-liberals position education at the forefront of national, and indeed international, competitiveness (McGregor, 2009) and therefore in need of evaluation through performative metrics such as *Programme for International Student Assessment* (PISA).

The link between performativity and neo-liberalism is illustrated in the resonances between Lyotard's work on the legitimation of scientific knowledge and Apple's (2006) examination of the neo-liberal market. Performative tools are employed to measure the performance of schools and teachers, for example through the use of General Certificate in Secondary Education (GCSE)[3] grades to indicate effectiveness (Nicholl and McLellan, 2008). Performativity as a neo-liberal policy technology also mediates what Rose called 'self-government' (1999: 264) where the state's accountability for its citizens is reduced, instead putting responsibility on the individual. For its proponents, therefore, neo-liberalism highlights the rise of the individual and the reduction of regulation, a point challenged by Jenny Ozga (2009: 150), who argues that neo-liberal and performative strategies such as inspection only mediate the appearance of the deregulation claimed by neo-liberal policy advocates.

The study

The five schools in which the key informants worked are located in the Midlands and South East of England[4] and are all state-funded secondary schools. Of the informants who volunteered for the study, only one of them was known to me previous to the research. Table 15.1 outlines the data relating to the key informants.

I employed reflexive interviewing (Hammersley and Atkinson, 1995) as the primary data generation tool. This model of interviewing was semi-structured (Kvale and Brinkman, 2009) in so far as master's PD and masterliness were the primary topics of conversation

Table 15.1 Key informant data

Informant	School	Completing MA	Completed MA	Not completed MA	Funding	Career trajectory
Harry	Winston	√	x	x	Joint funded with school	Beginning – 2nd-year Subject Teacher
Mary	Winston	√	x	x	School funded	Veteran – 25th-year SLT
Sammy	Sprowston	x	x	x	x	Beginning – 2nd year, 2nd in department
Chris	Sprowston	x	√	x	School funded	Middle years – 9th-year Head of Faculty
Ralph	Newbury	x	x	x	x	Veteran – 24th-year Head of Faculty
Asha	Newbury	x	x	x	x	Veteran – 21st-year SLT
Ria	Kings	x	√	x	Self-funded	Middle years – 11th-year Subject Teacher
Jo	Kings	x	x	x	x	Beginning – 3rd-year Head of Faculty
Gill	Woodside	x	x	x	x	Middle years – 16th-year Head of Year
Iesha	Woodside	x	√	x	Self-funded	Veteran – 25th-year Head of Faculty

between the informants and me. Prior to each interview, I prepared a script with key points for discussion which had emerged from my grounded theory analysis of previous interviews and the literature base. I was conscious that the script should not be strictly binding, and there were occasions where the informants' discussion opened up directions not included in the script.

As well as the key informants, interview data and field notes were also generated by a number of other actors. Members of staff would ask me what I was doing, and when I told them I was researching master's PD and masterliness, many would talk through their own thoughts on the subject. Rather than dismiss this data, I used this as a form of triangulation. For Denzin (1970: 310), using different methods to generate data indicates 'method triangulation'. I used data generated by actors in the settings as a method of verification, or refutation, of the key informants' claims through drawing on different data sources so as to develop a multi-layered view of the research setting. My analysis employed grounded theory (Glaser and Strauss, 1967) and I used open coding (amended from Charmaz, 2005) to yield concepts, which I grouped to make categories.

It is important to be 'up-front' with regard to some of the challenges facing this project. Indeed, a project such as this, which focused on a single researcher and a small number of key informants, requires acknowledgment of my subjectivity and reflexivity. My mobilisation of reflexivity is that it acknowledges 'past experiences and prior knowledge' (Wellington, 2000: 44) and challenges the notion that data can be 'free' from researcher influence. Consequently, my data analysis and interpretations were shared with the key informants for verification and to support the reflexive process.

The personal and the institutional

A focus of the chapter is how masterliness is considered by teachers at different points in their career trajectories. Day and Gu (2010) describe teachers as inhabiting 3 distinct phases of their career trajectories: beginning teachers, middle years teachers and veteran teachers.[5] I mobilised these three trajectory stages as 'filters' for the project as I wanted to explore associations, if any, between teachers at different points in their career and masterliness. What emerged from the data was that as much as links between master's PD and career trajectory, there was a distinction in the 'type' of master's PD engagement which I have called Personal Professional Development (PPD) and Institutional Professional Development (IPD). PPD is illustrated by informants who not only self-funded their master's but did not inform their schools of their studies. IPD can be seen in those informants who engaged in master's PD with the full knowledge of their schools, with some funding support from their schools and with regard to specific points which emerged from inspection reports and action plans.

I have used PPD and IPD in this chapter as a means of categorising, and understanding, what masterliness meant for the key informants. As Harry told me:

> I'm doing my MA a bit for me 'cause I want to run my own school, but mostly because I want to really do something for this school . . . I've had to sell why I'm doing this [the MA] to SLT [Senior Management Team] and that means it has to address the school's action plan . . . and that's fair. There might be things that I'm interested in, but it's about the school really.
>
> (Harry, interview)

For Harry, integral to masterliness was that it was part of the corporate structure of the school. Harry was completing an MA joint-funded by himself and his school and he clearly saw it as both contributing to the school's strategic plan and a vehicle for his career progression. Harry's thoughts were in stark contrast to Iesha, who had self-funded her MA over 18 years ago:

> I did my MA about something I passionately believed in. I did it as an action researcher but as a real action researcher . . . I mean that I wanted my research to change the school. I wasn't interested in the party line. I paid for it all myself and the Head didn't even know I was doing it.
>
> (Iesha, Field note)

It was from reflecting on Harry and Iesha's comments that it struck me the differences in the motivation for, and the audiences, these two teachers had in mind in relation to their masterliness engagement. Harry was clear that although he might want to do research into an area of his own interest, this was not the route he was going to pursue. For Harry masterliness was about contributing to his school's action plan and was therefore shaped by his school's, rather than his personal, priorities. Iesha, on the other hand, saw masterliness as a way of engaging with what she saw as a broken system and as she said 'shaking it up'. For Iesha, masterliness was an empowering of herself as a practitioner rather than a career move or corporate commitment.

From analysing this data it seemed that here were two distinct ends of a masterliness continuum. Harry inhabited the institutional end and Iesha the personal. What cannot be ignored here is that these two teachers are at different stages of their career trajectories and also participated in their master's during very different times for education. It was just this type of nuance that the project was designed to explore.

IPD engagers

Along with Harry, my analysis positions Mary and Chris also as IPD engagers. Chris was particularly vociferous in his thoughts as to what master's PD masterliness was and was not. For Chris, masterliness was all about impact:

> I don't see the point of doing research if you can't say what's actually happened. I understand that qualitative research is part of the social sciences . . . but I need to be able to tell my Head teacher that I have found *this* out. That's why I want to do RCTs [Random Control Trials]. These are a way of saying this was happening before, then we did this, and then we measured the difference. I have to talk about impact all the time . . . so research should be about impact.
>
> (Chris, interview)

What emerged from my interviews with Harry, Mary and Chris was that that PD should be developmental for the individual, but that the main drivers for such development were school-wide objectives. Mary suggested that when a member of staff came to her asking about master's PD, one of her first questions would be along the lines of 'what's in it for the school?' For Mary, the justification for master's PD that was fully or part-funded by the school was that there was a pay-back in relation to action plan targets. Indeed, a criterion for master's-level research at her school was that the measurable impact of an intervention was at the heart of any project.

This was not to say that Mary, Harry or Chris had a particular criticism of qualitative research in certain contexts. However, for these informants the ability to demonstrate impact was more readily afforded through the 'hard' data of quantitative methodologies. From interviews with these teachers there appeared an explicit assumption that any master's-level research would draw heavily on data-informed approaches:

> Doing a master's has to be about finding something out. I do the research methods bit and then I look at management and then I do the dissertation where I research something. But I've got to find something useful out . . . otherwise what's the point?
>
> (Harry, interview)

The key informants, whether IPD, PPD or master's non-engagers (MNE, see Table 15.1), all reported similarities in what constituted data. For these teachers data was very much part of the process of evidencing their practice as part of inspection processes. Where master's PD and masterliness sat in this was an important consideration for these teachers. Chris, having completed his master's, was clear that master's PD must inform the institution. Indeed, if master's PD was not institution-focused then it was, if not pointless, of questionable worth:

> I learnt a lot from my master's. I really enjoyed doing it. But if I were to do it now it would be completely different . . . of course I'm different, but the climate in schools has changed even over the last seven years. I wouldn't be happy doing my own little project. I would have to make sure that what I did was beneficial to the school as a whole.
>
> (Chris, interview)

All three IPD engagers described some of the issues which their schools were facing and where they felt masterliness fitted in with them. For these teachers their concerns were:

1   Inspection
2   Examination results
3   Progress/attainment
4   Data
5   Behaviour
6   Attendance.

Mary was concerned that the contents of this list, and her experiences of masterliness, did not necessarily match. She identified the importance of theory and practice and did not see a delineation between the two. Nonetheless, for Mary there was a mismatch between what master's PD meant in the confines of her university and what it meant in the highly pressured environment of her school. For all three IPD informants, masterliness was about applying the latest research-based evidence to the issues that their schools faced:

> I want to learn stuff that's going to help with kids' learning, behaviour, and attendance so that ultimately they [the students] get the best exam they can. In my school we do have an issue with some kid's behaviour . . . so I want to learn what research says about behaviour.
>
> (Mary, interview)

Ultimately, all three teachers wanted the best for their students and their school, were passionate about their subject, and wanted to be the best possible teacher that they could. What these key informants wanted from all PD and particularly master's PD and masterliness were strategies, learnings and understandings that they could take back and crucially *apply* to their school. For these teachers, theory was to be applied to context, research was a tool for finding things out and masterliness was fundamentally about making them, and their school, better.

PPD engagers

PPD engagers approached masterliness from a different perspective from Harry, Mary and Chris. Ria and Iesha saw their master's as a tool for self-reflection and informing their own practice. This is not to say they did not have a commitment toward their school as an organisation, but for these teachers masterliness was about them being the best teacher they could possibly be rather than addressing the school's action plans:

> I'm still a classroom teacher and that suits me fine. I've no interest in running departments or being on SLT. What I want to do is be as good as I can be. I read around education, I watch documentaries, I follow education tweets . . . teaching's such a mystery. My master's was about being a bit better equipped to try to make some sort of sense of it.
>
> (Iesha, interview)

Masterliness was located within a strong affinity PPD engagers had with specific issues which were close to them. Ria was passionate about special and inclusive education; for Iesha her passion was working with students at risk of permanent exclusion. Although both of these foci resonated with their school's action plans, they were not high priority. Indeed, it was the lack of priority given to her area of interest that motivated Ria to enrol in master's-level learning:

> I was working with lots of SEN [special educational needs] kids and I wanted to find out more about what this meant. I wasn't an SEN teacher or anything . . . and I didn't want to change to working in the SEN department! I just wanted to find out more.

> (Ria, interview)

What emerged from my conversations with these teachers was that both had self-funded their master's and, perhaps more importantly, had completed them covertly. I was intrigued by this notion of covert study and spent some time trying to unpick what this meant. Both informants felt that their school had not shown sufficient interest in these areas. Iesha had completed her MA in 2009 and Ria in 2012. Both teachers reported that the climate in their schools had detrimentally changed over their time working there, from one which might value their areas of interest to focusing on an inspection-facing model of school effectiveness.

The performative environment in English schools has wide-ranging implications for teachers' work (see Ball, 2003; Perryman, 2009; Clapham, 2014a). What was clear from the data for this project was that for all the informants the pressures facing schools and teachers were such that all PD, and with it masterliness, was located firmly within an 'impact' culture. Ria spoke about how she could not reconcile what she felt masterliness was for her and the need to demonstrate measurable outcomes:

> Measuring impact with SEN kids is so much against what I believe in. Getting some of these kids to school at all considering the chaotic and dysfunctional backgrounds some of them come from is a huge achievement. But a kid might still only have 40% attendance which in OfSTED speak is unsatisfactory. My MA was about trying to find out how we could support some of these kids . . . not measuring how much their attainment improves.

> (Ria, interview)

As the climate at their schools was not one these teachers felt supported the direction of their professional development, they took the decision to complete it independent of their school. I asked how this worked in relation to ethical clearance. Both teachers reported that they completed the necessary ethical procedures and that members of their school's SLT were aware that they were doing a master's but that they were, as Iesha put it, 'left to get on with it'.

My categorisation of IPD and PPD engagers raises a whole raft of questions regarding the direction of travel of masterliness and master's PD. On one hand there is Chris, who embraced the notion of PD being about a corporate commitment to improving the greater organisation, and his strident adoption of impact-measuring methodology such as RCTs. On the other hand is Iesha, who embarked on covert study rather than compromise her beliefs as to what her master's was about which, for her, was not measuring impact but exploring what might be the case.

Master's non-engagers (MNE)

When I define teachers as master's non-engagers it is important to stress this does not mean *masterliness* non-engagers. What was apparent from this cohort of key informants was that simply not having completed, or currently completing, master's-level PD did not preclude them from engaging with the concepts which La Velle (2012) uses to define masterliness (that is, critical thinking linked to action and informed by research). Jo, Gill, Ash and Ralph represented teachers representing all of Day and Gu's (2010) trajectory locations. What these informants shared were a common set of themes as to why a master's was not part of their PD agendas:

1   Work pressures stemming from inspection
2   Funding
3   Time.

All four of these teachers reported that the primary reason for not completing master's PD was directly linked to the performative and inspection-facing cultures at their schools. The pressures the informants described were related to the omnipresence of the inspector (see Foucault, 1977) and how this drove almost all of their work. The upshot of this culture was a lack of emotional and intellectual space with which to engage with meta-level educational issues beyond the next set of assessment checks.

Significantly, it was the lack of emotional space – what Gill called 'head space' – which all the MNE informants felt was necessary to do master's PD justice, which was of particular concern:

> I've thought about doing a master's . . . it really interests me . . . but I just don't see how I could get the space to think about the things I would need to think about.
>
> (Asha, interview)

The emotional and intellectual pressures of working in their schools left little space for these teachers to think about the constituent elements – such as research methodologies – of master's PD. Despite this, research was something which all four MNE informants reported really interested them. These teachers were intrigued by their practices and wanted to find out more about their work and they saw research as a valuable tool for helping with this. Unfortunately, what they could not resolve was how they would change their professional, and home, practices so as to fit in the work necessary to become a master's-level researcher.

Allied to this concern was that what these teachers might learn from master's PD might actually undermine even more the sometimes strained relationship between them and the direction of travel of their profession. This was an enthralling point. These teachers reported that the overriding mantra in their schools was 'inspection, inspection, inspection', a direction all were struggling to resolve. In many ways, being empowered to critique their schools through master's PD was a disconcerting prospect:

I don't bury my head in the sand. I really can't stand what's happening to schools. But . . . I really still love my job . . . I don't want to get angry and ill when I think about the madness of inspection and testing and league tables. I think that a master's would just highlight to me even more what's wrong with it all.

(Jo, field note)

What emerged here was that the MNE informants felt that the intellectual rigour of master's PD might highlight to them the large-scale challenges to their own professional identity and with it their feelings of disempowerment. This of course raises fundamental questions of power and power relationships which are outside of the scope of this chapter. Nonetheless, the tensions between what these teachers saw as their working environment, and the master's learning which might empower them to critique that environment, appeared to be a major player in their decision to be MNE.

Funding was also discussed by all four MNE informants with regard to their non-engagement. For their schools to contribute toward any master's PD, these teachers felt that they would be expected to produce deliverable outcomes which they might not necessarily be interested in. There were two strands to this concern: (a) the economic climate at the time of writing meant that schools were having their funding cut and (b) this resulted in 'measurable impact' on their school's action plans being a significant element of any funding that was available.

Paying for master's PD was seen as a large financial commitment by all the informants in this study. For those teachers, particularly part-funded IPD engagers, this commitment was part of buying into the cooperate requirements of their school's action plans first and then their own interests second. For PPD engagers, these teachers seemed to be both financially secure enough to make the self-funded commitment toward their own master's PD, and saw this as a worthwhile process primarily for their own development and then that of their schools. MNE informants seemed to be caught between the two. They saw the worth of master's PD but felt that they were not in a position to use what they might learn to empower themselves and their schools so they questioned the efficacy of making such a large financial outlay.

Integral to all of the MNE informants concerns regarding the feasibility of completing master's PD was time. All the informants in the study claimed they were time-poor. Those in relationships and with children found finding time for master's PD particularly challenging. This was not just a case of finding time to complete assignments – although this was a major concern – it was as much a case of finding time to think:

When I've got non-contact time I've found this little office, well a cupboard with no windows, and that's where I go to work and to think. No one knows about it and I've got a key!! I sit in there with the light off and do my work because I know I won't be disturbed.

(Gill, interview)

Despite their misgivings, all the MNE informants shared one final theme – they were interested in completing master's PD if circumstances were conducive. Of course, this could be a case of telling me what they think I wanted to hear. However, from the conversations I had with these informants, all talked passionately about their work, how much they loved what they did, and how they would relish the opportunity to understand more about their profession.

Conclusions

This chapter has been a whistle-stop tour of a small-scale research project. I am not making grand claims for what I have discussed. Having said that, the key informants I spoke to reported issues related to their master's PD which reflected challenges facing education systems at the macro-level. Foremost amongst these is how performativity, and performative tools such as inspection, are shaping the work of teachers and the environments they work in at fundamental levels. From the prevalence of 'impact' to teachers' disempowerment, this examination of why and how teachers engage with master's PD and masterliness has revealed some of the deep-seated challenges facing teachers way beyond the realm of professional development.

It seems to me that masterliness is ingrained in those teachers who are interested in what they do and want to find out more. This might seem an over-reduction of a complex set of themes and agendas. However, I argue that this chapter demonstrates some of the tensions and pressures facing teachers working in challenging schools and how these shaped their engagement with master's PD. In doing so, I suggest that performativity has had detrimental effects on how teachers choose to engage, or disengage, with master's PD. Space does not allow me to examine in the detail necessary some of the issues raised here. Having said that, the point of this book is to generate debate and thinking which I hope this chapter has done. However, I invite the reader to not just read. What I hope this chapter can do is to spark interest in others to think, read or research in the field of masterliness and master's PD.

To finish, I return to La Velle's (2012: 7) definition of masterliness as a 'state of advanced professional critical thinking linked to action and informed by research and evidence'. In reflecting upon La Velle's definition and with consideration of the data presented in this chapter, I maintain that if we are to develop our practice as educators then master's PD and masterliness should be a concern for students, parents, managers and policy makers alike. If it is not, then I suggest that the profession will become nothing but a performativity-driven production line where masterliness, and indeed critical and informed thinking in general, is relegated to a snatched activity carried out in dark windowless cupboards.

Notes

1 English schools are ranked as 'outstanding', 'good', 'requires improvement' or 'inadequate' (OfSTED, 2012: 17).
2 Master's PD has been considered in terms of performativity (see Bailey and Sorensen, 2012).
3 The end of compulsory schooling in England at Year 11 is signified by many students taking GCSE examinations. The number of A*–C GCSE grades attained by its students govern the position a school holds in national performance league tables and form part of the data set used by inspectors to rank effectiveness.
4 All schools and teachers have been renamed to preserve a level of anonymity.
5 Day and Gu (2010) suggest that there are two phases in each of the 3 categories of teachers' lives – beginning, 0–3 and 4–7 years; middle year teachers, 8–15 and 16–23 years; and veteran teachers, 24–30 and +31 years.

References

Apple, M. (2006) *Educating the 'right' way*. 2nd ed. New York: RoutledgeFalmer.

Bailey, M. and Sorensen, P. (2013) Reclaiming the ground of master's education for teachers: lessons to be learned from a case study of the East Midlands Masters in Teaching and Learning. *Journal of Education for Teaching: International Research and Pedagogy* 39, 1: 39–59.

Ball, S. (2003) The teacher's soul and the terrors of performativity. *Journal of Education Policy* 18 (2), 215–228.

Ball, S. (2007) *Education plc: understanding private sector participation in public sector education*. Abingdon: Routledge.

Clapham, A. (2013) Performativity, fabrication and trust: exploring computer-mediated moderation. *Ethnography and Education* 8, 3: 371–387.

Clapham, A. (2014a) Post-fabrication and putting on a show: examining the impact of short notice inspection. *British Educational Research Journal.* doi 10.1002/berj.3159

Clapham, A. (2014b) Producing the docile teacher: analysing Local Area Under-performance Inspection. *Cambridge Journal of Education.* doi 10.1080/0305764X.2014.955837

Clapham, A. (2014c) 'Answer your names please': a small-scale exploration of teachers technologically mediated 'new lives'. *Teachers and teaching: Theory and Practice* 21, 6. doi 10.1080/13540602.2014.968893

Day, C. and Gu, Q. (2010) *The new lives of teachers*. Abingdon: Routledge.

Foucault, M. (1991). *Discipline and punish: the birth of the prison*. London: Penguin.

Glaser, B. and Strauss, A. (1967) *The discovery of grounded theory: strategies for qualitative research*. Chicago: Aldine.

Hammersley, M. and Atkinson, P. (1995) *Ethnography: principles in practice* (2nd ed). London: Routledge.

Kvale, S. and Brinkman, S. (2008) *Interviews: learning the craft of qualitative research* (2nd ed). London: Sage.

La Velle, L. (2013) Masterliness in the teaching profession: global issues and local developments. *Journal of Education for Teaching: International Research and Pedagogy* 39, 1, 2–8.

Lyotard, J. (1979) *The postmodern condition: a report on knowledge* (G. Bennington and B. Massumi, Trans.). Manchester: Manchester University Press.

McGregor, M. (2009) Education for (whose) success? Schooling in an age of neo-liberalism. *British Journal of Sociology of Education* 30, 345–358.

Nicholl, B. and McLellan, R. (2008). 'We're all in this game whether we like it or not to get a number of As to Cs'. Design technology teachers' struggles to implement creativity and performativity policies. *British Educational Research Journal* 5, 585–600.

OfSTED (2012) *The framework for school inspection*. https://www.education.gov.uk/publications/eOrderingDownload/090019.pdf

Ozga, J. (2009) Governing education through data in England: from regulation to self-evaluation. *Journal of Education Policy* 24, 149–162.

Parsons, C. and Welsh, P. (2006) Public sector policies and practice, neo-liberal consumerism and freedom of choice in secondary education: a case study of one area in Kent. *Cambridge Journal of Education* 36, 237–256.

Perryman, J. (2009) Inspection and the fabrication of professional and personal processes. *Journal of Education Policy* 24, 609–629.

Wellington, J. (2000) *Educational research: contemporary issues and practical approaches*. London: Continuum.

16 Accountability

Trevor Cotterill

Historical perspective

Until recently the discourse surrounding schooling in England tended to focus upon issues such as pedagogy, allocation of resources and league tables (Allen and Burgess, 2010). Now, through quasi-marketisation, issues such as competition, deregulation and parental choice, along with the impact surrounding these changes nationally and globally, accountability has become a major force in current educational philosophy, policy and practice in the UK. The development of educational reforms and associated account-ability, starting with the Conservative government from 1979, through the New Labour government and the present Conservative-Liberal Democrat Coalition government, has led to the instigation of a 'quasi-market' with parents being viewed as 'consumers', who are provided with information about schools to make choices or 'preferences' of schools for their children (West et al., 2011). The introduction of market principles and greater autonomy for schools comes with the increased accountability for performance, supported by Ofsted reports and the publication of results in the form of league tables.

Under New Labour, alongside state-maintained schools, grant-maintained schools became foundation schools and independent academies were set up. Free from local authority control, they were controlled by a sponsor such as a business, voluntary organi-sation or Higher Education Institutions (West et al., 2011). The Conservative-Liberal Democrat Coalition government has extended this programme, introducing free schools where parents and other groups are encouraged to set up new state-funded schools (Cabinet Office, 2010). In the 1980s and 1990s the Conservative government introduced a number of policies with the intention of creating a market in education which sought to use private-sector and market incentives in state education (Hursh, 2005). For example, the Education Act (1980) began the process of giving more power to parents and the local management of schools, identified in the Education Reform Act of 1988, saw the head-teacher becoming an institutional manager. Pring (2012) describes an effective school as having a business model with precise targets along with performance indicators which are measurable and auditable. The language used in discourses surrounding education today is that of targets, performance indicators, audits, delivery, workforce, inputs and outputs, all of which originate from the business world.

The 1988 Education Reform Act (UK Parliament, 1988) allowed funding to follow the pupil and local authorities were required to allocate money to schools on a weighted per capita basis. Sanctions associated with market accountability were estab-lished, such as reduced funding for lower target numbers. Secondary schools in England and Wales were also given the power to opt out of local authority control, deriving funding from central government as they wished. The 1988 Act also introduced the National Curriculum and Key Stage testing at ages 7, 11 and 16; this became an important accounting measure. The Education Act 1992 saw parents taking a major role in the governance of schools and made head-teachers hierarchically accountable to parents. Schools were required to provide national test and examination results which were then made available to parents and published widely in the press as league tables. The Office for Standards in Education (Ofsted) was also established in this year, with responsibility for inspecting the quality of education in schools (House of Commons Children, Schools and Families Committee, 2009).

In 1995, the government approved the move to a value-added system of education, with prior achievement of pupils upon entering secondary school used to make adjustments from different intake achievements (Leckie and Goldstein, 2009). These value-added rankings were used between 2002 and 2005 but in 2006, contextual value-added systems were adopted. In addition to adjusting for individual student prior achievements, these models also attempted to adjust for factors such as the prior achievements of a student's peers, eligibility for free school meals, and lack of spoken English at home (Goldstein and Leckie, 2008). In 2009, the Labour government set out proposals, not adopted, for a School Report Card, which was to supersede the performance tables reporting on outcomes such as attainment, wellbeing, success in reducing the impact of disadvantage, parents' and pupils' views of the school and the support pupils received.

The current focus of the Coalition government

With a change of government in 2010, accountability became a more prominent feature within education with five key reforms outlined. These included ensuring that school governing bodies have the skills to hold their school to account, providing a greater variety of public information about each school and how it performs and the sharpening of the school performance with the addition of value-added measures accounting for prior attainment only. Also there was a more sophisticated minimum expectation for schools with the introduction of below the floor if fewer than 35% of pupils achieve 5 A*–C grade GCSEs (including English and mathematics), subsequently rising to 40%. Visits by Ofsted were changed, whereby schools judged to be Outstanding were only to be inspected if there was evidence of a decline in standards. In contrast, schools judged Inadequate would receive monitoring visits each term to assess improvement (Acquah, 2013). West et al. (2011) argued that these reforms were intended to create a quasi-market in education. This is much in evidence today, with new academies being created as well as the free schools programme enabling parents and other groups to set up state-funded schools, creating increased choice. However, Mattei (2012) suggests that this market operates in the shadow of a hierarchy with the results from national tests being available to parents to inform school choice, but that these indicators are also the focus of targets by the Treasury, the Department of Education (DfE) and Ofsted. The next section explores the general concept of accountability in education.

Accountability in education

The term 'accountability' is used in relation to a minimum expectation or standard regarding the effectiveness of a particular activity. An accountability system may be applied to something broad such as medical services, or restricted to specific initiatives such as truancy reduction (Stobart, 2007). Accountability in education is important as it is a publicly funded and universal state service. Education is therefore in the public interest and so the education system must be accountable both at the national and local level (House of Commons Children, Schools and Families Committee, 2009), because tax-payers have a right to expect that their money will be used effectively.

Accountability is also a multifaceted concept. West et al. (2011) present various types of accountability, conceptualised as professional, hierarchical, market, contract, legal, network and participative, distinguished in terms of who is accountable to whom, what they are accountable for, the various types of potential sanctions and the likelihood and severity of such sanctions. For example, professional accountability sees teachers at the centre of the process with accountability being based upon expertise developed through training and Continuing Professional Development (CPD) managed through codes of practice which are regulated by professional bodies and peers such as the Teaching Agency and the Education and Training Foundation. Other types of accountability relevant to education include contract accountability which is particularly relevant to academies who are accountable directly to the Secretary of State via a contractually binding funding agreement; legal accountability relating to how head-teachers and governing bodies have a legal responsibility for staffing, financial management, special educational needs and health and safety; and participatory accountability which sees the responsibility for education residing with parents, community stakeholders and students. I assert that two of the main types prominent in present educational policy and practice in England are hierarchical and market accountabilities.

Hierarchical and market accountabilities in education

Schools are held accountable through hierarchical structures for a number of aspects relating to their performance. For example, schools and their governing bodies are accountable to their local authority, DfE and Ofsted for their national test and examination results and how they spend resources. Sanctions in relation to hierarchical accountability take a number of forms, for example a negative Ofsted inspection could potentially have serious consequences for the viability of a school, including the issue of warning notices and the addition of new governors, or the replacement of a governing body with an interim executive board. Further reputational sanctions, such as publicly 'naming and shaming' schools and replacing management teams, are also associated with a hierarchical accountability regime (Acquah, 2013).

Market accountability has sought to make available a range of information by which consumers (parents) could hold English schools accountable. Information is available to parents in a variety of forms including the results of national tests and external exams taken at 11, 16 and 18, widely reported and commented upon in the media and reports of school inspections by Ofsted. The current Coalition government has made a commitment to provide comprehensive information available to parents about every school (Department for Education, 2010). Collectively, these different sources of information impact upon a school's reputation and inform consumer choice (West et al., 2011). Sanctions in relation to market accountability centre on the possibility of parental exit and school closure is possible if consumer demand declines significantly, but a more likely result is a reduction in funding.

Figlio and Loeb (2010) suggest that accountability in education is a broad concept that could be addressed in many ways. These include political processes to assure democratic accountability, the use of market-based accountability to inform parents and pupils or peer-based systems to increase the professional accountability of teachers. Accountability in education is aimed at increasing student achievement, and means evaluation and responsibility for all those involved. Education is the imparting of knowledge through a variety of means and Sahlberg (2010) suggests that we need to rethink accountability in a knowledge-based society. The advantage of such a system, with its trend towards competition and test-based accountability on predetermined knowledge, may do much to improve the performance of educational systems, but increased competition may not benefit the social capital of schools and the communities they serve.

International comparison

The fact that there is more choice for parents and that schools are accountable to either local or national government is important, but other factors also have an impact. Bradley and Taylor (2007) reported how schools in urban areas rather than in rural areas appear to improve their exam results in response to improvements in neighbouring school exam results. This was supported by Gibbons et al. (2008) who showed that secondary school progress is faster in areas of relatively dense population, but there was no overall effect of choice or competition on school performance.

The question of whether competition between private and public schools in Sweden has successfully raised standards has been debated. For example, Böhlmark and Lindahl's (2007) research on pupil performance showed a moderately positive impact of private school growth on academic performance but concluded that the advantages of school competition did not translate into any long-term gains. Morris (2012) concludes that school systems in which all students, regardless of their background, are offered simi-lar opportunities to learn, socio-economically advantaged and disadvantaged students attend the same schools, and students rarely repeat grades or are transferred out of schools because of behavioural problems, low academic achievement or special learning needs are more likely to perform above the OECD average and show below average socio-economic inequalities.

The educational system in Finland with its emphasis on cooperation rather than com-petition is often held up as an example whereby educational change does contribute to the social capital of schools. Interestingly, the Programme for International Student Assessment (PISA) (2012) average score for the 64 OECD countries showed that Finland was 519 (overall rank 12) compared with the United Kingdom 494 (overall rank 25) and the USA 481 (overall rank 36). At the top of the PISA league tables were Shanghai, China (613), Singapore (573) and Korea (554) (OECD, 2014). I suggest that the reason behind the high scores of many Asian countries such as China may lie not only in so-called rote learning but also a willingness to pair under-achieving schools with those that excel, a practice which is gaining favour in the English school sector.

The increasing emphasis on global measures of school effectiveness such as PISA results has gone a long way in legitimising government intervention in education. The previ-ous Coalition Secretary of State for Education, Michael Gove (2010–14), argued that the current education system is failing students in the core subjects of English, maths and science in comparison to other top-performing international countries (Department for

Education, 2011). He suggested that more attention should be paid to these core subjects as findings from international surveys, such as PISA, suggest that levels of attainment by UK students have rapidly decreased in the last ten years in literacy, maths and science (Department for Education, 2011). Such international findings were important in driving the Coalition government to address this so-called 'underperformance' and make education more accountable to central government.

However, Jerrim (2011) suggests that caution must be used when using the results of PISA exclusively as a basis for education reform. He argues that England's changing position in international performance tables neither supports nor refutes policymakers' calls for reform. He points out that while PISA indicates that England is slipping down the tables, another major study, TIMSS (Trends in International Maths and Science Study), reports that the maths scores of the country's 13 and 14-year-olds rose in comparison with other nations between 1999 and 2007. He has calculated that the disagreement between PISA and TIMSS over the change in English pupils' maths performance is much bigger than for any other country. Also, in contrast to Gove's focus on PISA, in 2013 one hundred academics wrote to the *Independent* newspaper arguing strongly against the reforms of the National Curriculum, suggesting that it would erode educational standards, and in a paragraph dedicated to PISA, suggested that he had clearly misunderstood England's decline in PISA international tests as schools in high-achieving countries such as Finland emphasise cognitive development, critical understanding and creativity, not rote learning (*Independent*, 2013). Pollard (2012) cited in Abrams (2012) shares a similar view; Pollard, who was elected as a member of the curriculum review team who produced recommendations for the reform, stated that the 2014 National Curriculum will increase inequality and reduce the quality of learning.

Nevertheless, there has been a move towards more radical market-based school reforms despite substantial rises in the number of pupils leaving school with five good GCSEs (DCSF, 2009), as UK schooling is not improving relative to other countries (OECD, 2007) and these improvements have been accompanied by even larger rises in educational spending, resulting in small falls in productivity across the sector (Wild et al., 2009). The PISA data suggests that a greater prevalence of school competition is related to a stronger relationship between a school's average socio-economic background and the school's average student performance and some would argue that PISA results apparently offer no support for the Government's attempt to extend the market approach in education, if the goal of education is to improve system performance and increase equity. Acquah (2013) reports that PISA 2009 also found there was no measurable relationship between the use of assessment data for accountability purposes and the performance of school systems. However, in Germany, Japan, Norway, Switzerland and the UK, having achievement data tracked by administrative authorities was positively related to student performance, and schools whose principals reported student achievement data publicly perform better than schools whose achievement data is not made publicly available in sixteen countries, but these tended to be socio-economically advantaged (Acquah, 2013). However, Burgess et al. (2011) concluded that publishing test results appears to be an extremely cost-effective policy for raising attainment and reducing inequalities.

Accountability and autonomy

I propose that education is more than performance indicators used for the purpose of accountability, and West (2010) supports this view by stating that such indicators do not meet the wider goals of education. Pring (2012) goes further when he suggests that the notion of performance against targets fails to treat young people as persons and that they become a means to some end in the production of league tables. However, DfE, citing the PISA research, has stated that there is strong evidence that using formal external assessment as the basis of accountability has significant benefits in how children perform, particularly for disadvantaged and minority groups. Whilst I agree that this may be the case, further longitudinal research as to the long-term benefits of such accountability measures is needed.

Keddie (2012) examines a key theme in the discussion on accountability and education, that of autonomy. On the one hand, she argues, it could be that schools have greater autonomy with respect to resource allocation, the linking of funding to student numbers and greater parental choice. The increased numbers of Academies (accelerated with the Academies Act in 2010) and Free Schools (from 2011) are clear examples of the government's prioritising of market-oriented school reforms, and the premise that parental choice, school diversity and competition between schools for their 'market' share of students will drive up school performance and outcomes. Currently half of all secondary schools in England (i.e. state schools originally the responsibility of the Local Education Authority [LEA]) have converted to Academy status. These schools are granted greater control and independence (than non-Academy status schools) through directly receiving state funding that would have previously been allocated to the LEA for oversight and support of schools in their jurisdiction (Glatter, 2012).

There is much debate about how academies are performing. DfE (2014) state that schools under the floor alongside a history of underperformance face being taken over by a sponsor with a track record of improving weak schools, a so-called Academy order, but critics including myself suggest that GCSE exam results in 2014 were lower than those for schools under local authority control. *The Guardian* (2014) stated that six out of nine of England's largest chains of academy schools only passed the government's minimum GCSE targets (40%) through success in other equivalent qualifications that are soon to be disqualified or downgraded in national league tables. Thus, I assert that an important measure of accountability, that of performance tables, can be manipulated by the addition or removal of vocational qualifications, or a change in the marking criteria such as that seen in the 2014 summer exams with the number asking for a review of marks increasing by 48% from 2013, with more than one in five challenges for both GCSEs and A-levels leading to new grades (Adams, 2014).

Free Schools extend the idea of the Academies programme; they are also independent, state-funded and not governed by the LEA but are established and run by parents, teachers, charities, businesses and other groups and are not bound to the national curriculum or by national union agreements (Hatcher, 2011). Supporters argue that they offer more choice to parents, whilst opponents suggest that they are taking resources away from established schools. There may have been a move towards greater autonomy, but equally, as far as state schools are concerned, there has been a move to a prescriptive National Curriculum and assessment framework where student performance is audited and converted to a public ranking of schools in the form of league tables, with school 'effectiveness' policed and regulated through Ofsted inspections (Glatter, 2012; Lawson et al., 2013).

Competition

A key factor in the discourse surrounding accountability is that of competition. In a market-based educational system parents choose a school and schools market themselves to maximise this potential, thus popular schools may grow and unpopular schools may close. This premise is that of a quasi-market system, based upon competition raising educational attainment. Key information sources used as performance indicators by parents acting as consumers include national tests, public exams reported through school achievement and attainment tables (so-called league tables by the media), as well as Ofsted inspection reports, but one could question the validity and reliability of such measures.

In August 2014 head-teachers in England put forward plans to publish their own school league tables, separate from official performance data published by the government used to generate school rankings. They wanted to include more information than exam results, such as music and sport results, with the aim of bypassing political involvement in school data. Published before the official tables, they argue that this would present an independent and more inclusive view of schools, with the emphasis on an objective, neutral and accurate view. The proposals have been put forward by the Association of School and College Leaders, the National Association of Head Teachers and the United Learning group, who run academies and independent schools. An interesting point relating to accountability is that they suggested that rather than criticising the government over league tables, it was time for the education profession to take responsibility for its own information. However, the government had already announced plans for an overhaul of how league tables are assembled. From 2016 they will show pupils' overall performance in eight subjects rather than currently focusing on five GCSEs at grade C or above. In addition there will be a move to ensure that all schools publish extensive information, including pupil progress. I feel that the time may have come for a meeting of minds to ensure that the outcomes measured take account of the pupil in a more holistic way, which includes indicators other than examination success.

Accountability and the teaching profession

Test and exam results are important indicators for how well a school is doing in comparison with others, but if a school does less well than another in the catchment area, there arises the debate as to who is accountable for these poor results. The 5 A*–C measure has been criticised for leading to a concentration of resources around 'C' grade, and reducing the educational gains of lower-achieving students, with issues surrounding equity (Burgess et al., 2005); there may be immense pressure for teachers to improve results and so-called teaching to the test or exam. The use of performance tables for accountability purposes has been identified as one of the factors influencing early entry policies at GCSE. Taylor (2012) examined trends in early entry between 2007 and 2011 using data from all the UK awarding bodies. There was a difference in entry patterns between subjects and he argued that this was likely to be a reflection of the perceived importance of different subjects in relation to the 5 A*–C measure as early entry was found to be most prevalent in English and Mathematics. DfE (2014) stated that from September 2013 a pupil's first entry in a particular subject will count towards the school's performance tables with the aim of discouraging preparation for examinations, the low progression onto A-levels from GCSE candidates with grades B and C and the 'banking' of results.

Conclusion

Economies of worth have changed what it means to be a teacher, with Ball (2013) suggesting that teachers are subject to a range of judgments, comparisons and targets linked to their capacities to drive up the performance indicators such as examination results, school retention and social participation. As the school is evaluated upon these priorities, teachers are drawn into an ethos of productivity by performance which may serve to undermine a teacher's autonomy and professionalism, leading to a culture of compliance. Teaching could be viewed as performance management against performance indicators and less about creativity, differentiation and student–centredness.

Accountability in education is here to stay and there continues to be a debate as to the value of current policy and practice, which relies heavily upon these measures. Sahlberg's (2010) 'intelligent accountability' combines internal accountability such as school processes, self-evaluations, critical reflection and school-community interaction with external accountability built on monitoring, sample-based student assessment and thematic evaluations. He argues that cooperation and networking, not competition, are necessary to create the conditions for young people to develop into well-educated and prepared people who have acquired the knowledge and skills to work in an innovative way (Sahlberg, 2010). Thus, education should not only be concerned with test results; there needs to be a broader focus upon the link between wellbeing and society with the focus upon social justice.

References

Abrams, F. (2012). Cultural literacy: Michael Gove's school of hard facts. [Online] Available from: http://www.bbc.co.uk/news/education-20041597 [Accessed: 21st August 2014].

Acquah, D. (2013). *School accountability in England: past, present and future.* Manchester: Assessment and Qualifications Alliance.

Adams, R. (2014). Fears over poor marking as appeals for A-level and GCSE exams hit new high. *The Guardian.* [Online] 21st October. Available from: http://theguardian.co.uk [Accessed: 21st October 2014].

Allen, R. and Burgess, S. (2010). *The future of competition and accountability in education.* London: 2020 Public Services Trust.

Ball, S. J. (2013). *Policy paper: Education, justice and democracy – the struggle over ignorance and opportunity.* Centre for Labour and Social Studies. London: CLASS.

Böhlmark, A. and Lindahl, M. (2007). *The impact of school choice on pupil achievement, segregation and costs: Swedish evidence.* IZA discussion paper 2786.

Bradley, S. and Taylor, J. (2007). *Diversity, choice and the quasi-market: an empirical analysis of secondary education policy in England.* Lancaster University Management School Working Paper, 038.38.

Burgess, S., Propper, C., Slater, H. and Wilson, D. (2005). *Who wins and who loses from school account-ability? The distribution of educational gain in English secondary schools.* CEPR Discussion Paper No. 5248.

Burgess, S., Wilson, D. and Worth, J. (2011). *A natural experiment in school accountability: the impact of school performance information on pupil progress and sorting* (CMPO Research Report). Bristol: University of Bristol, Centre for Market and Public Organisation.

Department for Children, Schools and Families (2009). *Your child, your schools, our future: building a 21st century schools system.* London: The Stationery Office.

Department for Education (2010). *The importance of teaching: the schools' White Paper.* London: DfE.

Department for Education (2011). *Review of the National Curriculum in England: what can we learn from the English, mathematics and science curricula of high-performing jurisdictions?* London: DFE.

Department for Education (2014). *Schools causing concern.* London: DfE.

Figlio, D. and Loeb, S. (2010). School accountability. In *Handbook of the economics of education,* edited by Hanushek, E.A., Machin, S. and Woessmann L. Amsterdam: Elsevier.

Gibbons, S., Silva, O. and Wilson, J. (2008). Urban density and pupil attainment, *Journal of Urban Economics,* 63(2), 631–650.

Glatter, R. (2012). Persistent preoccupations: the rise and rise of school autonomy and accountability in England, *Educational Management Administration & Leadership,* 40(5), 559–575.

Goldstein, H. and Leckie, G. (2008). School league tables: what can they really tell us? *Significance,* 5(2), 67–69.

Hatcher, R. (2011). The Conservative-Liberal Democrat Coalition government's 'free schools' in England, *Educational Review,* 63(4), 485–503.

House of Commons Children, Schools and Families Committee (2009). *School accountability.* London: The Stationery Office.

Hursh, D. (2005). Neo-liberalism, markets and accountability: transforming education and undermining democracy in the United States and England, *Policy Futures in Education,* 3(1), 3–15.

Independent (2013). *100 academics savage Education Secretary Michael Gove for 'conveyor-belt curriculum' for schools.* [Online] Available from: http://www.independent.co.uk/news/education/education-news/100-academics-savage-education-secretary-michael-gove-for-conveyorbelt-curriculum-for-schools-8541262.html [Accessed: 21st August 2014].

Jerrim, J. (2011). *England's 'plummeting' PISA test scores between 2000 and 2009: is the performance of our secondary school pupils really in relative decline?* IOE: DoQSS Working Paper No. 11 – 9 December 2011.

Keddie, A. (2012). *Matters of autonomy and accountability in the English schooling policy context: constraints and possibilities.* Brisbane: University of Queensland.

Lawson, H., Boyask, R. and Waite, S. (2013). Construction of difference and diversity within policy and practice in England, *Cambridge Journal of Education,* 43(1), 107–122.

Leckie, G. and Goldstein, H. (2009). The limitations of using school league tables to inform school choice, *Journal of the Royal Statistical Society: Series A* (Statistics in Society), 172(4), 835–851.

Mattei, P. (2012). Market accountability in schools: policy reforms in England, Germany, France and Italy, *Oxford Review of Education,* 38(3), 247–266.

Morris, P. (2012). Pick 'n' mix, select and project; policy borrowing and the quest for 'world class' schooling: an analysis of the 2010 schools' White Paper, *Journal of Education Policy,* 27(1), 89–107.

OECD (2007). *PISA 2006: science competencies for tomorrow's world.* Paris: OECD.

OECD (2014). *PISA 2012: results in focus – what 15-year-olds know and what they can do with what they know.* Paris: OECD.

Pring, R. (2012). Putting persons back into education, *Oxford Review of Education,* 38(6), 747–760.

Sahlberg, P. (2010). Rethinking accountability in a knowledge society, *Journal of Educational Change,* 11(1), 45–61.

Stobart, G. (2007). *Testing times: the uses and abuses of assessment.* London: Routledge.

Taylor, R. (2012). *Analysis of the trends in early entry at GCSE.* Manchester: Assessment and Qualifications Alliance.

UK Parliament (1988). *Education Reform Act 1988.* London: The Stationery Office.

West, A. (2010). High stakes testing, accountability, incentives and consequences in English schools, *Policy & Politics,* 38(1), 23–39.

West, A., Mattei, P. and Roberts, J. (2011). Accountability and sanctions in English schools, *British Journal of Educational Studies,* 59(1), 41–62.

Wild, R., Munro, F. and Ayoubkhani, D. (2009). *Public service output, input and productivity: education.* Newport: Office for National Statistics.

Part III

Practice

17 We are all critically reflective now

The politics of critical reflection in higher education and in the workplace

Ruby Oates

Look at any discipline within higher education these days and you will find some reference to the activity and concept of critical reflection. It seems that no matter what subject, discipline or vocation we study or practise, there is an expectation that we will be critically reflective in relation to the knowledge gained through higher education study, and through an application of it to our practice in the workplace. In my own field, early childhood studies, practitioners are required to use their learning to reflect upon their practice in the early childhood setting, to improve their performance and enhance their practice. In this chapter, I want to problematise the concept of critical reflection and consider its uses and limitations from a multi-disciplinary perspective. In doing so, I will question what it means to be critically reflective, what are its uses and limitations, and whose interests it serves.

What is critical reflection?

As students in postgraduate higher education, you are most likely familiar with the early contributors to the development of the terms 'reflection' and 'critically reflective practice'; in particular, the work and ideas of Dewey (1933) and Schön (1983). Ryan (2013: 145) notes that Schön's work on the '*reflective practitioner*' has been of particular interest to those of us who work with professionals, suggesting it is an approach that is 'steeped in practice, particularly in building theory from practice'. Ryan (2013: 144) notes that:

> Reflection is a common expectation for learners in higher education, both informally in the hope that learners will reflect and act upon feedback provided, but also in formal assessment tasks.

She suggests that despite the common and often undefined use of the term 'reflection', learners are rarely taught how to reflect, which results in superficial learning. Ryan (2013: 1344) argues:

> Indeed, attempts to include reflection in assessment tasks with little or no pedagogical scaffolding generally results in superficial reflections that have virtually no impact on learning or future practice.

Hickson (2011), writing from the perspective of a social worker, notes that many authors, for example Fook (2002; 2010), recognise it was the initial work of Dewey (1933) that was further developed by Schön (1983), Argyris and Schön (1996) and Mezirow (1990) that 'established the foundations of reflective practice' (Hickson, 2011: 831).

In defining 'reflection' Hickson (2011) suggests the terms 'reflection' and 'critical reflection' are contested ideas and there are various definitions, in part influenced by different practice experiences and the different disciplines and vocations. She notes Redmond's (2006) point that 'reflection' and 'critical reflection' are used interchangeably, without any explanation as to what makes them different.

Smith (2011), writing from a nurse training perspective, notes that what is striking about the concept of reflection and its uses is that very little is known about the difficulties, practicalities and methods of critical reflection and how it is taught in an academic context. He suggests that tutors should introduce students to the different theories and techniques to support their learning, otherwise

> students in HE could perceive critical reflection as elusive or idealistic rather than an essential set of learning tools.
>
> (Smith, 2011: 212)

We should not assume, however, that students move into higher education without any previous reflective skills. Taguchi (2007: 279) reminds us that in teacher education, students do not arrive

> with an empty toolbox needing to be filled with education theories and methods, but rather with a toolbox already filled (and continuously refilling itself), with tools needing to be unpacked, investigated, and reformulated.

To me, this understanding of higher education makes a lot of sense; it encapsulates its purpose as it emphasises the development of students' abilities and skills to think in a critical manner. Fook's (2006) point is useful here; he argues that we need to revisit our understanding of the 'critical' in critical reflection and the theoretical frameworks attached to it, if we are to fully understand it. Brookfield (2009) makes a similar point; he raises concerns about conflating the terms 'reflection' and 'critical reflection', suggesting that adding the qualifier 'critical' somehow makes the reflection more profound and deep. He suggests that while reflection has its uses in the workplace, if an activity is deemed critically reflective, it should question the power relationships that allow or promote one set of practices over another. For Brookfield (2009), the concept and definition of critical reflection incorporates a challenging and uncovering of power dynamics (Foucault, 1980) that frame practice, asking questions such as whose interests are served by a particular practice, as well as staying alert to ideas and behaviours that are subtly harmful to them and others (Brookfield, 2009).

Different understandings of critical reflection

My own interest in critical reflection in higher education and the workplace came about as a result of my role as programme leader and tutor to undergraduate students who made direct entry into the level six stage/final stage of the honours degree programme I led. Many of the direct entrants come via work-based awards underpinned by competency-based training. As an undergraduate teaching team we were concerned about how the rhetoric of 'critical reflection' was fully embedded within their writing, but the nature of the work was ritualistic (Mezirow, 1991), technical and narrow, simply reinforcing current thinking and practice within their own settings. It seemed as if work-based learning students were being denied knowledge and understanding of the theoretical backgrounds attached to the activity of reflection. They did not appear to be informed about how critical reflection might enable them to look beyond the day-to-day mechanics of an activity; it is in this sense that reflection can be seen as a technical act, most often confined to measuring outcomes that had been set by others.

In my own research (Oates, 2011) involving experienced early childhood practitioners, I interviewed participants about how they experienced and perceived their work-based training courses in terms of informing and developing their critically reflective practice. Two responses stood out:

> I found the whole thing mentally frustrating, the whole thing. It was too restrictive, the assignments seemed to be more about aligning the titles right and setting it out right . . . by the time you'd got the words in they wanted to read so you were writing to each objective and learning outcomes, then if you did that, you'd passed the assignment. The critical reflection was squeezed; it was edged out of the Foundation Degree.
>
> (Interview participant, higher-level teaching assistant, 14 years' experience: Oates, 2011: 133)

> The focus was about your practice rather than thinking and reading [the] ideas of others, practice was the benchmark, you found things that backed up what you thought but sometimes you tend to think your practice is right and you do not always question that enough perhaps.
>
> (Interview participant, higher-level teaching assistant, 18 years' experience: Oates, 2011: 133)

Barnett (2000) argues that the nature of university knowledge in recent years has changed from the pursuit of truth to the teaching of skills to enable workers to perform in the world of employment. In considering the limits of competence, he argues that genuine higher education is an open-ended process, not a delivery of pre-specified products. Tarrant (2000), in presenting a critique of competency-based training, suggests that such training denies students an opportunity to develop increasingly sophisticated ways of knowing and analysing society, and understanding their place within it:

> It halts the development of the mind by substituting it with a set of . . . behavioural performances.
>
> (Tarrant, 2000: 81)

It is important, however, to point out that it is the nature and context of work-based learning that is being criticised here and not work-based learning, which is acknowledged (Siebert and Walsh, 2013) as playing a very important role in widening participation in higher education for sections of society previously denied educational opportunities.

Moss's (2013: 233) contribution to debates about the role of the early childhood practitioner has been particularly useful in deconstructing the dominant discourses aligned to early childhood practice. He suggests that many practitioners have little option but to engage in a form of 'vulgar pragmatism' (Moss, 2013: 233) that reduces their work and any reflective practice attached to it to a narrow set of technical questions. He suggests it is 'critical pragmatism' (2013: 233) which provides the practitioner with opportunities to be involved in the making of ethical and aesthetic choices, creating a worker who is a reflective and dialogic practitioner, open to new, unexpected ideas, someone who is confident and can deal with change and uncertainty. Likewise, Osgood (2010), writing about early childhood practitioners and recent attempts to professionalise this workforce, notes how undergraduate degree courses such as Early Childhood Studies provide a space for students/practitioners to reflect upon the ways in which theory relates to practice and, as a result of their growing professional confidence, practitioners are able to engage in critical reflections. This provides practitioners with

> alternative positionings available to them through the articulation and performance of alternative discourses of professionalism.
>
> (Osgood, 2010: 13)

Fendler (in Pihlaja and Holst, 2013: 183), as a cultural feminist, argues that reflection takes part within a discourse and knowledge base that has been 'socialised by masculinist technical rationality'. Likewise, Osgood (2010) argues that neo-liberal discourse promotes a form of professionalism underpinned by masculinist values and cultures, noting how childcare is a highly gendered, employment sector strongly associated with caring and nurturance. Childcare work then is often seen as lacking in professionalism because it is deemed to be hyper-feminine (Cameron et al., 2001; Osgood, 2010). In my own research (Oates, 2011) with early childhood practitioners, many of the participants talked about the passion they had for their work. Osgood (2010) suggests what is required is an alternative discourse about childcare work and the professionalism associated with it. She suggests that a 'critically reflective emotional professional' (Osgood, 2010: 119) is required for the sector, one that recognises the pedagogic practices in nurseries and acknowledges the emotional labour (Colley et al., 2003) attached to such work, and celebrates rather than denigrates emotional professionalism.

Pihlaja and Holst (2013) suggest that Habermas's (1972) levels of knowledge are an excellent starting point for any study of reflectivity; this includes three levels of reflection: technical, practical and emancipator. They used these three levels to undertake their research of early childhood teachers' working in Finnish day-care settings, investigating how they used reflexivity. Their findings show teachers reflecting upon their work mainly at a technical level and conclude that the low levels of reflectivity in Finnish day-care are a matter of concern. Their research raises questions about what factors hinder practitioners' abilities to reflect critically and how, and if, a culture of reflexivity is possible within these settings, given the constraints and pressures placed upon day-care workers.

My own research (Oates, 2011) found evidence that the early childhood practitioners' critical thinking had increased during their time in higher education, providing them with 'new agency' (Francis, 2001: 166) to change their lives, even though their previous work-based programmes left them initially unprepared for the deep thinking skills required at honours-level study. For me, this raises ethical questions about the role work-based learning plays in the continuation of a gendered, 'vocational habitus' (Colley et al., 2003: 471) in the early childhood workplace. However, like Pihlaja and Holst (2013),

I am also concerned about how opportunities for practitioners to reflect individually and with colleagues are embedded within the practice setting; I, too, recognise that a cultural shift in working practices is required if we are to move beyond the rhetoric of critical reflection in students' work and in the workplace.

MacNaughton et al. (2002), writing from a feminist, post-structuralist position, argue that it is imperative that early childhood workers incorporate criticality into their daily practice. They believe this should constitute a form of critical activism whereby practitioners should be encouraged to contest, reflect on and explore different truths about childhood. MacNaughton (2005: 38) builds upon the ideas of Foucault (in Dreyfus and Rabinow, 1982) suggesting that child-centred pedagogies constitute a 'regime of truth' which presents child development in a particular way and through a particular set of discourses. MacNaughton argues that through critically reflective questioning it is possible to analyse the micro-politics of power in early childhood education and care settings to bring about change. However, others (for example, Penn, 2007) would question whether individual practitioners hold sufficient power to change things, given the power held by governments and the private sector, in particular the increasing multinational ownership of the private day-care in this country and in other parts of the world.

Brookfield's (2009) writing is a useful starting point for those interested in appreciating and understanding the theoretical background to the emergence of critical reflection in many subject areas. He sets the scene by recognising the technical aspects of reflection and how a number of intellectual traditions coming from philosophy, psychoanalysis, constructivism and pragmatism inform these aspects. He makes a useful comment:

> When professionals talk about reflective practice it is these traditions that usually lurk at the periphery.
>
> (Brookfield, 2009: 296)

Brookfield (2009) suggests that there are four intellectual traditions informing the use of the term 'critical reflection' in academia. These are neo-Marxism and the work of the Frankfurt School of critical social theory; psychoanalysis and psychotherapy; analytical philosophy and logic; and pragmatist constructivism. Readers are encouraged to seek out their own interests dependent on their discipline and vocational backgrounds, to place critical reflection within an intellectual framework, using the reference list at the end of this chapter.

Given the differing theoretical traditions shaping the concept of critical reflection, it is important to appreciate and recognise that the concept itself can mean very different things, and it is in this way that reflection is a contested (Brookfield, 2009) and socially constructed idea. I strongly believe that students in higher education should seek out and formulate their own position on what constitutes critical reflection to inform their practice in any context of education.

The uses of critical reflection

Moore and Ash (2002: 5–6) explored the value of reflective practice to new teachers, noting that they will inevitably think critically about what they are doing; however, if left unsupported such thinking can become negative, perfunctory and destructive. In defining reflective practice they say it must be critical, challenge existing presuppositions, seek alternatives and contribute significantly to development or change. They identified four forms of reflection; one they call 'ritualistic reflection', which they say is often linked to discourses of competence and performance, in some ways similar to Moss's (2013) 'vulgar pragmatism'. A second form they call 'pseudo-reflection'; this involves a genuine intention to consider important issues but it does not lead to change or development. A third form they call 'constructive' which seeks to problematise a situation and challenge existing beliefs. A fourth and final term is 'reflexivity'; here reflection moves beyond the immediate situation to consider social, cultural and emotional aspects and their impact upon practice. Their findings show that their participants value reflection even at an early stage of their professional development. Moore and Ash (2002: 18) conclude that the development of reflective practice should be restored to the centre of teacher education programmes and not form something peripheral to it.

Morley and Dunstan (2013), in exploring social work education and the role of critical reflection, express concern about the recent ascendance of competency-based initiatives that they suggest are leading to deprofessionalisation of social work, through a separating of theory from practice. They suggest that such initiatives 'undermine more sophisticated approaches to theorised practice' (Morley and Dunstan, 2013: 142) and create divisions between academics and the field of practice. Their social work education programme uses critical reflection as a pedagogical tool to enable students to deconstruct their practice and the implicit values and actions within it. Writing about their students' use of critical reflection, they note:

> Once they have used deconstruction to uncover multiple interpretations of their practice incident, they draw on critical and postmodern theoretical principles to reconstruct their practice.
>
> (Morley and Dunstan, 2013: 149)

Their research findings show that critical reflection helps students to manage their responses to conflict better, it provides students with opportunities to deconstruct dominant understandings of their role as a student in practice, and provides the participants with an 'empowered sense of identity' (Morley and Dunstan, 2013: 152). They argue that critical reflection is a powerful learning tool for students and that critical reflection alongside a critical pedagogy can act as practices of resistance and provide tools for students to question and rethink social work discourses to promote individual agency. They conclude:

> Finding the agency to exercise such practices of resistance may be important in creating alternative ways of engaging in and with field education, and may ultimately be crucial to our capacity to maintain and protect the quality of field education and social work programmes into the future.
>
> (Morley and Dunstan, 2013: 153)

Callens and Elen (2011) studied how students in Belgium on a pre-teacher training course used critical reflection. They found that students' reflections do not reach a critical level and they question whether it is too ambitious to expect all students to reflect critically. They suggest that students are allowed control over their assignment tasks, their layout and competencies, if they are required to engage in critical reflection in a meaningful way.

Smith (2011) notes the huge variation in how critical reflection is put into practice in higher education. For example, this can range from informal discussions to highly structured forms of assessment and may include journals, interactive forms and service–user involvement. This means that the focus of learning is on the technique itself rather than on the intended purpose of critical reflection. She suggests that in educational contexts reflection can therefore become inward–looking and allows self-inspection to dominate. She notes how Clegg (1999) suggests that this extreme self-reflection can become internalised, subjecting the student to an adherence to a way of being without conscious scrutiny; the focus then is the self rather than the social contexts in which the individual studies, works and practises.

In a Foucauldian sense (Foucault, 1977) critical reflection can be seen as a form of disciplinary technology (Oates, in Oates and Hey 2014) whereby workers subjugate themselves through their own surveillance and self-scrutiny. In this way, reflection is a normalising process whereby workers believe they are exercising some control over their working lives and practices when in fact they are not. The way in which higher education supports students' critical thinking and reflection, then, becomes even more important. Morley and Dunstan (2013) suggest one solution is to build reflective tools into course structures; these provide students with a framework that enables them to reflect upon their autonomy, self-direction, critical reflection and transformation, as well as knowledge and power formations.

The problem remains, however, that the subject of reflection continues to monitor and assess him or herself in front of others, usually their tutors. This then raises ethical questions about if and how much of the self should be scrutinised by others. Siebert and Walsh (2013) argue that work–based learning in particular exposes the student to public scrutiny and self-surveillance; it becomes a new and modern form of 'confession' (Usher and Edwards, 1994: 95). This form of practice is now commonly seen in work-based learning, through which the individual exercise of reflection is an illusion, but the actual benefit is to the organisation as the individual learns to self-regulate their behaviour and practice.

Other criticisms of the role of critical reflection also address the increase in students reflecting upon their 'emotional performativity' (MacFarlane and Gourlay, 2009: 455) in a similar way to the 'confessional' aspect of such writing already discussed in this chapter. Reflective student assignments in higher education often include students reflecting upon themselves in a manner that is often overly self-critical and guilt-ridden, again exposing the student to public scrutiny. MacFarlane and Gourlay (2009) argue that this devalues the authenticity of reflection because students are very aware that their reflections are judged by others.

In a similar vein, Siebert and Walsh (2013) argue that the most contested aspect of reflection in education is assessment, particularly when students have to expose themselves to the scrutiny of others, usually their higher education tutor. They note how the tutor has the power to judge another's reflections so that a true partnership is not possible. This may lead to students providing a particular answer to present an image of him or herself, which raises further questions about the authenticity of the work and the student's position within it. This suggests that academic disciplines and assessment requirements constitute an exercise of power over students and practitioners. In a Foucauldian sense, the process and action of assessment constitutes yet another form of disciplinary technology. Siebert and Walsh (2013: 171) also suggest that in exposing the content of reflection to the scrutiny of others who have authority over them, the learner/worker risks a negative judgement, either from the academy or from their employing organisation. Trust is essential in making the exercise meaningful; however, our experiences of facilitating work-based learning in higher education suggest that lack of trust in the workplace and the managers' intentions hinders learning from reflection. 'Self-censored' reflective accounts may not be perceived as meaningful learning.

However, it is important not to over-simplify the relational aspect of critical reflection and the power relations attached to it. In my own research with experienced early childhood practitioners (Oates, 2011: 176), I found that exposing students to theories and tools of critical reflection has the potential to promote individual agency. For example, one focus group member's comments, shown below, reflect a general finding from the participants. On discussing her experience on her BA (Hons) Early Childhood Studies degree, one participant said it

> allows you to be quite radical in your thinking because you can start to question your approach to a situation and think about how you influence children . . . you start to question stuff, so you think from the margins rather than just going along with what the government tells you to do.
>
> (Oates 2011, participant no. 9, focus group 1)

I argue that critical reflection, when well taught, has the potential to provide students and practitioners with opportunities to question practice and provision. However, I recognise that a question mark remains in relation to how much power individuals possess to effect change. Brookfield (2009) notes how professional women in the workforce face subtle but real and effective forms of discrimination and that critical reflective opportunities can provide women with alternative ways of seeing and questioning their position within the workforce. He notes how some employers claim to be an equal opportunities organisation yet women's experience of it are anything other than equal; critical reflection, then, provides women with insight into the contradictions within a given context. Brookfield (2009: 174) also suggests that increased autonomy and self-reflection may provide the tools to negotiate discourses of power more effectively. One way to do this (see Oates, in Oates and Hey, 2014) is to provide students with opportunities to take a critical stance to negotiate powerful discourses through challenging them and the practices that emerge from them, at a macro and micro level in the workplace and in wider society as an active citizen.

Critical reflection also provides opportunities to practitioners to disturb pedagogic practice because of higher education learning, which increases knowledge and skills, as well as developing confidence to challenge dominant discourses that inform normalised practices in the workplace. Siebert and Walsh (2013) note that their teaching experience in higher education has shown how significant numbers of students undertaking work-based learning find the activity of reflection beneficial. This is through the way it consolidates students' learning; it enables good practice to be replicated and provides a platform for open and honest discussion. Education in itself has the capacity to change lives as most of you reading this book will no doubt know. Siebert and Walsh (2013) note that reflection in higher education has the capacity to be a useful tool that can be used to individual advantage. Critical reflection, therefore, can be helpful in alerting practitioners to the existence of difference and opportunities in the workplace and in society, and in this sense it is a positive aspect of learning for personal and professional growth.

Conclusion

I hope in this chapter I have provided you with some 'food for thought' about the use of critical reflection in the workplace and higher education. I hope I have provided you with a platform to engage in further reading about reflection and the contested nature of it, perhaps by exploring how critical theory (for example, Habermas, 1974; 1978; 1987) may inform your understanding of critical reflection and its uses and abuses. I also hope this reading provides you with confidence and a belief in your right to question why, when, where, how and with whom you are expected to be critically reflective, taking care not to expose yourself to forms of public scrutiny without your informed consent. I urge you to construct and develop forms of reflection based upon your wide and informed reading, appropriate to you as an individual with agency and as a professional practitioner and student in higher education and in your relationships with others, knowing yourself to be an active, confident, assertive and contributing member of society.

References

Argyris, C. and Schön, D. (1996) *Organisational learning II: theory, method and practice*. Reading, MA: Addison-Wesley.

Barnett, R. (2000) *Realizing the university in the age of supercomplexity*. Buckingham: The Society for Research into Higher Education and The Open University.

Brookfield, S. (2009) The concept of critical reflection: promises and contradictions. *European Journal of Social Work*, 12:3, 293–304.

Callens, J.C. and Elen, J. (2011) The impact of approaches to reflection and learner control upon critical reflection. *Reflective Practice: International and Multidisciplinary Perspectives*, 12:4, 495–506. (Online) Available from http://dx.doi.org/10.1080/14623943.2011.590338 (Accessed 29 May 2014).

Cameron, C., Owen, C. and Moss, P. (2001) *Entry, retention and loss: a study of childcare students and workers*. London: Thomas Coram Research Unit, Institute of Education, University of London and also DfES Research Report No. 275.

Clegg, S. (1999) Professional education, reflective practice and feminism. *International Journal of Inclusive Education*, 3:2, 167–179.

Colley, H., James, D., Tedder, M. and Diment, K. (2003) Learning as becoming in vocational education and training: class, gender and the role of vocational habitus. *Journal of Vocational Education and Training*, 55:1, 471–498. (Online) Available from http://dx.doi.org/10.1080/13636820300200240 (Accessed 2 July 2010).

Dewey, J. (1933) *How we think*. Buffalo, NY: Prometheus Books. Original edition 1910.

Dreyfus, H.L. and Rabinow, P. (1982) *Michel Foucault: beyond structuralism and hermeneutics – with an afterword by Michel Foucault*. London: Harvester Wheatsheaf.

Fook, J. (2002) *Social work: critical theory and practice*. London: Sage.

Fook, J. (2006) Beyond reflective practice: reworking the 'critical' in critical reflection. Keynote for 'Professional Lifelong Learning: Beyond Reflective Practice', 3 July 2006. (Online) Available from http://www.leeds.ac.uk/educol/documents/155665.pdf (Accessed 29 May 2014).

Fook, J. (2010) Beyond reflective practice: reworking the 'critical' in critical reflection. In H. Bradbury, N. Frost, S. Kilminster and M. Zukas (Eds) *Beyond reflective practice approaches to professional lifelong learning* (pp. 37–51). London: Routledge.

Foucault, M. (1977) *Discipline and power: the birth of the prison*. Harmondsworth: Penguin Books.

162   *Ruby Oates*

Foucault, M. (1980) *Power/knowledge: selected interviews and other writings, 1972–1977* (Ed) C. Gordon. London: Harvester Wheatsheaf.

Francis, B. (2001) Commonality and difference? Attempts to escape from theoretical dualisms in emancipatory research in education. *International Studies in the Sociology of Education*, 11(2), 157–172.

Habermas, J. (1972) *Knowledge and the human interests.*1st ed. London: Heinemann.

Habermas, J. (1974) *Theory and practice.* London: Heinemann.

Habermas, J. (1978) *Knowledge and the human interests.* 2nd ed. London: Heinemann.

Habermas, J. (1987) *The theory of communicative action: volume two, lifeworld and system – a critique of functionalist reason.* Boston, MA: Beacon Press.

Hickson, H. (2011) Critical reflection: reflecting on learning to be reflective. *Reflective Practice: International and Multidisciplinary Perspectives*, 12:6 829–839. (Online) Available from http://dx.doi.org/10.1080/14623943.2011.616687 (Accessed 29 May 2014).

MacFarlane, B. and Gourlay, L. (2009) The reflection game: enacting the penitent self. *Teaching In Higher Education*, 14:4, 455–459.

MacNaughton, G. with Campbell, S. and Page, J. (2002) Curriculum contexts: becoming an early childhood professional. In MacNaughton, G. (Ed) *Shaping early childhood: learners, curriculum and context*, Maidenhead: Open University Press.

MacNaughton, G. (2005) *Doing Foucault in early childhood studies.* London: Routledge Falmer.

Mezirow, J. (1990) *Fostering critical reflection in adulthood: a guide to transformative and emancipatory learning.* San Francisco: Jossey Bass.

Mezirow, J. (1991) *Transformative dimensions in adult learning.* San Francisco: Jossey Bass.

Moore, A. and Ash, A. (2002) *Reflective practice in beginning teachers: helps, hindrances and the role of the critical other.* Paper presented at the Annual Conference of the British Educational Research Association, University of Exeter, 12–14 September 2002. (Online) Available from http://www.leeds.ac.uk/educol/documents/00002531.htm (Accessed 29 May 2014).

Morley, C. and Dunstan, J. (2013) Critical reflection: a response to neoliberal challenges to field education? *Social Work Education: The International Journal*, 32:2, 141–156. Available from http://dx.doi.org/10.1080/02615479.2012.730141 (Accessed 29 May 2014).

Moss, P. (2013) Meetings across the paradigmatic divide. *Educational Philosophy and Theory*, 39:3, 229–245. (Online) Available from http://dx.doi.org/10.1111/j.1469-5812.2007.00325.x (Accessed 29 May 2014).

Oates, R.A. (2011) *Constructing the early childhood professional: a research project capturing the voice of early childhood practitioners, their experiences of the workplace during a period of professionalization, and the impact of higher education.* Unpublished doctoral thesis. Derby: University of Derby.

Oates, R.A. and Hey, C. (2014) (Eds) *The student practitioner in early childhood studies: an essential guide to working with children.* London: Routledge.

Osgood, J. (2010) Reconstructing professionalism in ECEC: the case for the 'critically reflective emotional professional'. *Early Years: An International Research Journal*, 30:2, 119–133. (Online) Available from http://dx.soi.oef.10.1080/09575146.2010.490905 (Accessed 9 July 2014).

Penn, H. (2007) Childcare market and managements: how the United Kingdom Government has reshaped its role in developing early childhood education and care. *Contemporary Issues in Early Childhood*, 8(3), 192–207. (Online) Available from http://dx.doi.org/10.230/ciec.2007.8.3.192 (Accessed 14 August 2014).

Pihlaja, M.P. and Holst, T.K. (2013) How reflective are teachers? A study of kindergarten teachers' and special teachers' levels of reflection in day care. *Scandinavian Journal of Education Research*, 57:2, 182–198. (Online) Available from http://dx.doi.org/10.1080/00313831.2011.628691 (Accessed 29 May 2014).

Redmond, B. (2006) *Reflection in action: developing reflective practice in health and social services* (2nd ed). Aldershot: Ashgate.

Ryan, M. (2013) The pedagogical balancing act: teaching reflection in higher education. *Teaching in Higher Education*, 18:2, 144–155. (Online) Available from http://dx.doi.org/10.1080/13562517.2012.694104 (Accessed 29 May 2014).

Schön, D. (1983) *The reflective practitioner: how professionals think in action.* New York: Basic Books.

Siebert, S. and Walsh, A. (2013) Reflection in work-based learning: self-regulation or self-liberation? *Teaching in Higher Education,* 18:2, 167–178. (Online) Available from http://dx.doi.org/10.1080/13 562517.2012.696539 (Accessed 29 May 2014).

Smith, E. (2011) Teaching critical reflection. *Teaching in Higher Education,* 16:2, 211–223. (Online) Available from http://dx.doi.org/10.1080/13562517.2010.515022 (Accessed 29 May 2014).

Taguchi, H.L. (2007) Deconstructing and transgressing the theory-practice dichotomy in early childhood education. *Educational Philosophy and Theory.* (Online) Available from http://dx.doi.org/10.1111/j.1469-5812.2007.00324.x (Accessed 9 July 2014).

Tarrant, J. (2000) What is wrong with competence? *Journal of Further and Higher Education,* 24:1, 77–83. London: NATFHE.

Usher, R. and Edwards, R. (1994) *Postmodernism and education: different voices, different worlds.* London: Routledge.

18 Children's places

Jon White

There are as many different childhoods as there are children. Each has an environment generated for them over which they have little or no control and it is from this constructed world that they are required to make some sense. They need to begin to understand where they fit into the place or places that they experience. It may come as a surprise to some to realise that children are found in places other than school.

Of course, authorities (Sheridan, 2014) propose that by certain ages, children ought to be able to have developed the skills that are expected of an individual of their age; it is the contention here that many of our early childhood environments are organised on this false contention and singularly fail to take into account the nature of childhood being experienced. Rather than proposing a linear model of child development, another direction is considered by Bronfenbrenner (1979), who proposed that children tend to understand their world as a network of experiences. Through different systems, from the immediate to the extended family, through community activities and to chance encounters with the unfamiliar, the world of most children is formed by a mixture of personal and community experience. The key idea here is that with each experience they begin to construct a way of understanding their places through a rich and complex framework.

Some children will thus begin to see the world as a place populated by people who have their best interests at heart, while others will see it as a cold and threatening place. Therefore their development is largely dependent on both their inherited temperament and their perceived ability to react to the different environments in which they are operating.

The immediate family is the place where children will first spend their time. This is a confusing place, often with siblings and a range of adults coming and going. Featherstone (2004) proposes that family structures may change over time, with new adults often integrating to existing structures. Constructing an understanding of who fits where is a tough challenge, accomplished over a relatively short period of time even in the most complex of families. However, the nature of childhood, and the key focus of this reflection, is how children begin to understand their other places – often encountered unexpectedly and under challenging circumstances. Adults often do all they can to prepare children for the expected changes in their lives, supporting the development of resilience. It is the strength of this characteristic that can contribute to the successful management of the unexpected events that all children will need to face at some point in their lives. Developing the resilience to manage change would, therefore, appear to be an essential feature of early childhood development.

One place in which resilience will need to be shown is a hospital visit. This may occur because a child is in need of care (expectedly or unexpectedly) or to visit a relative or friend. Whatever the reason, the nature of this experience can be traumatising. The ways in which the health care professionals can prepare children for this kind of visit are well documented, but it is evident that there is a far from consistent strategy applied across the health care sector when it plans for meeting the needs of children.

A quite different experience will be felt as a result of a visit to a leisure environment such as a theme park. A dedicated child-friendly place, the focus is on the experience of the child: this may encompass every aspect of the visit, from before their arrival (with advertising and promotion materials) to the marketing of toys and playthings to take away. The creation of places for children's leisure is a testimony to what can be achieved when commercial interests are being served.

Children are also found in the care of the state. National agencies exist to look after children, in the event of their family no longer being able to manage this role. As children move from home into care, they are asked to adjust to potentially alarming revisions of their daily routine. This transition into a looked-after environment requires children to demonstrate the ability to be both patient and compliant. The extent to which decisions are made about them without their involvement is a measure of the engagement adults have with the welfare of the individual. Kelly and Gilligan (2002) proposed that their ability to adapt and be resilient is a testimony to the competence of many children when facing difficult circumstances.

In summary, it appears that as children move between the places we have created for them, we need to ensure that these environments are truly fit for purpose and the transitions that occur between them are made as straightforward as possible. For if children learn to cope with expected changes when they are young, there is every possibility that they will develop the resilience to manage unexpected change when they are older.

So it has been established that very young children will experience a range of places in a relatively short period of time. As such, they will come into contact with a wide range of adults who are working in these environments as the range and level of qualifications is very broad. There will be many practitioners qualified to level 3, with many settings staffed by graduates who, according to Urban and Dalli (2012), are critically aware of the pressures and conflicts they face. All will have Disability and Barring Service clearance as well as a basic knowledge of paediatric first aid. Recent changes in the entry levels for awards at level 3 and above require both English and Maths GCSEs to have been acquired. Children's places appear to be inhabited by adults with a wide range of expertise.

With such a range of backgrounds, it is hardly a surprise that there is variety in what the places are trying to achieve for the children in their care. A historical perspective takes us to the early work of the Victorian pioneers in England, such as Margaret McMillan and Italian luminaries such as Maria Montessori. This early work saw the creation of places for children to play and experience a childhood, perhaps for the first time. It was recognised that children had specific needs that should be met if they were to thrive. In major industrialised cities, child labour was seen as a resource to be exploited; the Victorian pioneers perhaps had their own vested interest at heart, but were certainly able to enhance the quality of life for many children. There is a continuation of this early work today, exemplified by organisations such as the Thomas Coram Centre and Barnardo's, and it was much later that we arrived at Aries' (1960) proposition of the concept of the socially and historically constructed childhood.

However, the magnanimity of charitable organisations was often driven by a range of values. For example, the last Victorian workhouse in England is located in Southwell,

Nottinghamshire. When visiting, you can see the care that went into designing a building that required the community to work hard and accept the manager's disciplinary strategies. It was a business, undoubtedly aiming to generate a profit, but through the profits poor children would have their physical, social and spiritual needs met. It is the contention here that many privately run children's places' primary goal is to provide a living for their employees. There is much to be said for a business model through which high-quality provision can be delivered. Every parent is aware of the high cost of childcare. However, some parents are unable to access provision, even with government support. It is argued that a cultural divide is developing, in which better-off parents can access high-quality child care and better employment, being then in a position to provide an enriched home environment, which improves the child's experience at nursery. This is in contrast to parents who are caught in the cycle of seeing childcare as unaffordable so they are unable to make themselves available for work. This is exacerbated by government cuts, for example the closure of many Surestart Children's Centres who were supporting the most economically vulnerable children and families.

Bourdieu and Passeron (2000) saw this as a process through which inequalities of cultural capital are reinforced through state provision. In the later years of the first decade of this century, the State made a series of interventions into childcare with a view to eradicating child poverty, e.g. *Every Child Matters* (2003) and *The Children's Plan* (2008). However, with economic constraints currently limiting the role of central Government, the traditional inequalities are in danger of returning and the growth of private day nursery provision may be a factor reinforcing inequality.

This economic pressure on children's places is very real and impacts on both children and their families. As a consequence, arrival at a new place might see some children being well prepared and confident, with others feeling insecure and suspicious of the new authority figures with whom they are confronted. How can they be prepared? The contention here is that there are likely to be a range of predictable events in the lives of most children. To support such movement between places, there is much to support the development of a listening culture within children's places, providing an understanding of the perspectives of children and the lived experience of childhood. Dahlberg et al. (2007) propose that by doing this effectively, there is a greater opportunity to really see the world from the point of view of the children who we are trying to support.

Loris Malaguzzi (1994) coined the phrase 'The Hundred Voices of Children' in relation to the work being carried out at the Malaguzzi Centre in Reggio Emilia. This was further developed through the use of the Mosaic Approach (Clark and Moss, 2011) and related to a landmark critique *The Otherness of Reggio* (Moss, 2007). In this multi-method approach, adults are encouraged to participate reflexively with children in an exploration of their feelings towards their environment. The children are asked about their world, observed in their world, invited to take pictures of their world and provide adults with guided tours of their world.

In compiling the findings from this research, it has become clear that children are accomplished social actors, able to negotiate their way through the minefield of challenges that comprise a typical nursery environment. However, it is also evident that the adults with whom the children share these spaces have the challenge of consulting with the children to create a co-created shared space in which learning can happen. This may require a de-construction of the meanings that the adults may associate with particular activities and a new look at how children's places are operated. Derrida (1992) considered there to be a requirement to consider children's places in quite new ways, incorporating social–political, legal and ethical dimensions. The power structures and the meaning of perceived truths are being challenged in new and radical ways.

So how do practitioners respond to this shifting paradigm?

The UN Convention on the Rights of the Child (Article 13) states that:

> The child shall have the right to freedom of expression; this right shall include the freedom to seek, receive and impart information and ideas of all kinds, regardless of frontiers, either orally, in writing or in print, in the form of art or through any other medium of the child's choice.

If we are serious about implementing this Article (and successive governments have been committed to this since its inception in 1948), then we have the responsibility to be open to seeing children as democratic partners. In children's places, we may begin to see the importance of the pedagogy of listening. This neither sees children as entirely powerless nor as fully empowered. What it helps us to understand, as proposed by Sinclair et al. (2008), is that children need to be listened to because they are part of the whole community, both involved in and contributing to community activities and initiatives. This might involve a community arts project, or a well dressing (very popular in Derbyshire), or a fete or carnival. The involvement across generations helps to create a sense of belonging and social cohesion, working across generations and giving children a voice in their world. David (2006) cites examples of this, with a particular recognition of the work done by local and national museums, who are often seen to be taking the lead in involving children and families in projects and liaisons with schools to create valuable, sustainable partnerships.

It is to the question of how technology is enabling the creation of children's places that we now turn. There was a view held not very many years ago that television was going to bring families together. This provided a basis for much research into the impact of this medium on children. The debate over how TV influences learning, health and social interaction continues, but it appears that childhood has not died and neither has TV damaged the development of a generation. In fact, children and parents can be better informed than ever before and profoundly aware of the world beyond their immediate community. As such, it appears that TV has not become the monster it was predicted to be. The parallel between historical developments is clear: Plato predicted that writing information down would lead to people losing their ability to remember things, while learning to read has not always led to the poor becoming revolutionaries (Pearson, 1999).

In an influential report published in 2008, Byron explored the issues and challenges surrounding children and technology. Her conclusions promoted the theme that children are surprisingly competent when it comes to both using and managing technology in an appropriate way. The slightly patronising attitude exemplified by pundits with regard to the use (and impact) of technology appears to be challenged. The romanticised view of the child being vulnerable and isolated, potentially a victim of technological abuse (or even as promulgated by the Alliance for Childhood, a view that technology heralds the death of childhood), has been largely refuted as technology now incorporates an ever-widening range of sophisticated devices.

It is to these devices that children are turning to create their own spaces. Through a familiarity that makes the older generation gasp, very young children are able to navigate through an increasingly complex virtual landscape, from which adults may be largely excluded. Plowman and Stephen (2008) propose that it is in these virtual worlds that children are able to find spaces and places to call their own, managing the peer-to-peer interactions and relationships that come from their networks and interests. They are 'out there', enjoying the freedoms in which many are engrossed. As the nature of child and machine interactions progresses, this trend is likely to become even more deeply entrenched.

So, in conclusion, to the future of children's places. What will their places be like in the near and in the not-so-near future? This is a challenge to which the trainers of early years practitioners will need to rise, with no-one underestimating the difficulty of pre-dicting the future in an increasingly uncertain world. There do, however, appear to be some themes of which we can be reasonably certain.

The first certainly is that the children of the next generation will have a more global view than their parents or grandparents. They will be citizens of communities that extend far beyond their immediate geography. They will be able to share and benefit from their engagement with an ecological framework, similar to but much broader than the one envisioned by Bronfenbrenner in the 1970s. The extent to which this new network of loose alliances is able to reinforce existing barriers or whether it will lead to wider under-standings remains to be seen.

Another certainty is that the communities of childhood will become further divided, with poverty or wealth being reinforcers as the key determinants of engagement. Those who are in a position to become global children will continue to streak ahead of those who do not have access to these resources. The inequalities of childhood continue therefore to be exacerbated by unequal distribution of wealth. A series of reports following a UNICEF conference in 1996 (Penn and Molteno, 1997) challenge the universality of provision, expressing concern that the reality of such a goal is actually the imposition of Western social and cultural norms. There is no such thing as best practice and as children communicate in more sophisticated and complex ways, they are certainly going to see that there is more than one truth in the adult world.

Woodhead (1997), writing on cultural imperialism, proposes that the very nature of childhood is viewed with a Western norm in mind. As such, the inequalities that are appearing are in reality a failure of Western culture to acknowledge the values of a non-Western pedagogical construction. The truth appears to revolve around ideas of what childhood is seen to be: of what is expected of children as they grow and experience the richness of life around them, and it is to this subject that we now turn.

Conclusion

We have a duty to prepare children for the world that they will find when they are older. There is a need to be prepared for uncertainty and the reality that their world will be very different from the world of their parents. My question has been whether our current provision of children's places is fit for this purpose, and my conclusion is that they only partially achieve this goal.

The imposition of the top-down quality framework in the form of the Early Years Foundation Stage, plus the rigorous inspection regime, create an atmosphere of running to keep up with the demands made externally. This has the potential to encourage introversion and to stifle innovation, driving children's places through the mechanism of performativity (Ball, 2003), exploring the contest between being child-centred and meeting external targets.

Supporting the youngest children with activities which allow the promotion and strengthening of their resilience would appear to be a priority. Involving parents, wider communities and international collaborations has the potential to prepare children for their life in an exciting but uncertain world.

Is this the real challenge to those who are in a position to influence the activities of children's places?

References

4Children (2012) Surestart children's centre census 2012, www.4children.org/uk/resources. Accessed: 5 November 2014.

Aries, P. ([1960] 1986) *Centuries of childhood: a social history of family life*. Harmondsworth: Penguin.

Ball, S. (2003) The teacher's soul and the terrors of performativity. *Journal of Education Policy*, 18: 2, 215–228.

Bourdieu, P. and Passeron, J. (2000) *Reproduction in education, society and culture*. London: Sage.

Bronfenbrenner, U. (1979) *The ecology of human development: experiments by nature and design*. Cambridge: Harvard University Press.

Byron Review (2008) *Safer children in a digital world*. London: IoE.

Clark, A. and Moss, P. (2011) *Listening to young children: the mosaic approach*. 2nd edition. London: NCB.

Dahlberg, G., Moss, P. and Pence, A. (2007) *Beyond quality in early childhood education and care: languages of evaluation*. Abingdon: Routledge.

David, M. (2006) The world picture in Pugh, G. and Duffy, B. (eds) *Contemporary issues in early years*. 4th edn. London: Sage.

Department for Children, Schools and Families (2008) *The Byron review action plan*. London: HMSO.

Department for Education and Skills (2003) *Every child matters*. London: HMSO.

Derrida, J. (1992) The force of law, in Cornell D., Rosenfeld, M. and Carlson, D. (eds) *Deconstruction and the possibility of justice*. New York: Routledge.

Featherstone, B. (2004) *Family life and family support: a feminist analysis*. London: Palgrave.

Kelly, G. and Gilligan, R. (2002) *Issues in foster care: policy, practice and research*. London: Kingsley.

Malaguzzi, L. (1994) The bill of three rights: innovations in early education. *The International Reggio Exchange*, 2(1), 9.

Moss, P. (2007) *The otherness of Reggio: experiencing Reggio Emelia – implications for pre-school provision*. Oxford: Oxford University Press.

Pearson, J. (1999) *Women's reading in Britain 1750–1835: a dangerous recreation*. Cambridge: Cambridge University Press.

Penn, H. and Molteno, M. (1997) *Sustainability in early childhood development projects*. Unpublished UNICEF paper.

Plowman, L. and Stephen, C. (2008) The big picture: video and the representation of interaction. *British Educational Research Journal*, 34:4, 542–544.

Sheridan, M. (2014) *From birth to five years: children's developmental progress*. Abingdon: Routledge.

Sinclair, J., Diduck, A. and Fitzpatrick, P. (2008) Conceptualizing learning for sustainability through environmental assessment: critical reflections. *Environmental Impact Assessment Review*, 28(7), 415–428.

Urban, M. and Dalli, C. (2012) A profession thinking and speaking for itself, in Miller, L. Dalli, C. and Urban, M. (eds) *Early childhood grows up: towards a critical ecology of the profession*. Dordrecht: Springer.

Woodhead, M. (1997) Psychology and the cultural construction on children's needs, in James, A. and Prout, A. (eds) *Constructing and deconstructing the child: contemporary issues in the sociological study of childhood*. London: Falmer.

19 Behaviour in schools

Is it as bad as they say – or is it worse?

Ang Davey

Introduction

Behaviour management is a key issue in schools and has been high on government agendas since 1988 when the Elton Report *Discipline in Schools* was commissioned by the then Department of Education and Science. Managing behaviour is important in schools for many reasons. There is a clearly established link between behaviour and learning (Powell and Tod 2004) and one of the main aims of schools is for children to have the opportunity to learn. A good standard of behaviour in a classroom allows the children to have the opportunity to learn without distraction whilst children who are actively engaged in learning have less inclination or opportunity to behave inappropriately and this allows teachers to teach. Schools are the training ground for work and for playing a full role in society. Developing appropriate behaviour allows children to learn both practical and social skills and qualities that will be required when they enter the workforce, where inappropriate behaviour will not be tolerated, and enable them to enjoy both their time at work and in their leisure. Appropriate behaviour in schools promotes a safe environment for both children and teachers, thus contributing to their wellbeing and enjoyment of the school experience which can have a positive effect on the quality of teaching and learning.

Impact of inappropriate behaviour on the teaching profession

The Importance of Teaching (2010), a government White Paper which led to the Education Act (2011), claimed:

> We know that among undergraduates considering teaching, fear of bad behaviour and violence is the most common reason for choosing an alternative career.
>
> (DfE 2010: 3)

DfE (2010) also claimed that a very common reason experienced teachers have for leaving teaching is inappropriate behaviour by pupils. Against statistics produced by DfE (2014) that rising birth rates since 2002 will require an additional 400,000 state-funded places for primary children by 2023 with a similar increase expected for state-funded secondary school places, this raises a real concern that if prospective teachers are deterred from applying for teaching posts and current teachers are leaving the profession, there will be a shortage of teachers in the next decade. This also raises another concern that the decline in behaviour in schools with an increasing fear of violence is affecting pupils' opportunities to learn in a conducive, safe environment.

A further claim by DfE (2010) is that two thirds of teachers say their colleagues are being driven out of the profession because of poor pupil behaviour, generally identified as a lack of respect shown by pupils to teachers but, of course, this does not mean that two thirds of teachers are leaving or want to leave the profession, just that two thirds thought it was a reason why some teachers were leaving or wanted to leave.

Undergraduates and postgraduates considering teaching as a career will be aware of some of the claims made about poor behaviour in schools, often from the media which generally report on the most serious incidents in schools involving violence, even death. These prospective teachers need to ensure that they are fully aware of the facts regarding behaviour in schools to decide for themselves whether behaviour in schools is as bad as suggested, or whether it might be even worse. They need also to consider whether there are other reasons why teachers might be leaving or considering leaving the profession.

Recent reports (Brown and Winterton 2010, Haydn 2014 and Ofsted 2014) suggest the situation remains a major concern, with DfE (2013) confirming that it is poor pupil behaviour that continues to be the greatest concern of new teachers and why experienced teachers leave the profession.

There seems to be a difference in perceptions of prospective teachers and practising teachers. DfE (2011) agrees that poor pupil behaviour has caused teachers to either leave the profession or consider leaving the profession but points out that it is actually only in fourth place of the reasons for leaving the profession, the top three being workload, initiative overload and target-driven cultures in schools. Ratcliffe (2014) supports this view by citing workload and Ofsted inspections as the principal reasons why a third of all teachers consider leaving the profession. However, to put this into context Saunders (2013) reported that three quarters of all workers in both professional and non-professional occupations regret their career choices for one reason or another. A poll of undergraduates by DfE in 2008 was highlighted by DfE (2011) claiming that prospective teachers were most likely to be deterred from teaching because of feeling unsafe in the classroom. However, if these prospective teachers are forming their opinions from what they have seen in the media, they perhaps need to weigh up the evidence, taking into account their own first-hand experiences in the classroom on placement as all prospective teachers will have had placement experience.

Impact of inappropriate behaviour on pupils

There is a wide-ranging debate on inequality in the classroom based on gender, race, social background and other factors, but it is interesting that Haydn (2014) considers that one of the biggest inequalities of opportunity in our classrooms arises from those pupils who are in classes that are well managed and controlled by their teachers and those who are not. He considers that there is not just a difference in standards of behaviour between schools but also within schools. Anyone interested in education can reflect on their own experience at school to consider those classes where behaviour was good and those where it was less than good and think about any reasons that might have led to that behaviour.

The effect of inappropriate behaviour on pupils is very important. Inappropriate behaviour prevents the perpetrator from learning as well as impacting on the learning of others in a negative way, and indeed Haydn (2014) considers that it has been clearly established that attainment is negatively impacted upon by inappropriate behaviour. Poor levels of behaviour can create an environment which feels unsafe for many pupils and this could lead to disengagement from learning and even truancy (Ferguson et al. 2005). However, Brown and Winterton (2010) found in their study that although poor behaviour is present in schools, its impact is not as great as may be thought, particularly when the teacher is present.

Government intervention

In November 1987, the Professional Association of Teachers had written to the then Prime Minister, Margaret Thatcher, requesting that a Committee of Enquiry be set up to look at behaviour in schools based on their own survey findings that most teachers considered that behaviour in schools was declining and a third of its members had been physically attacked by pupils. This reported poor behaviour caused considerable unease in Parliament and in the public's eye, and led to the government's first intervention into behaviour in schools in England and Wales when they commissioned the Elton Report (1989) chaired by the Rt Hon Kenneth Baker, the then Secretary of State for the Department of Education and Science. The Elton Committee carried out the largest structured survey on teacher perceptions of behaviour in schools ever undertaken in Britain.

The conclusions of the Elton Report (1989) were that behaviour in schools cannot be measured with quantitative data and therefore they could not draw a conclusion that behaviour was actually getting worse, but recognised teacher perceptions that behaviour was getting worse year on year in their careers. One of the important findings of the Elton Report (1989) was that inappropriate behaviour was not recorded by schools in terms of types of inappropriate behaviour or the number of incidents, although exclusions were recorded by some local education authorities (LEAs), but not all. This was restated by DfE (2011) that data collected by them did not evidence the state of behaviour in schools or the commonality of its occurrence. If the evidence then of declining behaviour is based on teachers' perceptions rather than statistical data, perhaps behaviour has not actually declined but teachers just feel it has – maybe because of now having to manage classrooms against a background of higher workloads, initiative overload and target-driven cultures.

Ofsted's views

A general overview of behaviour in schools is provided by Ofsted in their Annual Reports and in 2010, behaviour was deemed to be good or better than good in 89% of primary schools and 70% of secondary schools (Ofsted 2010), continuing a trend of Ofsted reports claiming that behaviour was not a serious issue. DfE (2011), however, found that teachers considered Ofsted reports did not reflect their own experiences and that head teachers were not always honest with Ofsted inspectors. Head teachers were reported to employ two strategies to avoid inspectors observing inappropriate behaviour – first, suspending badly behaved pupils during inspections and second, appointing supply teachers whom Ofsted would not observe. DfE (2011) also criticised Steer (the Steer Report, 2005 and 2009) for relying too heavily on Ofsted reports for his own findings on the state of behaviour in schools, and concluding that such behaviour was improving without considering sufficiently other available evidence. However, the latest Ofsted report (2014: 4) raises concerns that behaviour in schools is 'deeply worrying' because pupils' learning and their life chances are being negatively impacted on and, again, concern that very good teachers are being driven away from the profession.

It seems, therefore, that the official reports from Ofsted until 2014 and government commissioned reports by Elton (1989) and Steer (2005, 2009 and 2010) paint a picture that behaviour in schools is improving and looking good; whereas the media, politicians and teachers suggest otherwise, and this latter view is finally echoed by Ofsted in their 2014 report. It is the disparity between these two sets of sources that needs to be explored by prospective teachers for them to make up their own minds on the current scale of the problem, or if the problem exists at all. The current state of behaviour in schools is not known because it is based on the subjective views of teachers based on their anecdotes and experiences (DfE 2011).

Teachers' views

Poor behaviour in schools ranges from low-level disruption to more serious incidents including violence, although there is no clear guideline as to what constitutes low-level disruption, what constitutes serious incidents and how often they are occurring.

The biggest dataset on behaviour in schools is produced by Ofsted inspectors in their reports when inspecting schools. However, they can only report on what they see and what they are told. With the pressures head teachers are under from performance tables to the marketisation of schools, it is not surprising that they try to present as positive a picture as they can to inspectors and the parents of prospective pupils. Teachers too may not wish to admit they have problems controlling their pupils as this challenges their own professional skills and qualities. On the other hand, teachers may exaggerate the seriousness of behaviour to gain school and public support outside the Ofsted arena for not achieving higher attainment levels.

Steer (2010) purports that behaviour standards in primary and secondary schools are high for most children with only a few of the 7 million children in schools behaving poorly. He considers that standards have risen since the Elton Report (1989) and negative views are promoted by media reports of rare major incidents. *The Guardian* (2014) reports that Michael Gove (the then Education Secretary) similarly believed that there has been considerable improvement in the standards of behaviour in schools, but also echoed Steer (2010) that there is still more to be done.

Recent views

The Association of Teachers and Lecturers undertook a survey of its members in 2011 and concluded that there was no clear research that behaviour in schools was worse, the same or better, but that its members felt that behaviour was deteriorating. It is difficult to quantify inappropriate behaviour without a clear definition of what constitutes inappropriate behaviour or possible boundaries to what it might be. Children talking in class whilst they are working on set tasks might be seen by one teacher as inappropriate behaviour whilst another teacher might consider that talking helps the learning process.

Haydn (2014) considers that the true extent of disruptive behaviour is underestimated in terms of the scale of the problem, the nature of the problem and the complexity of the problem. By including the complexity, he develops the discussion by adding the issue of children who might lack social skills and those who do not want to learn, or both. This develops the teacher's role from trying to manage behaviour to trying to understand the causes of it and echoes the conceptual framework developed by Powell and Tod (2004) who consider that identifying the underlying causes of inappropriate behaviour is necessary to support a change in that behaviour through a range of behaviour management strategies.

Ofsted produce annual reports on schools and the consistent message being given over the last few years up to 2014 is that behaviour is improving. In 2012, behaviour was satisfactory or above in 99.7% of schools. If behaviour is satisfactory or better in 99.7% of schools, this means behaviour is unsatisfactory (or inadequate in Ofsted terms) in only 0.3% of schools. This is looking good and cause for celebration, but might have a different meaning. Ofsted grades are outstanding, good, requires improvement (formerly satisfactory) and inadequate. So today Ofsted would say that behaviour is requiring improvement or better in 99.7% of schools which paints quite a different picture. Ofsted (2010) declared that behaviour was good or better in 89% of primary schools and 70% of secondary schools. The percentages have increased but the criterion has changed from good or better to requiring improvement (satisfactory) or better. And so it is argued that behaviour has declined and Ofsted was masking the problem. Of course, Ofsted (2014: 4) has now changed their position and declared behaviour in schools to be 'deeply worrying'.

Ofsted (2013) focused on teaching and learning in good schools and made the link with good behaviour at several points, but made very little mention of schools where inappropriate behaviour occurred – this suggests that Ofsted was avoiding discussing inappropriate behaviour in schools which bucked the trend from earlier reports where they positively portrayed behaviour in schools. To the reader, it suggested that inappropriate behaviour in schools may no longer have been an issue. However, Ofsted (2014) has clearly articulated that the problem still exists and is worse than previously portrayed.

Elton (1989) drew on press comments that physical attacks on teachers were commonplace, but their findings were that teachers did not consider such attacks were a major problem and certainly not the most difficult behaviour that they had to deal with (Elton 1989). Elton (1989: 11) further recognised that major incidents were not the problem but that the most difficult behaviour, according to the teachers consulted, was the high level of 'trivial but persistent' behaviour including talking out of turn, hindering the learning of other pupils and deliberate task-avoidance whilst physical violence was ranked only 10th in order of concern. This state of behaviour was found in both primary and secondary schools and the list can go on – children tapping their pens on the desk, walking round the room, talking to each other, passing notes to each other, using their phones, poking each other, pulling silly faces at each other – all arguably minor infringements of behaviour that could perhaps be ignored in small doses. However, as Elton (1989) points out, there is a high level of this behaviour and this starts to impact on learning in the classroom as children cannot concentrate amid this type of disruption, teachers spend too much time dealing with inappropriate behaviour and of course the miscreants themselves cannot be learning whilst they are focusing on their 'off-task' behaviour.

Defining inappropriate behaviour

Low-level disruption was identified as the most persistent form of inappropriate behaviour in the Elton Report (1989) and Ofsted (2006), and was echoed more recently by DfE (2011) and Ofsted (2014) to include name calling, swearing, not listening, interrupting and fighting, although it is questionable whether fighting can be considered low-level disruption. Low-level disruption is increasing and is the biggest challenge to teachers (Brown and Winterton 2010) and cyber bullying, particularly among teenage girls, is also increasing. Verbal aggression is commonplace between pupils and physical attacks are more likely to be against boys. It is interesting that whilst Brown and Winterton (2010) were writing about violence in schools, they too found that it was the low-level disruption that was the biggest challenge facing teachers.

Steer (2005) recognises that persistent low-level disruption affects both pupils and teachers — pupils' learning is interrupted, staff are stressed and importantly, low-level disruption can be the breeding ground for more serious issues to occur. A letter from Tony Blair, the then Prime Minister, to Steer in 2005 added his voice to the definition of inappropriate behaviour including 'backchat and disrespect' (Steer 2005: 86). In 2009, Steer revisited behaviour in schools and repeated that inappropriate behaviour in schools could not be tolerated but that there is

> strong evidence from a range of sources that the overall standard of behaviour achieved by schools is good and has improved in recent years.
>
> (Steer 2009: 4)

Again, this must now be considered in light of the 2014 Ofsted report.

Earlier reports generally focused on the views of teachers and the observations of Ofsted inspections, but Haydn (2014) collated pupils' views on behaviour in schools that diverts them from their learning and found recurring themes — children being disruptive of their own and others' learning, throwing things around in class and being off task — all issues of low-level disruption but on a scale that makes it a high-level problem. Here, the pupil voice is telling us that there is a problem and that they are feeling its effects.

Elton (1989) also considered physical aggression in schools and found that contrary to media and government concerns that there was violence in the classroom and teachers fear this violence, there is in fact little violence in schools and what there is generally involves children fighting with each other, and any physical harm occurring to teachers is incidentally caused by intervening in children fighting, and not by pupils attacking teachers. However, whilst this might be reassuring for prospective teachers, perhaps it is not so for pupils and their parents.

Ofsted (2005) provided examples of challenging behaviour which go beyond low-level disruption to include physical attacks such as pinching other children and throwing furniture.

Brown and Winterton (2010: 12) report that definitions of violence vary widely but drew on the work of Benbenishty and Astor (2005) who defined school violence as:

> behaviour intended to harm, physically or emotionally, persons in school as well as their property and school property.
>
> (Benbenishty and Astor (2005) cited in Brown and Winterton (2010: 12))

This would include physical attacks on pupils and teachers, fighting, damaging property, bullying, cyber bullying and verbal aggression.

Extreme violence including that leading to death is very rare in the UK and carrying weapons is also rare (Brown and Winterton 2010). There are media reports about inappropriate conduct in schools carried out by both pupils and teachers but fortunately very serious cases of violence are rare, two prominent and extreme cases being the murders of Philip Lawrence in 1995 and Ann Maguire in 2014.

Inappropriate behaviour from outside the school

Serious issues do not just arise from pupils and teachers but also from parents. According to Brown and Winterton (2010), 40% of teachers reported that they had had to deal with aggressive parents and it is common now to see notices outside both primary and secondary schools warning parents that staff at the schools will not tolerate abuse or aggression from parents or other carers.

Haydn (2014) reports that in 2010, the Prime Minister David Cameron cited that there were 17,000 assaults on teachers each year and he highlighted that 330,000 pupils were excluded from school in 2010–2011, 5,080 being permanent exclusions. With just under 7 million children in the school system, this equates to 1 in 20 children being excluded which seems a high number – at least one child per class is excluded each year? However, these are all exclusions and the majority of these are fixed term, but it still suggests that behaviour in schools is such that exclusions are necessary, whether fixed term or permanent, and therefore the government reports and Ofsted before 2014 were masking a real problem.

Inappropriate behaviour from teachers

Having considered inappropriate behaviour by pupils, there is another strand here – inappropriate behaviour by teachers. Haydn (2014) found that pupils reported that their learning was affected by teachers who could not control their classes and did not deal with inappropriate behaviour when it occurred. Haydn (2014) also concluded that whilst there were variations in the standards of behaviour between schools, there were also variations in standards of behaviour within schools. This reflects the pupils' views that individual teachers are responsible for whether their classes are well behaved or not (Haydn 2014). Haydn (2014) cites Gove (2010) who looked at the issue from a different perspective when he recognised that learning could be disrupted where discipline had broken down. This suggests that it is not the behaviour that is the problem but rather the lack of appropriate strategies being implemented by teachers, and this could be viewed as inappropriate behaviour by teachers. Powell and Tod (2004) explored the notion that two possible underlying causes of inappropriate behaviour can be relationship with others and relationship with the curriculum. How teachers behave and interact with pupils alongside their level of teaching skills can affect pupils' levels of engagement or disengagement with school or individual lessons, possibly leading to inappropriate behaviour as a means of avoiding the learning process.

This suggests that inappropriate behaviour is not the disease but is the symptom of other underlying causes. Whilst government and Ofsted reports are generally silent on inappropriate behaviour by teachers (with the exception of the link between good teaching and good behaviour), the media are not so silent and report on inappropriate behaviour by teachers including misuse of social network sites.

Solution still needed

Considering the diverse evidence available on the scale of the problem of inappropriate behaviour in schools and the lack of agreement on the definition of low-level disruption and serious misbehaviour, it is difficult to be absolutely conclusive about whether behaviour has declined, stayed the same or improved over the last 25 years since the Elton Report (1989) was produced. The publication of the Ofsted report (2014) suggests a U-turn as it now declares there is a serious problem in schools, contradicting previous reports based on different criteria. However, prospective teachers will have been in schools prior to seeking a teaching position, either as part of their B Ed placement or as part of voluntary placements in preparation for the PGCE interview, and so should have an understanding of what behaviour is like in schools. Prospective teachers will also perhaps consider whether they can rise to the challenge of being an inspirational teacher who can win the hearts and minds of pupils so that they will want to engage in the learning process and thus have no time for inappropriate behaviour. From the government's point of view, there needs to be recognition that children are being adversely affected by inappropriate behaviour in class. Ofsted (2014) recommend that the main issue is teachers being inconsistent with setting behaviour management rules and dealing with inappropriate behaviour. A whole-school approach led by the head teacher and senior leadership team as recommended by Elton (1989), Steer (2005) and DfE (2010) should lead teachers in that aim of consistency and support them in managing inappropriate behaviour.

References

Association of Teachers and Lecturers (2011) *Managing classroom behaviour.* London: ATL.

Brown, J. and Winterton, M. (2010) *Violence in UK schools: what is really happening?* London: BERA.

Department for Children, Schools and Families (2010) *Behaviour and the role of Home-School Agreements.* Nottingham: HMSO.

Department for Education (2011) *Behaviour and discipline in schools.* London: HMSO.

Department for Education (2013) *Improving behaviour and attendance in school.* London: HMSO.

Department for Education (2014) *Statistical first release: schools, pupils and their characteristics.* January 2014, Available at: https://www.gov.uk/government/uploads/system/uploads/attachment_data/file/319028/SFR15_2014_main_text_v2.pdf, Accessed July 2014.

Department of Education and Science (1989) *Discipline in schools* (The Elton Report). London: HMSO.

Department for Education and Skills (2005) *Learning behaviour: the report of the practitioners on school behaviour and discipline* (The Steer Report). London: HMSO.

Department for Education and Skills (2009) *Learning behaviour: lessons learned* (The Steer Report). Nottingham: HMSO.

Ferguson, B., Tilleczek, K., Boydell, K., Rummens, J.A., Cote, D. and Roth-Edney, D. (2005) *Early school leavers: understanding the lived reality of student disengagement from secondary school.* Final Report submitted to the Ontario Ministry of Education, May 31, 2005.

Guardian (2014) Michael Gove urges 'traditional' punishments for school misbehaviour. *The Guardian,* 2 February.

Harris, N.S. (1991) Discipline in schools: the Elton Report. *Journal of Social Welfare and Family Law,* 13(2), 110–127.

Haydn, T. (2014) To what extent is behaviour a problem in English schools? Exploring the scale and prevalence of deficits in classroom climate. *Review of Education,* 2(1), 31–64.

House of Commons (2010) *The importance of teaching.* London: DfE.

Office for Standards in Education (2005) *Managing challenging behaviour*. London: HMSO.

Office for Standards in Education (2006) *Improving behaviour*. London: HMSO.

Office for Standards in Education (2010) *The annual report of Her Majesty's Chief Inspector of Education, Children's Services and Skills 2009/10*. London: HMSO.

Office for Standards in Education (2013) *The report of HM Chief Inspector of Education, Children's Services and Skills*. London: HMSO.

Office for Standards in Education (2014) *Below the radar: low-level disruption in the country's classrooms*. London: HMSO.

Powell, S. and Tod, J. (2004) *A systematic review of how theories explain learning behaviour in school contexts*. Research Evidence in Education Library. London: EPPI-Centre, Social Science Research Unit, Institute of Education, University of London.

Ratcliffe, R. (2014) *A third of teachers would consider an alternative career*, available at: http://www.theguardian.com/teacher-network/teacher-blog/2014/apr/29/teachers-alternative-careers-school-recruitment, accessed April 2014.

Saunders, A. (2013) *Three quarters regret career choice, a third bored at work, says survey* (online). Available at http://www.managementtoday.ac.o.uk/news/1187016, accessed March 2014.

20 Developing critical thought about SEN

A complementary approach

Mike Flay

What are special educational needs (SEN) and how could they concern us? The term might comprise conditions ranging from acute autism to states of physical malfunction or states of emotional and mental disturbance, depression and even anorexia. What kind of bearing could literature have on such conditions, and isn't it mistaken to claim that non-fictional modes have more useful relevance?

There exist numerous guides to SEN conditions and advice for education practitioners. These have value. However, for a more complex involvement, the development of critical and imaginative responses, and awareness of a wider context, other kinds of text need reading. This chapter aims to demonstrate how these 'other' texts are relevant to perspectives about SEN via their imagined narratives, and to discuss examples that add to our awareness.

Before autism was identified as a distinct condition, Joseph Conrad was writing about it. In his short story *The Idiots* (Conrad, 1973; first published in 1898) he investigates a possible effect on a married couple of having a series of disabled children. In this way the SEN issue is located in a family context and explored in unusual ways that have current relevance to any thinking about autism spectrum disorder (ASD). The mother is described with a new child:

> That child, like the other two, never smiled, never stretched its hands to her, never spoke; never had a glance of recognition for her in its big, black eyes which could only stare fixedly at any glitter, but failed hopelessly to follow the brilliance of a sunray slipping slowly along the floor.
>
> (Conrad, 1973: 62)

Here are characteristics of autism clearly presented: the baby, like the others before it, is nonresponsive, fails to develop speech, affiliation and recognition and is habitually preoccupied or obsessed with some features of light ('stare fixedly at any glitter').

Conrad shows ways in which the autistic children in this case damage the relation between husband and wife. Jean Pierre's awareness that something is wrong with the children isn't immediate. His sudden query, brutal, to his wife after months have elapsed, looking at his twins – 'What's the matter with those children?' – leads her to respond in pain 'with a fond wail' (Conrad, 1973: 63). He then examines the children as they sleep: 'When his wife returned he never looked up . . . and remarked in a dull manner – "When they sleep they are like other people's children"' (Conrad, 1973: 75). The husband's trajectory leads him to wish to prove he can have children like other people's. He forces himself sexually on his wife repeatedly at intervals, leaving her to resist, in the hope of other, normal babies.

Conrad points to a genetic problem and the disruption to a family successive births of autistic children may cause. Interestingly, he complicates the depiction by introducing a character for whom the children's conditions aren't over-troubling in the shape of the children's maternal grandmother. She runs a small shipping business and considers there are 'worse misfortunes' (Conrad, 1973: 75), and that her daughter Susan is bad at coping. Susan complains that she is ostracised by other women who regard her as the 'mother of idiots', and she dislikes the burden of looking after children who 'would never know me, never speak to me. They would know nothing'. She refuses sex with her husband in case she ends up with her house 'full of these things' (Conrad, 1973: 74).

Significantly, Conrad's story presents many themes that are current. The parents at first consult experts about the children, then pass into obsessive, depressed, aggressive/ passive modes. Interestingly too, the children are presented, at the start of the narrative, in the fiction as adolescents, left to roam on the grandmother's farm, the parents being dead. Their activities comprise lying in the roadside dust, staring at any traffic that passes, doing as they please. This raises an issue of non-confinement; the children move in an unstructured environment and take their chances with natural hazards. There is no suggestion they'd be better off in a school (if one existed) or an asylum.

Conrad also presents a case of what would later be categorised as Asperger's Syndrome in his novel *The Secret Agent* (Conrad, 1963). Again he opts for a family context to thematise his case. Stevie is cared for by his grown-up sister who is impelled into marriage with the aim of providing security for the boy. Stevie is literal-minded; he sets off dangerous fireworks at his low-level office boy job location because of tales of injustice other junior employees tell him. He sees a cab pulling an ill horse and believes the police should be called. Ill horses in the street become a fixed interest. He often forgets his own address and gets lost. His obsessional activities at home consist of repeatedly drawing circles on paper with a pencil.

In relation to 'vulnerability' – an important SEN theme – Stevie is led to his own destruction as a result of his literal-minded sense of social justice. His stepfather, Verloc, is a minor figure in pre-Soviet agitation organisations in London and takes Stevie to political discussion meetings. Verloc uses Stevie, exploiting his trust, as a bomb carrier in a London park near the London observatory. Stevie stumbles and is killed in the subsequent explosion. In a modification of the parental reaction depicted in *The Idiots*, Winnie as sister-mother is entirely outraged; her whole existence as shown in the novel has been to care for and support the brother, seen by Verloc as 'half witted, irresponsible . . . Only fit for the asylum' (Conrad, 1973: 173).

An advantage Conrad's novel has over non-fictional accounts of this variety of autism is that it presents associated issues in a full way, not steering clear of complexities. The widespread exclusion of fictional writing from 'critical writing' about SEN issues and conditions is a strange phenomenon; fiction could usefully be central to such reflectings, an intriguing complement to the usual kind of account.

A risk in non-fictional writing is that it can over-rationalise, simplify and reduce. In contrast, fiction can resonate with wider social contexts and raise relevant questions. People with disorders, for example, are vulnerable to many kinds of exploitation – seduction into bomb carrying is, Conrad proposes, one kind of risk in a context he specifies, an individual situation.

It is important to note that unlike in many journalistic articles or fact books about autism, Conrad doesn't sentimentalise problematics or make out care is easy or rewarding. *The Idiots* works as an incisive, imaginative account of a family problematic. Immersion in its narrative provides a useful insight into how a critical–imaginative approach to an SEN issue might work. Significant too is the realisation that what is being presented is a human issue that could affect anyone, not a compartmentalised 'this is SEN' thematic.

A 'human' issue will also be a social one. Foucault, for example, has written well about the 'frontier of abnormality', pointing out that society tends to 'establish an overall rule':

> the rule must be made to function as a minimal threshold, as an average to be respected or as an optimum towards which one must move. It measures in quantitative terms and hierarchizes in terms of value, the abilities, the level, the 'nature' of individuals. It introduces, through this 'value giving' measure, the constraint of a conformity that must be achieved. Lastly, it traces the limit that will define difference in relation to other differences, the external frontier of the abnormal.
>
> (Foucault, 1991: 183)

Foucault's writing is inventive and original here and represents a non–fiction mode that has a relation to fiction. The same can be said of Freud's work which students can usefully read in connection with 'SEN issues', especially those of anxiety, depression and hysteria. Freud presents these disorders imaginatively, his case studies having close relations to short story writing.

Foucault proposes that the tendency towards rule making is routine in educational establishments, hospitals and elsewhere. By implication it also applies to staff themselves, also in corporations or, for example, universities. There is a constant surveillance of behaviours and outputs and a 'perpetual penalty' that can be 'put into operation to exclude' when things get too abnormal. The social tendency is to homogenise.

The issue of this kind of surveillance and setting of norms is central to any consideration of SEN functions. Pupils have to be observed to be effectively supported. However, is there a possibility that one motivation behind multiple assessments and watchings is a wish for a type of unannounced constraint?

A Danish writer, Peter Hoeg, has investigated the issue in his novel *Borderliners*, published in 1996. This text focuses on young people who are disabled emotionally, often by dint of personal history, factors over which they have no control, sometimes also by genetic disposition. Hoeg is critical of a Danish system consisting of institutions in which support merges with Foucault's identified 'perpetual penalty'. For example, pupils categorised as having 'social adjustment problems with neurotic or other pathological characteristics' were in danger of being put in care with the 'mental retardation services' where the baseline was 'permanent residential care, in a locked ward, strapped down' (Hoeg, 1996: 30).

A risk too of being 'supported' is becoming invisible: 'Because, for an orphan in Denmark, everything was very strictly regulated. Across the country ran certain tunnels that were invisible; they ran alongside each other, absolutely parallel' (Hoeg, 1996: 28). A paradox exists that in spite of the numerous assessments, observations, and support systems, the pupils gradually vanish, the public being generally unaware of them and such provision. The pupils also vanish from each other as they are sent to separate institutions for treatments and then residential education. The novel shows them trying to keep in contact, struggling to know what is being done to them and if necessary to counter that.

The issue of risk-taking or self-harming behaviour is central to SEN concerns. Hoeg shows how in a Danish residential school there are many casualties. The son of a teacher is found in a locker by his father: 'he had tried to cut out his tongue with a razor blade' (Hoeg, 1996: 51). Another pupil, treated violently by his parents, breaks the fingers of a teacher. The same pupil stops eating and becomes addicted to sniffing gas as a self-anaesthetic. Hoeg outlines certain dangerous behaviours of the pupils. All of these pupils would be categorised in the SEN lexicon as having Emotional and Behavioural Difficulties (EBD). One aspect of these is risk-taking behaviour. For example, boys at the residential school swing out on a rope fixed to a tree and hang in front of approaching trains on the railway adjacent to the school. At the last minute, they move. The narrator pupil's best friend is killed when his moving goes wrong. The novel suggests causes for the behaviour. One of the pupils says the game is a way of clearing his mind, making it go blank and out of time. The relation to addiction, the seeking out of modes that produce a feeling of oblivion, is made clear in the text. The search for a state of non-feeling, nullity, is a feature.

An underlying theme is for certain of the pupils to counter this nullity seeking by an opposite effort in which they attempt to re-assemble their own identities by finding out about their own pasts and revealing them to each other, gaining access to reports, assessments, and psychiatric gradings that have been made about each but kept confidential by experts, psychiatrists, medical staff, and teachers. The hierarchic authorities resist and block attempts.

In spite, too, of the acutely regulated system the pupils are inserted into, and the high level of surveillance, there are other risks for the pupils. At times the institutional participants shown in Hoeg's novel suffer sexual abuse such as homosexual attacks from a teacher of Danish. The attacks are based on a compulsory routine of an individual pupil cutting the lawn below the teacher's apartment and then going up to his rooms there. The teacher also carries out assaults in phone boxes under the guise of giving instructions about use of phone books. Again, it is the accumulation of specific and individual detail that makes Hoeg's novel useful for developing a critical and informed sense of the social and human problems involved in what are often bracketed off as SEN issues.

Hoeg's narrator observes that if your life has been broken early enough (neglectful parents, traumas etc.) then a disability arises in which efforts that an 'average' person could make are impossible for you. Instead, strategies of self-reduction take compensatory place in the shape of risk games, gas sniffing, eating disorders, self-harm, and attempted suicides.

Hoeg shows how a high incidence of neurosis remains untreated and unsupported in the 'EBD' pupils he presents. On an actual level this raises the problematic of the current (and previous) inadequacy of UK mental health services in dealing with children, adolescents and adults in relation to the widespread incidence of psychological disorders. This is a pressing SEN issue. Foucault suggests an element of social fear is a part cause: 'the existence of a whole set of techniques and institutions for measuring, supervising and correcting the abnormal brings into play the disciplinary mechanisms to which the fear of the plague gave rise'. As a result there are 'mechanisms of power', 'disposed around the abnormal individual' (Foucault, 1991: 199). These might also include non or minimal and unsuitable provision of treatment.

At an extreme 'the abnormal' individual may be shut away, rendered invisible to the outside world. The pupils in Hoeg's novel are in that situation. Other systems of control might entail ostensible measures to help, such as 'inclusion', but these are essentially measures of containment, evasion or denial. Of course the balance between containing volatilities, physical malfunction or malformation and support is difficult to strike. In terms of mental health, many pupils at mainstream schools receive sparse support for problematics, or none at all. For all age groups NHS provision in this area is inadequate. It is the case, too, that many self-styled advanced and expensive residential schools for pupils with acute autism also have very advanced systems for confinement, door locking and surveillance, a kind of 'benevolent' incarceration (e.g. Prior's Court School, Hermitage, Berks) with the balance tipped away from freedom. At the other end of the scale, Conrad shows in *The Idiots* the autistic adolescents left to roam about their grandmother's farm-land, lie in the dust as they choose, and possibly meet with accident. Surveillance and confinement are zero. The two extremes haunt thinking about SEN issues.

Quayson has argued that in the gaze of the able bodied at the disabled 'there is a flow of affectivity' that includes 'guilt, bewilderment and even fear' (Quayson, 1999: 55). In relation to the physically disabled he suggests an international context exists in which some disabilities are a consequence of war. Given that physical disability is considered part of an SEN spectrum, this is a further area to include in a process of developing critical reflection. Again, fiction is helpful. Quayson proposes that the encounter with the disabled in post-colonial writing is as much an attempt to transcend 'the nightmare' of history and he points to wars in underdeveloped zones as making disability 'part of everyday life'. He suggests that for post-colonial writers the problem is 'how to confront a traumatic history of disability at the personal as well as social level' (Quayson, 1999: 66).

Physical disability can take surprising turns. The issue of sexuality and SEN is relevant here. Often a taboo or elided area, the question of the sexual identity of individuals with disorders, neuroses, physical malfunctions or all of these needs raising. For example, recently there was press outrage at the notion of men in wheelchairs hiring prostitutes; legal cases occur in which mothers claim their daughters should be sterilised (or refrain from sex altogether) because of low IQ. The theme of child sexuality and its relation to adult behaviour is current. Sexuality is an area of unease within cultures in any case and to consider it in an SEN context involves going far beyond the designated 'education/ SEN' area.

An example of such transcending presentation comes in Coetzee's novel *Waiting for the Barbarians* (2000). A Magistrate takes in a blind and maimed young woman. The girl's previous defilement – she has been tortured and had her feet broken – becomes a source of erotic impetus. Coetzee shows that the colonial magistrate is genuinely empathising in his relationship with her but his interest is intensified by her maimings. It is also conveyed that she is attractive even though she is partially blind and cannot walk well. Interestingly, a Morrissey song approaches a related taboo area of sex and disability. In 'November Spawns a Monster' the singer raises the idea of sex with a disabled, unprepossessing person, offering it as a possible positive experience for both. The unease conventional morality expresses over such situations is revealed in press outrage that the late Jimmy Saville 'even' caressed the physically disabled. Such press coverage assumes that disabled people lack a sexual identity.

A theme that arises in relation to SEN-defined pupils in school settings is that of child abuse. What sort of person abuses a child? An example in fiction comes in John Harvey's recent novel, published in 2014, *The Subject of a Portrait*. The demonstrated point of this chapter, that fiction has great value in presenting detailed and individualised cases of disturbed states of mind and body, is borne out by this novel. A version of Ruskin, the

Victorian art and social critic, is presented. Ruskin is only able to relate to the female in the shape of pre-adolescent girls. His marriage to an adult woman is annulled because it was never consummated. Adult women disgust him except in terms of spiritual interchange. He sees their bodies as deformed.

However, pre-adolescent girls are his preference, partly because they have no breasts and their other sexual features are in his opinion less obvious. Such girls constitute for him aesthetic objects of beauty. The Ruskin figure in the novel has a collection of pictures, early photographs of naked, breastless young girls. On occasions he looks at these and simultaneously masturbates. He has a range of other neuroses. Significantly, he met his wife when she was twelve and married her when she was sixteen. By sixteen she had become disgusting to him, but he believed the marriage could be spiritual only.

Here are some aspects that resonate currently. In particular, the Ruskin possession of images of nude young girls has its link to images of young girls available online. The thematic of exploitation (who are the girls, why and when did they pose for the pictures?) is implicit. How did they react to having posed; was there coercion? A historical perspective is also established, it being plain that vulnerability was rife in a non-compulsory school attendance era just as it currently is in 2014; sexual problematics seem to be humanly endemic at any period. Here SEN issues surface in relation to the emotional and physical consequences of being abused, as disturbingly shown in the current Rotherham case. It is also important to identify psychiatric characteristics of the abusers which can be very varied.

The novel, in its presentation of one case, focuses the point that is often skipped over in non-fictional, apparently scientific or factual texts, that issues are usually multiple and multi-faceted. There may be many reasons for, and types of, child abuse and many consequences and symptoms displayed by victims. To reflect on these within an SEN category only is too limiting – interested students would need here to ask very wide questions about the various attitudes to sexuality that prevail currently in the UK and elsewhere, and the social contribution to attitudes.

A novel by Michael Flay (2009), *The Watchers*, also has as a theme the problematic of vulnerability and abuse. Here a pupil with acute autism is groomed and then used by a school caretaker and his wife, also exploited for pornographic film purposes. The boy is rented out to an upper circle of figures who use him via the caretaker in prostitution. Here there are graphic presentations also of the difficulties of dealing with such a pupil in an education environment, the autistic boy's habits of violence, soiling and sexual behaviours.

To conclude, D.H. Lawrence is another writer who has contributed both non-fictionally and fictionally and in fact to thematics associated with SEN. Without naming the condition (it had no name then), Lawrence was also a non-fictional commentator on autism via his friend Lady Cynthia Asquith and her son John, born in 1911 and so two years old when Lawrence first knew him in 1913. In 1918 Lawrence wrote about John that 'something has got locked in his psychic mechanism' (Lawrence, 1962: 537). An earlier letter in response to Lady Cynthia's complaint that John doesn't respond to her advice: 'Put yourself aside with regard to him. You have no right to his love. Care only for his good and well-being; make no demands on him' (Lawrence, 1962: 342).

The non-responding aspect of autism, the fact that John responds better to his nurse than to his mother, troubles Lady Cynthia and she struggles to make sense of the condition, writing not only to Lawrence but other people she feels might have a solution. In his book *The Asquiths* Colin Clifford comments that in May 1915 Cynthia, 'in a "cold terror" about John, consulted friends, family members, even two "specialists", all of whom suggested different diagnoses and different solutions'. The consulting of 'experts' is a theme in Conrad's short story too and research also shows that currently a reaction to having a child with autistic symptoms can be a desperate parental seeking for guidance.

Lawrence's views about the causes of John's condition, and his tendency to see flaws in the relation between John's parents as causative, are speculative. His practical advice, not to look for personal responses, to provide for John's immediate needs only, seems sound enough. Lawrence even offered to have John with him for a period to attempt a cure. The offer wasn't taken up.

The outcome for John was unfortunate. In spite of the expert advice sought, John displayed ferocious temper tantrums according to his mother, scaring his brother. Cynthia records in her diary he is 'very silent and unresponsive'. A series of exclusions followed. In 1916 he had a separate governess to keep him apart from his brother whom he attacked and scared and from then on 'had a series of keepers'. In 1920 he was sent to a special school at the age of 9. Clifford records he was then confined to a series of institutions until he eventually died in 1957 (Clifford, 2003: 354–5).

A problematic is raised here of what happens to individuals with acute autism as they age. The pattern outlined above, with movement over time into increasingly separated-off institutions, is also current. The adult individual with SEN characteristics is likely to be moved over time into increasingly institutionalised care settings. The political problematic – many of these settings are privatised, staff may be untrained – of economics arises here. Recent cases of abuse in such settings don't generate confidence in existing provision.

It is important to note that Lawrence also wrote fictionally about disability. The story *England, My England*, for example, presents a child whose leg is maimed in an accident in her garden. Her situation is presented in the context of her family and outcomes for her are determined by the nature of the relation between her parents as well as the physical nature of her injury, together with capacities to pay for medical attention. A further social political context is set by the evolving European crisis that resulted in the First World War which Lawrence lucidly opposed and criticised. Situations spread out and are not easily compartmentalised. Any 'SEN disorder' constitutes a human situation and as such its ramifications will be complicated and widespread. For example, Professor Ghahramanlou Holloway has well presented the wave of effects that a mental disorder ending in suicide will have not just on the victim but also a whole grouping of individuals, family members and so on. And a suicide and its prelude will also involve social and political factors in relation to diagnosis, therapies tried, availability of mental health services and sums allocated by governmental decision (Brown et al., 2008). Holloway's suggestions for preventative provision for individuals at risk of suicide are relevant to SEN and other education contexts, and represent a useful area of psychiatric discussion, non-fictional, to complement the fiction mode.

Hopefully this chapter will have provided useful justifications for adding the reading of relevant fiction to that of non-fiction texts in relation to developing a critical and enlightened approach to SEN-categorised themes. Slavoj Žižek, for example, has proposed that 'a thing to fight for' is to make 'people, the experts in certain domains, be aware of not just accepting that there are problems, but of thinking more deeply. It is an attempt to make them see more'. A 'main task' for universities and elsewhere, as Žižek sees it, should be 'to prevent the narrow production of experts' (Žižek, 2013: 54). To consider SEN themes effectively, a wide context is valuable and fiction can be useful, even essential, in developing this. It is to be restated too that such fictional insights are to be considered in conjunction with those from other sources. There is a need for fictional evidence to be instated as acceptable and in no way inferior to the conventional, non-fiction kind, to run as a complement in developing SEN skills.

References

Brown G., Beck A. and Ghahramanlou-Holloway, M. (2008) 'Suicide', in *Adapting Cognitive Therapy for Depression,* ed. M. Whisman, New York and London, Guilford Press.

Clifford C., (2003) *The Asquiths*, London, John Murray.

Coetzee J.M., (2000) *Waiting for the Barbarians*, London, Vintage.

Conrad J., (1973) 'The Idiots' in *Tales of Unrest*, Harmondsworth, Penguin.

Conrad J., (1963) *The Secret Agent*, Harmondsworth, Penguin.

Flay M., (2009) *The Watchers*, Cheltenham, Polar Books.

Foucault M., (1991) *Discipline and Punish*, Harmondsworth, Penguin.

Harvey J., (2014) *The Subject of a Portrait*, Cheltenham, Polar Books.

Hoeg P., (1996) *The Borderliners*, London, Harvill.

Lawrence D.H., (1962) *The Collected Letters of D.H. Lawrence*, ed. H.T. Moore, London, Heinemann, p537, Letter to Lady Cynthia Asquith, 28.1.1918.

Quayson A., (1999) 'Looking Awry: Tropes of Disability in Post-colonial Writing' in *An Introduction to Contemporary Fiction*, ed. Mengham R., Cambridge, Polity.

Žižek S., (2013) 'The Subversive Use of Theory' in *Demanding the Impossible*, Cambridge, Polity.

21 Educational leadership

Developing insight into practice

Melody Harrogate

Developing leadership capacity within the different contexts of education has been highly focused on over the last few decades. Research findings from Leithwood et al. (2004) led them to declare that leadership was second only to classroom instruction. Much of the literature published has stemmed from four particular leadership landscape studies; Earley et al. (2002), Stephens et al. (2005), PricewaterhouseCoopers (2007) and Earley et al. (2012). The works of Wallace et al. (2011) focus particularly on the issue of developing leadership capacity in schools and universities; developing leadership is seen as a soft policy lever in the attempt to 'secure competitive national advantage in the global economy' (p. 21). Their work questions how far the investment in developing educational leadership is capable of achieving the 'envisioned return' (p. 25). The perceived need to focus on developing leadership skills has been the driving force of many continuing professional development programmes in an attempt to meet this political agenda.

There is no single all-encompassing 'theory of educational leadership' (Bush 2011: 9); the array of contexts and leadership roles that emerge from these contexts are endlessly diverse. It would not be possible to argue that one particular leadership model is more favourable to use than another. It is necessary, however, for the variety of theories of leadership and leadership models to be understood by a potential leader. It is more productive for the emerging leader to build an understanding of the historical and contemporary leadership models and choose the most effective approach either for the situation they are dealing with or to steer or implement their vision. Developing the skills to learn about leadership is not only fundamental (Swaffield and MacBearth 2009), but vital. The complex issues involved in leadership are things that anyone aspiring to leadership needs to understand; the level of understanding they reach can 'determine whether a leader can succeed with the task in hand and sustain themselves over a period of time' (Crawford 2014: 4). It is also vital that the potential leader has good background knowledge to the extrinsic and intrinsic context of the organisation they will be leading and strong subject currency, with lots of enthusiasm and passion.

There are many theories on the timeline of leadership development. Some academics have grouped them into categories; Bush and Glover (2002), Leithwood et al. (1999), and Bush (2011) give us: Managerial Leadership, Transformational Leadership, Participative Leadership, Interpersonal Leadership, Transactional Leadership, Postmodern Leadership, Moral Leadership, Instructional Leadership and Contingent Leadership, which makes each theory easier to correlate with a variety of leadership roles. It is beyond the scope of this chapter to discuss these in detail, and it is well worth further research and reading. Bush (2011) clearly identifies particular types of leadership or management roles for each of these categories. However, there are some leadership theories which have adopted different names for similar processes, for example Direct Instructional and Transactional Leadership are often interchangeably used, as are Transformational and Charismatic and Visionary Leadership; in these cases, the emerging leader would be wise not to expect clear-cut and separate identities by the name of the leadership theory but to be more mindful of the process it purports to follow.

'Throughout the years, researchers have searched for the relationship between school leadership, school effectiveness and school improvement and for the impact of leadership on student achievements' (Kruger 2009: 110). The leadership theories which have gained most attention in educational leadership over the last 10 years are: Transactional Leadership and Transformational Leadership, Participative Leadership and Distributive Leadership. These leadership theories will be explored and current debates relating to them considered; I believe these particular theories have all been used as a reaction to meet the requirements of education reforms and Government agendas.

Transactional and Transformational Leadership theory are often discussed together and seen by Hartog (2003) not as separate dimensions but as two extremes of a continuum. Transactional leadership is seen as a *model most closely aligned with micro politics* (Bush 2011: 119); it is a model of an exchange dimension (Northhouse 2013) and has factors such as contingent reward, management by exception being active or passive and results in expected outcomes. Transactional leadership is seen when there is a focus on the main task and the standards to be achieved (Bass and Riggio 2006); transactional leaders do not change quickly, they are not easily deviated from the goal and use rewards as motives (Smith and Bell 2014). I believe that Transactional Leadership is a more behaviouristic approach to leadership and correlates with reward and punishment philosophy, whereas Transformational Leadership is more aligned with a constructivist approach in relation to scaffolding, evolving, and growing. I believe there can be situations where it is necessary and productive to use both approaches.

Transformational Leadership is not a new theory; it was originally identified through the works of Downton (1973) and Burns (1978) and developed by Bass (1985) and Avolio and Bass (1994, 2002). It is seen as a process that can change and transform people, and hence organisations, for the better. It focuses on values, emotions, standards, and ethics; it looks at long-term goals and how to work with followers' motivation drivers; it is seen as humanistic and strives to fulfil needs and develop followers to accomplish more than is expected of them (Northhouse 2013). Transformational leadership generates respect through communication of values, purpose and the organisation's overall aim and mission (Bush 2011). Transformational leadership is seen when the leader is fluid and flexible, inspirational, vision-focused, encouraging development and able to change and promote changes (Smith and Bell 2014).

A very similarly described theory is Direct Instructional Leadership, which encompasses all activities that may have an impact on student learning, and indirect instructional leadership which can encompass developing leadership in others (Larson and Rieckhoff 2013). Instructional and Transformational Leadership have been investigated and findings from Robinson et al. (2008) suggest that the average effect of Instructional Leadership on students' outcomes was three or four times higher than that of Transformational Leadership; this is also supported by the research of Shatzer et al. (2014). However, Transformation Leadership is seen to be more effective at developing staff (Bush 2011).

Educational reforms have led to educational leaders having to align their role with effective outcomes (Larson and Rieckhoff 2013), and to do this within a collaborative structure creating a need for collegial leadership models to be used. The two collegial approaches to leadership in education have been Participative Leadership and Distributive Leadership. Participative Leadership enhances the opportunities that staff have to 'engage in the process of organisation decision making' (Leithwood et al. 1999: 12). Distributive Leadership is seen as leadership practice in an integrated framework; it involves multiple agents participating and contributing to the process of leadership (Crowther et al. 2008), and is seen as a move away from the heroic individual leadership approach (Gronn 2010). It has been 'one of the most influential ideas to emerge in the field of educational leadership' (Harris 2010: 55), and has become necessary because in the current climate the 'job is far too challenging for any one individual' (West-Burnham 2004: 2). Performance beyond expectations happens only when leadership is 'with and through others' (Hargreaves and Harris 2010: 36; Stone-Johnson 2014: 648). The main concern with this type of leadership approach is that not all leaders are happy to seemingly dilute the level of their leadership autonomy through redistribution of power; this model needs acceptance of collaboration to be successful (Gronn 2010; Harris 2010; Bottery 2004).

For any person in any leadership role to grow to their full potential, developing a process of reflection and reflexion (Bourdieu 1990; Brubaker 1993) brings about introspective insight and opportunities to grow and move. Developing leadership skills can be enhanced by coaching and mentoring, systematic reflection and action learning (Hammond et al. 2009; Earley and Jones 2009; Earley 2013). It is also necessary when applying leadership strategies to be aware of the extrinsic context such as the unique culture of the organisation (Claxton et al. 2011). I also believe that the mindset (Dweck 2006) of the person leading is paramount to the effectiveness of their leadership approach, that when you are 'working in the world of growth-mindset leaders, everything changes. It brightens, it expands, it fills with energy, with possibilities' (Dweck 2006: 225).

This leads me to look at the next part of this chapter: what can be used to help the potential leader to have more self-knowledge, seen as a central element to leadership development (Sieff 2009), reflect and become more reflexive? How useful is the following tool at helping the potential leader to achieve that?

Psychological testing: Myers and Briggs

How effective is psychological testing at providing insightful information to potential leaders, about themselves and their colleagues? In this part of the chapter I have analysed literature around this question.

The psychological-type questionnaire I am looking at here is the Myers and Briggs Type Indicator (MBTI).

The MBTI was launched in 1962, and although it has been established for a number of years it is still a very popular tool for establishing the way someone prefers to be. Completing the questionnaire results in one of 16 types, with titles like 'ESTJ' and 'INFP' being identified as the preferred habitual leadership MBTI type. These refer to four polarities based on the works of Carl Jung in the 1920s such as extroversion, introversion, where we get our energy from, externally to ourselves (extroversion) or from within, introversion. Sensing and intuition relate to how we prefer to process information through our senses, or looking at the bigger picture. Thinking and feeling are about how we make our decisions, with our heads or our hearts. Judging and perceiving; do we prefer structure and order or are we happy to go with the flow? The questionnaire is used to assess preferences, not judge performance or skills. MBTI preferences and combinations of preferences might influence the types of life experiences a person is exposed to or the way in which such experiences are perceived and responded to (Vincent et al. 2013). If the questionnaire is completed by the whole team, it is possible to formulate a team profile and from that analyse the way the team may be operating. So it is useful for both individual and group profiling.

MBTI can be used as part of the learning process not only for leadership but for also individual personal reflection; learning how a person prefers to do something, or the way a person thinks about something or might react to something, is always going to be very useful and help to develop accurate self-perception. Of course, it has to hold some value to the person completing the process otherwise it would just become pointless. Research has been completed to prove the validity of the outcome of the questionnaire (Myers and McCaulley 1985) and there has been much refining of the process over the years; the questionnaire has been used for over 50 years now. I believe gaining insight into your own preferences is very useful and would help with decision making regarding leadership approaches and styles. Research has shown that having accurate self-perception can improve leadership effectiveness (Roush and Atwater 1992) and is also seen an a component of Authentic Leadership (Hickman 2015).

There has been research around using the MBTI and Transformational Leadership. The research undertaken by Roush and Atwater (1992: 1) showed that the MBTI 'could be used to understand transformational and transactional leadership behaviours as well as the leader's self-perception accuracy'. Their research showed that an individual whose perception of their own leadership was similar to the perceptions that others had of them were more successful leaders. It was also noted that followers identified transformational leaders as those who had sensing rather than intuition preference and feeling rather than thinking preference, which goes against what the theory suggests: that intuition would be a close match for what is expected from a transformational leader. Another interesting point was that extroverts were no more transformational than the introverts, questioning the presumption that leaders should have an extrovert preference. There are many of the MBTI preference-type profiles which are claimed to be seen in many leaders which are both introvert and extrovert, the main ones being ENTJ and INTJ. Research from Brown and Reilly (2008: 927) is also based around the MBTI and transformational leadership results were the opposite of Roush and Atwater (1992) and Hautala (2006). In this study follower perceptions' of leadership effectiveness were independent of the leader's psychological type.

I believe that the MBTI could be used with other tools to aid insight and development of self-perception. Wagner (2003) argues that MBTI should not be used in isolation as there are a large amount of management styles that go far beyond the sixteen types identified by Myers and Briggs. It should be 'used with caution'. However, if used under 'close scrutiny' it can be a tool which provides an opportunity for increased self-awareness of a person's decision-making preferences and behaviour (2003: 78). I completely support that for accurate and complete feedback, the MBTI should only ever be distributed and analysed by a qualified practitioner.

Conclusion

Understanding the effects of educational reforms and the social policy that shape the educational landscapes is vitally important and helps us to see why the leadership approaches that are so popular today are being used: we are enlightened by Bush (2011).

It is equally important that potential leaders have the opportunity to learn about leadership theories and the debates around them, to understand that there is no 'overall valid truth to what good leadership is as it is dependent . . . on what individual, social and cultural constructions are present which may vary considerably between groups of people' (Schyns et al. 2011: 406). Whether the choice of approach is Transactional, Transformational, Distributive, Moral, Ethical (Shapiro and Stefkovich 2011) or Responsible Leadership (Stone-Johnson 2014), developing a growth mindset (Dwek 2006) and wanting to reflect and be reflexive can enhance self-perception and levels of accuracy in the leader understanding themselves and the decisions they make. Using a tool such as the MBTI questionnaires gives the opportunity for insight to develop accurate self-perception. I agree with Allio (2009: 9) that we can teach leadership theory and philosophy, but 'leadership behaviour must be learned . . . individuals evolve into leaders as they experiment with alternative approaches to new challenges'. Leaders have to be able to understand their own and others' perspectives to 'take ownership of their work, make a stand for their beliefs and manage enormous ambiguity and complexity' (Drago-Severson and Blum-DeStefano 2013: 7).

References

Allio, R. J. (2009) Leadership: The Big Five Ideas. *Strategy and Leadership* 37(2), 4–12.

Bass, B. and Avolio, B. J. (1994) *Improving Organisational Effectiveness Through Transformational Leadership*. Thousand Oaks, CA: Sage.

Bass, B. and Riggio, R. (2006) *Transformational Leadership*. 2nd Edition. Mahwah, NJ: Lawrence Erlbaum Associates

Bligh, M. C. (2009) Personalities and Theories of Leadership. In *Encyclopaedia of Group Processes and Intergroup Relations*. London: Sage.

Bono, J. E. and Judge, T. A. (2004) Personality and Transformational and Transactional Leadership a Meta-analysis. *Journal of Applied Psychology* 89, 901–910.

Bottery, M. (2004) *The Challenges of Educational Leadership*. London: Paul Chapman.

Bourdieu, P. (1990) *In Other Words: Essays Towards a Reflexive Sociology*. Stanford, CA: Stanford University.

Brubaker, R. (1993) Social Theory as Habitus. In C. Calboun, E. LiPuma and M. Postone (eds), *Bourdieu: Critical Perspectives* (Chicago: University of Chicago Press).

Burns, J. M. (1978) *Leadership*. New York: Harper & Row.

Bush, T. (2011) *Theories of Educational Leadership and Management*. London: Sage.

Bush, T. and Glover, D. (2002) *School Leadership: Concepts and Evidence*. Nottingham: NCSL.

Claxton, G., Chambers, M., Powell, G. and Lucas, B. (2011) *The Learning Powered School: Pioneering 21st Century Education*. Bristol: TLO.

Crawford, M. (2014) *Developing as an Educational Leader and Manager*. London: Sage.

Crowther, F., Ferguson, M. and Hann, L. (2008) *Developing Teacher Leaders: How Teacher Leadership Enhances School Success*. Thousand Oaks, CA: Corwin Press.

Day, C. and Gurr, D. (eds) (2014) *Leading Schools Successfully: Stories from the Field*. London: Routledge.

Downton, J. V. (1973) *Rebel Leadership: Commitment and Charisma in a Revolutionary Process*. New York: Free Press.

Drago-Severson, E. and Blum-DeStefano, J. (2013) A New Approach for New Demands: The Promise of Learning-Oriented School Leadership, *International Journal of Leadership in Education: Theory and Practice*, 16(1), 1–33.

Dweck, C. S. (2006) *Mindset: The New Psychology of Success – How We Can Learn To Fulfill Our Potential*. New York: Ballantine Books.

Earley, P. (2013) *Exploring the School Leadership Landscape: Changing Demands, Changing Realities*. London: Bloomsbury Press.

Earley, P., Higham, R., Allen, T., Howsen, J., Nelson, R., Rawar, S., Lynch, S., Morton, L., Metha, P. and Sims, D. (2012) *Review of the School Leadership Landscape*. Nottingham: National College for School Leadership.

Earley, P. and Jones, J. (2009) Leadership Development in Schools. In Davies, B. (ed) *The Essentials of School Leadership* (2nd ed.). London: Sage.

Gronn, P. (2010) Where to Next for Educational Leadership? In T. Bush, I. Bell and D. Middlewood (eds) *The Principles of Educational Leadership and Management*. London: Sage.

Hammond, L., Meyerson, D., LaPointe, A. and Orr, M. (2009) *Preparing Principals for a Changing World: Lessons from Effective School Leadership Programmes*. New York: John Wiley.

Hargreaves, A. and Harris, A. (2011) *Performance Beyond Expectations*. Nottingham: National College for School Leadership.

Harris, A. (2010) Distributed Leadership: Evidence and Implications. In T. Bush, I. Bell and D. Middlewood (eds) *The Principles of Educational Leadership and Management* (2nd edn). London: Sage.

Hartog, D. (2003) Trusting Others in Organisations: Leaders, Management and Coworkers. In Nooteboom, B. and Six, F. (eds) *The Trust Process in Organizations: Empirical Studies of the Determinants and the Process of Trust Development*. Cheltenham: Edward Elgar.

Hautala, T. M. (2006) The Relationship between Personality and Transformational Leadership. *Journal of Management Development* 25(8), 777–794.

Hickman, G. R. (2015) *Leading Organizations*. London: Sage.

Judge, T. A., Bono, J. E., Ilies, R. and Gerhart, M. W. (2002) Personality and Leadership: A Qualitative and Quantitative Review. *Journal of Applied Psychology* 87(4), 765–780.

Kruger, M. (2009) The Big Five of School Leadership Competencies in the Netherlands. *School Leadership and Management: Formerly School Organisations* 29(2), 109–127.

Larson, C. and Rieckhoff B. S. (2013) Distributed Leadership: Principals Describe Shared Roles in a PDS. *International Journal of Leadership in Education: Theory and Practice* 17(3), 304–326.

Leithwood, K. Jantzi, D. and Steinback, R. (1999) *Changing Leadership for Changing Times*. Buckingham: Open University Press.

Leithwood, L., Anderson, S. and Wahlstrom, K. (2004) *How Leadership Influences Student Learning*. New York: Wallace Foundation.

Myers, I. B. and McCaulley, M. H. (1985) *Manual: A Guide to the Development and Use of the Myers-Briggs Type Indicator*. Palo Alto, CA: Consulting Psychologists Press.

Northhouse, P. (2013) *Leadership: Theory and Practice* (6th ed.). London: Sage.

PricewaterhouseCoopers (2007) *Independent Study into School Leadership*. Department of Education and Skills, research report RR818A. London: HMSO.

Roush, P. E. and Atwater, L. (1992) Using the MBTI to Understand Transformational Leadership and Self-Perception Accuracy. *Military Psychology* 4(1), 17–34.

Schyns, B., Keifer, T., Kerschreiter, R. and Tymor, A. (2011) Teaching Implicit Leadership Theories to Develop Leaders and Leadership: How and Why it Can Make a Difference. *Academy of Management Learning and Education* 10(3), 397–408.

Sieff, G. (2009) Personality Type and Leadership Focus: Relationship between Self and Line Manager Perceptions. *SA Journal of Human Resource Management* 7(1), 63–73.

Shapiro, J. P. and Stefkovich, J. A. (2011) *Ethical Leadership and Decision Making in Education* (3rd ed). London: Routledge.

Shatzer, R. H., Caldarella, P., Hallam, R. and Brown, B. (2014) Comparing the Effects of Instructional and Transformational Leadership on Student Achievement: Implications for Practice. *Educational Management Administration and Leadership* 42(4), 445–459.

Smith, P. and Bell, L. (2014) *Leading Schools in Challenging Circumstances: Strategies for Success*. London: Bloomsbury Press.

Stephens, J., Brown, J., Knibbs, S. and Smith, J. (2005) *Follow-up Research into the State of School Leadership in England*. London: DfES.

Stone-Johnson, C. (2014) Responsible Leadership. *Education Administration Quarterly* 50(4), 645–674.

Swaffield, S. and MacBearth, J. (2009) Leadership for Learning. In J. MacBearth and N. Dempster (eds), *Connecting Leadership and Learning Principles for Practice*. London: Routledge.

Vincent, N., Ward, L. and Denson, L. (2013) Personality Preferences and Their Relationship to Ego Development in Australia Leadership Program Participants. *Journal of Adult Development* 20, 197–211.

Wagner, J. M. (2003) Using the Myers-Briggs Type Indicators as a Tool for Leadership Development? Apply with Caution. *Journal of Leadership and Organisational Studies* 10(1), 68–81.

Wallace, M., Deen, R., O'Reilly D. and Tomlinson, M. (2011) Developing Leadership Capacity in English Secondary Schools and Universities: Global Positioning and Local Mediation. *British Journal of Educational Studies* 59(1), 21–40.

West-Burnham, J. (2004) *Building Leadership Capacity: Helping Leaders Learn*. London: National College for School Leadership.

22 The refuge of relativism

Dennis Hayes and Ruth Mieschbuehler

In educational thought, relativism is rife. Hardly anyone believes in knowledge and statements such as 'all truth is relative' pass without comment or criticism. The ubiquitous nature of relativism today is a result of a new phenomenon, 'cultural relativism', the widely accepted belief that all 'cultures' must be respected and have their own value systems, which is also accepted without comment or criticism.

Relativism and cultural relativism constitute an attack on knowledge and universal moral values. They persist in part because the discipline of philosophy, which was once in the vanguard of the study of education, is no longer a required area of study for education professionals. Philosophers might think that a revival of the subject of philosophy would help repel the attack on knowledge, but a fuller explanation of their persistence and the strength and dominance of relativism since the latter half of the twentieth century shows it to be more of a pessimistic self-loathing, a sociological and cultural mood in the post-colonial period that is set against Enlightenment values of reason, science and progress (Gross and Levitt 1998; Malik 2014).

Moving between philosophical and sociological analysis makes it possible to see how cultural trends which constitute an attack on knowledge draw on philosophy, and how philosophy offers logical criticisms which can undermine the so-called philosophical 'foundation' of cultural trends.

The power of philosophical arguments to undermine contemporary cultural trends is weakened by the claims made by cultural relativists that they 'empower' minority and oppressed groups by celebrating their 'cultures', but not only are their approaches based on self-contradictory arguments, they also disempower and disadvantage minority and oppressed groups by denying the universal element in knowledge and morals that extends across 'cultures'.

Philosophy alone may not be enough to reverse cultural trends but it can provide a foundation for educationalists to feel confident enough to seek to bring powerful and empowering knowledge back into education.

Relativism is rife

We present some philosophical arguments here but the main thrust of our argument is an attempt to say *why* educationalists need to *do* some philosophy. Our aim is to advance a sociological or political understanding of the urgent need for philosophy and why philosophical arguments today are very weak and have little impact.

The clearest explanation of why philosophy is necessary in education today can be taken from Allan Bloom's powerful polemic, *The Closing of the American Mind*.

The sub-title of this best-selling-book is 'How higher education has failed democracy and impoverished the souls of today's students'. He opens his polemic with an attack on 'openness'. 'Openness and being open-minded might seem to be a good thing, and indeed, it once was: Openness used to be the virtue that permitted us to seek the good by using reason but today it means the opposite, accepting everything and denying reason's power' (Bloom 1987: 38). 'Openness' has become the dominant value in education but not in the old way:

> There are two kinds of openness, the openness of indifference – promoted with the twin purposes of humbling our intellectual pride and letting us be whatever we want to be, just as long as we don't want to be knowers – and the openness that invites us to the quest for knowledge and certitude. . . . The second kind of openness encourages the desire that animates and makes interesting every serious student . . . while the former stunts that desire.
>
> (Bloom 1987: 41)

'True openness' for Bloom was 'the accompaniment of the desire to know, hence of the awareness of ignorance' (Bloom 1987: 40). The new openness means that we must be open to, and respectful of, everything and anything. This sense of 'openness' is closely connected with relativism and 'relativism is necessary to openness; and this is the virtue, the only virtue, which all primary education for more than fifty years has dedicated itself to inculcating' (Bloom 1987: 25–26). The consequence is that: 'There is one thing a professor can be absolutely certain of: almost every student entering the university believes, or says he believes, that truth is relative' (Bloom 1987: 25).

Faced with an awareness of various claims to truth and different opinions about what constitutes a good or a bad way of living, a relativistic 'openness' seems to be the most important and democratic value. It is a value that rejects intolerance and absolutist views about the truth of any particular set of beliefs. It also produces a particular kind of student, one that Bloom characterises as 'nice':

> Students these days are, in general, nice. I choose the word carefully. They are not particularly moral or noble. Such niceness is a facet of democratic character when times are good. Neither war nor tyranny nor want has hardened them or made demands on them. The wounds and rivalries caused by class distinction have disappeared along with any strong sense of class. . . . Students are free of most constraints, and their families make sacrifices for them without asking for much in the way of obedience or respect. Religion and national origin have almost no noticeable effect on their social life or their career prospects. Although few really believe in 'the system', they do not have any burning sentiment that injustice is being done to them. . . . Students these days are pleasant, friendly and, if not great-souled, at least not particularly mean-spirited. Their primary preoccupation is themselves, understood in the narrowest sense.
>
> (Bloom 1987: 82–83)

What Bloom said about students nearly three decades ago now also applies to many academics and to those who have graduated in the era of niceness. Relativism is rife but despite the seeming niceness that results from relativism, niceness is not a moral position. It results in an amoral and narcissistic indifference to what constitutes truth or goodness.

Bloom condemns educationalists for producing students who are 'not particularly moral or noble' and whose primary 'value' is a relativistic openness that is damaging to intellectual and moral life. In contrast, readers may find they are sympathetic to being 'open' in this new sense. What may be surprising is the condemnation of this position by some rather than the celebration of it. Roger Scruton even goes so far as to describe relativism about moral problems as the 'first refuge of the scoundrel' (Scruton 1994: 32).

Condemning the ubiquity and persistence of relativism today should not be necessary if philosophical arguments alone had the power of persuasion as well as the power of refutation. Relativism is not a new perspective and for over 2,000 years there have been philosophical refutations of relativism that show it to be untenable. In the next section, these arguments are discussed before turning to a more detailed consideration of why relativism, particularly in the form of 'cultural relativism', persists in spite of its easy philosophical refutation.

The philosophical critique of relativism

The most famous quick refutation of relativism is over 2,000 years old. It is found in a passage in Plato's *Theaetetus* (s. 170a–171d) where Socrates is arguing against the relativistic ideas put forward by Protagoras in his book *The Truth*. In this book, Protagoras argues that every person's judgements are true for them although thousands may disagree with their opinions. Many people may also disagree with Protagoras' opinion that every person's opinions are true for them:

Socrates:	Protagoras admits, I presume, that the contrary opinion about his own opinion (namely, that it is false) must be true, seeing as he agrees that all men judge what is.
Theodorus:	Undoubtedly.
Socrates:	And in conceding the truth of the opinion of those who think him wrong, he is really admitting the falsity of his own opinion?
Theodorus:	Yes, inevitably.
Socrates:	But for their part the others do not admit that they are wrong?
Theodorus:	No.
Socrates:	But Protagoras again admits *this* judgement to be true, according to his written doctrine?
Theodorus:	So it appears.
Socrates:	It will be disputed, then, by everyone, beginning with Protagoras – or rather, it will be admitted by him, when he grants to the person who contradicts him that he judges truly – when he does that, even Protagoras himself will be granting that neither a dog nor the 'man in the street' is the measure of anything at all which he has not learned. Isn't that so?
Theodorus:	It is so.
Socrates:	Then since it is disputed by everyone, the *Truth* of Protagoras is not true for anyone at all, not even for himself?

(Burnyeat 1990: 298)

A vast literature on Plato and this argument exists but it will not be discussed here because arguments of a similar sort are still used today. Nozick refers to one argument as a 'quick refutation' of relativism. If someone argues that 'All truth is relative', this assertion is easily dismissed by asking 'Is that view relative?' (Nozick 2001: 15). These quick refutations are well known. All show statements asserting the relativity of truth are self-refuting.

Siegel provides a clear example which he calls the 'self-refutation' argument against relativism. Siegel even suggests that a statement be put on the white board, or more likely on a PowerPoint slide in today's higher education world, which reflects the students' relativistic views and makes them think about the logical coherence or incoherence of relativism. Siegel suggests the following statement:

> *Statement A:* 'There is no right or wrong concerning the constitution of good reasons. Such judgements are just opinions; probative force is in the eye of the reasoner'.

Then ask: 'Is [statement] A right, or just your opinion?'

(Siegel 1997: 21)

Siegel's pedagogic suggestion would be welcomed by Bloom, who sees all undergraduates as being predisposed to relativism as if it were a 'moral postulate' (Bloom 1987: 25).

If educationalists and researchers were familiar with these arguments, then they would perhaps be less inclined to adopt relativism and be more inclined to debate and discuss. Relativists, however, face a yet more general problem. When relativists utter any statements, they must engage in 'truth talk'. For example, when relativists assert propositions like 'there is no universal truth to which our construction is a more or less good approximation', they engage in 'truth talk' (Bridges 1999: 610). Beyond simple self-contradictory statements, relativists also engage in 'truth talk' through their work; for example, when they state beliefs or discuss evidence. This propositional 'truth talk' also self-refutes the claim that all 'truth talk' is relative.

These knock-down arguments are, of course, subject to criticism. Siegel is sanguine about them (Siegel 1987, 1997), whereas Nozick is uncomfortable with quick refutations (Nozick 2001). One of the many attempts to escape self-refutation is that of Rorty who would argue that statements of relativism are not the same as those in 'normal discourse' but belong in 'hermeneutic discourse' and are not true or false statements (Putnam 1992: 71). However, this is a rejection of the idea that relativism reveals a metaphysical truth about the world. If 'All truth is relative' is not a proposition with a truth value, it is simply rhetoric aimed to get us to 'change our ways, to give up talk about truth and falsity' (Putnam 1992: 71).

Writing in 1992, Putnam declared that 'first-person relativism', the view that truth is what I agree with, or would agree with if I investigated it for sufficient time, was 'virtually unfindable on today's philosophical scene' (Putnam 1992: 73). But over twenty years on, that view is everywhere in academic scenes, if not in philosophical scenes. Part of the reason for this return is, as we have argued, the popularity of 'cultural relativism', or relativism with a 'we' rather than an 'I'. For Putnam, both collapse into solipsism: the view that 'truth' is merely a disposition to believe on the part of the relativist. Putnam argues that truth, or the language game of truth, is something that is 'not simply conventional, is not simply determined by consensus, but something that requires evaluation' (Putnam 1992: 77). He recognises that this is 'troubling to many a contemporary sensibility' and that 'the distrust of the normative in present-day philosophy is evidenced above all by the lengths to which philosophers will go to avoid admitting that truth – that is, the rightness of what is said – *is* a normative notion' (Putnam 1992: 77).

The arguments against relativism have to be refined as relativists refine their arguments. Take, as an example of a more sophisticated relativism, the view that our truth statements are only true relative to a theory that we accept. The acceptance of a theory is a statement about some absolute facts about our beliefs so it does allow some absolute facts. Furthermore, if truth is in fact only relative to a theory we accept, how does the relativist deal with this fact? He must argue that 'According to a theory that we accept, there is a theory that we accept, and according to this latter theory, there is a theory that we accept and . . . there have been dinosaurs' (Boghossian 2007: 56). We are in an infinite regress and relativism comes down to an unintelligible infinite statement.

This brief discussion shows that relativism is self-contradictory and incoherent. It survives in philosophy because of what Putnam calls the 'distrust of the normative' which we can place in a wider context of what Boghossian calls 'fear of knowledge' or what Bailey calls 'veriphobia' or 'fear of truth' (Bailey 2001, 2004). These are not primarily philosophical but political and cultural states.

A familiar example of relativism

Students and teachers may not come across such philosophical arguments directly but relativism is there in textbooks and in course materials. Unfortunately, on education courses this is often philosophy at fourth or fifth hand. A philosopher of education reads a philosophical work and writes about it. A teacher educator reads the philosopher of education and writes about it in a course textbook and then a lecturer takes from the textbook something that has almost been distilled into an unproblematic truth. It takes a philosopher or a philosopher of education to show that these statements are neither unproblematic nor unquestionable.

As an example of how a philosopher of education can search out a whiff of relativism and provide a criticism, consider Richard Pring's discussion of an influential book by Guba and Lincoln from 1989 (Pring 2000; see also Pring 2004).

Pring points out that Guba and Lincoln in *Fourth Generation Evaluation* state that 'realities' are not objectively 'out there' but 'constructed' by people as they attempt 'to make sense' of their surrounds (which surrounds do not exist independently of them anyway) (Pring 2000: 250). This is a popular view that has been adopted by many educationalists. Although they may not go as far as saying there are 'multiple realities' they, like Guba and Lincoln, believe that 'there are different ways in which reality is conceived, and those differences may well reflect different practical interests and different traditions' (Pring 2000: 254). The difficulties faced by Guba and Lincoln are those faced by the relativists discussed above. As Pring says, 'although Guba and Lincoln must necessarily fight shy of claiming "the truth" of what they argue, they are obliged to have recourse to words and phrases which, more obscurely, imply much the same' (Pring 2000: 252). They argue that 'through a hermeneutic dialectic process, a new construction will emerge that is not "better" or "truer" than its predecessors, but simply more informed and sophisticated than either' (Guba and Lincoln 1989: 17 cited in Pring 2000: 252). The constant process of construction and reconstruction of 'reality' through negotiation, they claim, 'creates a constructed reality that is as informed and seems (not "is") more *reasonable* and *appropriate* to those in the *best* position to make that judgement'

(Pring 2000: 252). Using terms like 'better informed', 'more sophisticated', 'more reasonable', and 'more appropriate' are desperate attempts to avoid 'truth talk' and we can see them as clever sleights of hand.

Why not go all the way and take a realist rather than a relativist position? Realists affirm the notion of objective truth (knowledge) and assert that there is 'a single way of being or truth' (Anderson 1962a; Anderson 1962b; Baker 1986: 20; Bridges 1999; Swann and Pratt 1999). They believe that there is 'a reality, a world, which exists independently of the researcher and which is to be discovered' (Pring 2004: 59). Is this not what most teachers and educationalists believe?

We would argue that it is probably the case that most people are realists in their daily lives but when they begin research or thinking about education, they adopt a relativist position and focus on people's experiences, or their perceptions of reality, and may even claim that multiple 'realities' exist and that equal validity must be attributed to each person's socially constructed reality (Berger and Luckmann 1967; Smith and Lusthaus 1995; Lyotard 1999; Bryman 2004; Pring 2004).

What this reluctance about realism reflects has nothing to do with coherent arguments. Relativism is self-contradictory and therefore false. Gross and Levitt in their discussion and demolition of the arguments against the struggle to explain the world and understand reality through science show that what lies behind them is 'an astonishingly general mood swing' in society (Gross and Levitt 1998: 217). The arguments put forward for 'social constructivist' or 'feminist' views of science can be demolished but the antagonism to science is widespread. It is linked to Western self-loathing, the fear that science is in the hands of capitalists and war-mongers, and the belief that Enlightenment values are oppressive. The failure to separate out this sentimental mush of politics from science is partly explained by careerism as there is currently some support and some status attached to attacking 'Western' values in the academy. There are career benefits for many, particularly for the academic left who oppose science and see their work in the academy as political. What they want is political change, not truth, and their arguments are not opposed by management who use relativism to avoid criticism of their (different) political objectives.

Why doesn't the philosophical critique simply do away with relativism?

It is easy, because of the academic culture of 'openness', to see the persistence of relativism and the attack on scientific knowledge as a psychological problem. Epistemology is the study of knowledge, of what it means when we say we know something. It is a core discipline of the subject of philosophy. In many ways it *is* philosophy. If there is a 'fear of knowledge' we could talk about 'epistemophobia' as a label for fear of knowledge and 'veriphobia' as the label for fear of truth (Bailey 2001; 2004). Epistemophobia and veriphobia affect philosophy although they are cultural 'phobias' or trends which need sociological explanation. The terms 'veriphobia' and 'epistemophobia' try to capture something of what you might call a contemporary fear of knowing. There is a danger in seeing the attack on knowledge as a psychological problem.

Relativism, despite being self-contradictory and incoherent, persists. It persists, according to Putnam, because relativism, like scepticism, is eternal, a part of the human condition:

Relativism and scepticism are all too easily refutable when they are stated as positions; but they never die, because the attitude of alienation from the world and from the community is not just a theory, and cannot be overcome by purely intellectual argument.

(Putnam 1992: 178)

It is debatable whether the alienation Putnam mentions is an eternal condition. Assuming it is, for the sake of argument, it has expressions that are particular to historically specific circumstances.

One reason why relativism persists in education at the present time is the emphasis on cultural differences and the way this emphasis seems empowering because it is accepting and non-judgemental. This non-judgementalism is not empowering at all; it actually diminishes our human being simply by attacking our ability to judge. In the twenty-first century all judgements of aesthetic, moral, social and political value have become anathema or as Kennedy put it, 'the irony of the state of culture today is that society fears the individual expression of judgement' (Kennedy 2014: 6). This fear of judgement is the contemporary state of Western culture which is 'uncomfortable with making value judgements' (Furedi 2011: 80). 'Western culture' is usually the focus for these discussions, although the discussion could arguably be extended to the state of all cultures in a global world.

Cultural relativism feeds off and supports relativism by avoiding judgements about the value of particular beliefs, customs and practices and by adopting the general cultural condition of non-judgementalism. By doing so, cultural relativism appears to empower a multiplicity of 'cultures' against dominance by other cultures, yet it merely avoids judgement. Therefore, what is commonly seen as recognition and respect for different cultures, which are incommensurable and cannot be challenged from without, is an appeal to the non-judgementalism that constitutes the culture of relativism. But there are damaging consequences to non-judgementalism.

Non-judgementalism gives, in fact, a false sense of empowerment. Bailey has pointed out that Foucault, in his denial of 'truth', suggests that 'truth' has to be understood in the context of power relations (Bailey 2004). However, identifying regimes of truth and describing them as tools of domination, power and control without making the distinction between truth and falsity 'disempowers the very people it claims to represent' (Bailey 2004: 205). This is because if, as relativists argue, there are multiple 'truths' and socially constructed 'realities' and 'truths' and 'realities' are equally valued, relativists are eroding the very basis on which power relations could be challenged. If socially constructed 'realities' are equally valid, 'truths' presented by groups identified as powerful are equally valid as 'truths' presented by minoritised groups and cannot be challenged (Scruton 1994; Bailey 2004). In other words, non-judgementalism appears to 'protect oppressed cultures' as 'the powerful can't criticise the oppressed', while in fact it censors 'the oppressed' as the 'oppressed can't criticise the powerful' either if the same logic is applied (Boghossian 2007: 130).

Boghossian makes the point that relativism seems to empower even after refuting both relativism and related social constructivist views of knowledge. Boghossian argues that if all knowledge is relative then 'any claim to knowledge can be dispatched if we do not happen to share the values on which it allegedly depends' and this appears to 'protect oppressed cultures from the charge of holding false or unjustified views' (Boghossian 2007: 130). The problem is, it does just the opposite. It does not silence criticism by the powerful of minorities and the oppressed:

If the powerful can't criticise the oppressed, because the central epistemological categories are inexorably tied to particular perspectives, it also follows that the oppressed can't criticise the powerful. The only remedy, so far as I can see, for what threatens to be a strongly conservative upshot, is to accept an overt double standard: allow a questionable idea to be criticised if it is held by those in a position of power – Christian creationism, for example – but not if it is held by those whom the powerful oppress – Zuni creationism, for example.

(Boghossian 2007: 130)

The 'strongly conservative' outcome would be that the powerful would be beyond criticism and the oppressed could do nothing about their views. Of course, there is no need to accommodate to relativism in Boghossian's censorious and unworkable way. It would be far better to allow everyone to criticise everything.

The false sense of empowerment appeals to people's moral sense of justice. It is this emotional appeal that makes relativism and its offshoots persist in education irrespective of the fact that they are intellectually quite easily refutable.

Cultural relativism has been criticised by many for its claim that 'there is no common standard by which cultures, and the practices embedded in them, can be evaluated' (Barry 2001: 252). These critiques emphasise the universal enlightenment values of morality and open discussion and debate against those who censor judgements in the name of non-judgementalism (Barry 2001; Pring 2004; Furedi 2011; Malik 1996, 2008, 2014; Kennedy 2014). Although the debates are heated, the facts about universality have been stated in more moderate ways in Pring's discussion of educational research:

Educational practices are conducted or engaged in within societies of shared values and understandings. There are national, indeed global debates, which create common understandings. And there are generalisations about how people are motivated and learn, however tentative these must be and in need of testing in the circumstances of particular classrooms.

(Pring 2004: 140–141)

Pring draws attention to the fact of globally shared understanding, communication, generalisation and discussion which is often forgotten in debates about incommensurable cultures. Forgetting facts about the world is a feature of the debates on relativism which strengthens the appeal of cultural relativism.

'Experience' and the threat to higher education

Another way of understanding why relativism persists which may be familiar is the emphasis in education on 'experience'. Talking about and interpreting experiences is a defining feature of cultural relativism in its search for cultural differences and the endless discussion in educational and professional literature on people's 'perceptions' of their work and their world.

It is particularly in higher education where the preoccupation with 'experience' was encouraged by a shift which abandoned a focus on subject-based teaching in favour of student–centred and learning process-oriented teaching. This ideological shift in education was officially introduced into British higher education by the *Dearing Report*

(Report of the National Committee of Inquiry into Higher Education) in 1997. Recommendation eight of the report entreated that 'all institutions of higher education give priority to developing and implementing learning and teaching strategies which focus on the promotion of students' learning' (Dearing 1997). The shift away from subject-based teaching towards student-centred education and learning process-oriented teaching prompted a growing concern with the student experience, to the extent that today 'student experience' has become an integral part of education policy and practice. It is this change in approach to higher education and teaching that facilitates the spread of relativist ideas in education, without any questioning or discussion about the validity and implications of this approach.

Another reason why relativism is widely absorbed into academic thinking is the relativist tendency to conflate experience with knowledge. Failing to draw the conceptual distinction between experience (people's perceptions) and knowledge (objective truth) can lead to equating knowledge with experience. When these two terms are conflated, knowledge is reduced 'to what is known by different groups, the power relations between them and their different experiences', but it says little about knowledge (Young 2008: 27). The tendency to conflate experience with knowledge undermines knowledge, but to relativists it gives them the confidence (though in reality a false belief) that they have knowledge.

As we have argued, in social and educational studies the terms 'knowledge' and 'objective truth' refer to 'inherited understandings' about the social world (Pring 2004: 60–61). These understandings refer to a reality through which 'we understand what is happening independently of us' without being 'our creation', even though inherited understandings 'have evolved over the millennia through intricate social interactions' (Pring 2004: 61). This conceptualisation allows for social forces and structures, whether people are conscious of them or not, to shape relationships, but contests that people can 'simply create another way of conceiving the social world' (Pring 2004: 60). Individual creations of the social world are not possible because the 'world is constituted' and already shaped by inherited understandings which evolved over time rather than being constructed individually at a specific point in time (Pring 2004: 61).

The idea of 'inherited understandings' equally applies to studies which involve cultural aspects because 'however culturally specific any one description or reality is, such a description has to come up against the hard facts of reality' (Pring 2004: 62). 'Different cultures might mark out different ways of conceptualising reality. But the viability of those distinctions depends upon features of the world which make them possible' (Pring 2004: 62). This means that there is a reality that is based on what Pring calls 'inherited understandings' which evolved to become 'hard facts of reality' that apply universally rather than being culturally or ethnically specific (Pring 2004: 62).

Equating experiences and different ways in which reality is perceived with knowledge has consequences for education. It suppresses the intellect in education.

What is missing is the universal, the human

Cultural relativists express an attitude of dislike for the values of the university which revolve around the pursuit of knowledge and understanding without fear or favour. This attitude is sometimes seen as a 'radical' position but what this really does is take away the power of criticism. To have the power of criticism, it is necessary to hold to the values of liberal universalism in higher education. These Enlightenment values or 'liberal universalism' are essentially a commitment to reason, the pursuit of truth and a belief in human potential.

The university is the embodiment of Enlightenment values and has the unique educational function of advancing knowledge as well as teaching existing knowledge, although schools and colleges may also have that commitment. The way in which knowledge is passed between generations or advanced is through 'liberal', 'knowledge-based' or 'subject-based' education. Teaching in a university is concerned with the acquisition of knowledge for its own sake and the development of the mind that results from knowledge (Hirst 1965). As Matthew Arnold famously wrote, the aim of this teaching is to learn 'the best that is known and thought in the world' (Arnold [1864] 2003: 50). In knowledge-based education all teaching must be rational, and whatever is taught must be based on reason and logically consistent intelligent justifications (Newman [1873] 1960; Hirst 1965; Oakeshott 1989; Halstead 2005).

The modern university has replaced liberal education and the pursuit of knowledge and understanding with 'other values', among which relativism and cultural relativism thrive. Any rejection of 'liberal universalism' by cultural relativists is appealing because it has the 'other purpose' of seeming to empower people when in reality it leaves people intellectually powerless.

Relativism survives because of an academic culture that is favourable to it. Relativism can be undermined, however, particularly in the university, by pointing out its self-contradictions. And relativism should be undermined in universities because these are special places that embody Enlightenment values; and it is these Enlightenment values, particularly the openness to criticism, which allow universities to house those who reject these values.

It is important to reassert liberal educational values in British higher education because this sector is under threat, both from political forces outside of mainstream university life and from current university policies and practices within it. There is a growing literature which reflects concern about these threats which constitutes a substantial, if defensive, defence of 'liberal education' and the idea of the university as the site of liberal higher education (Graham 2002; Maskell and Robinson 2002; Hayes and Wynyard 2002; Evans 2004; Collini 2012; Williams 2013). These declinist works talk about 'the university in ruins' or 'the death of the universities' and the need to set about the 'recovery' of the university (Readings 1996; Graham 2002; Evans 2004). Challenging relativism is the first and most essential step in that recovery.

Bringing the universal back in

The philosopher Kenan Malik argues that 'at the heart of the discourse of cultural relativism . . . there lies a hostility to Enlightenment universalism' (Malik 1996: 145). Restoring the belief in universalism as embodied in the liberal university is the prerequisite to restoring the power of philosophy. One way of doing this is to take note of historical examples which show that relativism does not follow from recognition of particular difference. We offer one here.

In 1952, Frantz Fanon, writing in *Black Skin, White Masks*, made his attitude to the conflict between the universal and particular very clear. He was conscious of being a 'black man' but also a 'man' and of not trying to be one particular 'black' or more disastrously trying to be 'white', but to recognise the universal in himself and his thought, something that was a constant struggle (see Malik 2014: 275–278). Fanon expresses this view, for example, when he writes that 'the negro, however sincere, is the slave of the past. None the less I am a man, and in this sense the Peloponnesian War is as much mine as the invention of the compass' (Fanon [1952] 1993: 225).

Fanon was a psychiatrist, writer and revolutionary in the time of colonial struggle, who did not succumb to relativism but recognised the universal in human history, science and culture. His example is a powerful one against those who would restrict anyone to their local and given identity. His work is also important as a critique of the easy relativistic rejections of 'Western' Enlightenment values that have come to dominate cultural and educational thinking in the 'post-colonial' period.

All this will need to be argued over and over because relativism is stronger now than at any time in history because of the loss of a belief in moral universals (see Malik 2014). The 'quick refutations' we discussed, although they do away with relativism as a philosophical position, cannot be convincingly employed unless, through continual debate and discussion, an attempt is made to win the case for the universal, for knowledge.

Finally, there is one more reason why the case for realism, objective truth and knowledge and particularly scientific knowledge has to be made. In educational thought and research there is a danger that because adopting a 'open' position avoids the intellectual difficulties involved in judgement, it seems to make thinking easy and relativism can become the first refuge of a lazy mind.

References

Anderson, J. (1962a) The knower and the known, *Studies in Empirical Philosophy*. Sydney: Angus and Robertson.

Anderson, J. (1962b) Realism and some of its critics, *Studies in Empirical Philosophy*. Sydney: Angus and Robertson.

Arnold, M. ([1864] 2003) The function of criticism at the present time, in Collini, S. (Ed.) *Culture and Anarchy and Other Writings*. Cambridge: Cambridge University Press.

Bailey, R. P. (2001) Overcoming veriphobia: learning to love truth again, *British Journal of Educational Studies*. 49 (2): 159–172.

Bailey, R. P. (2004) Why does truth matter? in Hayes, D. (Ed.) *The Routledge Falmer Guide to Key Debates in Education*. London: Taylor and Francis Group.

Baker, A. J. (1986) *Australian Realism: The Systematic Philosophy of John Anderson*. Cambridge: Cambridge University Press.

Barry, B. (2001) *Culture and Equality*. Cambridge: Polity Press.

Berger, P. L. and Luckmann, T. (1967) *The Social Construction of Reality: A Treatise in the Sociology of Knowledge*. London: Penguin Books.

Bloom, A. (1987) *The Closing of the American Mind: How Higher Education Has Failed Democracy and Impoverished the Souls of Today's Students*. New York: Simon and Schuster.

Boghossian, P. (2007) *Fear of Knowledge: Against Relativism and Constructivism*. Oxford: Oxford University Press.

Bridges, D. (1999) Educational research: pursuit of truth or flight into fancy? *British Educational Research Journal*. 25 (5): 597–616.

Bryman, A. (2004) *Social Research Methods* (2nd Edition). Oxford: Oxford University Press.

Burnyeat, M. (1990) *The Theaetetus of Plato* (translated by M. J. Levett). Indianapolis, IN: Hackett.

Collini, S. (2012) *What Are Universities For?* London: Penguin Books.

Dearing R. (1997) *Report of the National Committee of Inquiry into Higher Education*. London: Department for Education and Employment.

Evans, M. (2004) *Killing Thinking: The Death of the Universities*. London: Continuum.

Fanon, F. ([1952] 1993) *Black Skin, White Masks*. London: Pluto Press.

Furedi, F. (2011) *On Tolerance: A Defence of Moral Independence*. London: Continuum.

Graham, G. (2002) *Universities: The Recovery of an Idea*. Exeter: Imprint Academic.

Gross, P. R. and Levitt, N. (1998) *Higher Superstition: The Academic Left and its Quarrel with Science*. Baltimore and London: The Johns Hopkins University Press.

Guba, E. G. and Lincoln, V. S. (1989) *Fourth Generation Evaluation*. London: Sage.

Halstead, M. (2005) Liberal values and liberal education, in Carr, W. (Ed.) *The Routledge Falmer Reader in Philosophy of Education*. London: Routledge.

Hayes, D. and Wynyard, R. (Eds) (2002) *The McDonaldization of Higher Education*. London: Bergin and Garvey.

Hirst, P. H. (1965) Liberal education and the nature of knowledge, in Archambault, R. D. (Ed.) *Philosophical Analysis and Education*. London: Routledge and Kegan Paul.

Kennedy, A. (2014) *Being Cultured: In Defence of Discrimination*. Exeter: Imprint Academic.

Lyotard, J. ([1986] 1999) *The Postmodern Condition: A Report on Knowledge*. Manchester: Manchester University Press.

Malik, K. (1996) *The Meaning of Race: Race, History and Culture in Western Society*. New York: New York University Press.

Malik, K. (2008) *Strange Fruit: Why Both Sides Are Wrong in the Race Debate*. Oxford: One World.

Malik, K. (2014) *The Quest for a Moral Compass: A Global History of Ethics*. London: Atlantic Books.

Maskell, D. and Robinson, I. (2002) *The New Idea of a University*. Exeter: Imprint Academic.

Newman, J. H. ([1873] 1960) *The Idea of a University*. Notre Dame, IN: The University of Notre Dame Press.

Nozick, R. (2001) *Invariances: The Structure of the Objective World*. London: Harvard University Press.

Oakeshott, M. (1989) *The Voice of Liberal Education*. London: Yale University Press.

Pring, R. (2000) The 'false dualism' of educational research. *Journal of Philosophy of Education*. 34 (2): 247–260.

Pring, R. (2004) *Philosophy of Educational Research* (2nd Edition). London: Continuum.

Putnam, H. (1992) *Renewing Philosophy*. London: Harvard University Press.

Readings, B. (1996) *The University in Ruins*. London: Harvard University Press.

Ross, P. R. and Levitt, N. (1998) *Higher Superstition: The Academic Left and Its Quarrels with Science*. Baltimore and London: Johns Hopkins University Press.

Scruton, R. ([1994] 2004) *Modern Philosophy: An Introduction and Survey*. London: The Random House Group.

Siegel, H. (1987) *Relativism Refuted: A Critique of Contemporary Epistemological Relativism*. Dordrecht: D. Reidel.

Siegel, H. (1997) *Rationality Redeemed? Further Dialogues on an Educational Ideal*. New York and London: Routledge.

Smith, W. J. and Lusthaus, C. (1995) The nexus of equality and quality in education: a framework for debate. *Canadian Journal of Education*. 20 (3): 378–391.

Swann, J. and Pratt, J. (1999) *Improving Education: Realist Approaches to Method and Research*. London: Cassell Publications.

Williams, J. (2013) *Consuming Higher Education: Why Leaning Can't Be Bought*. London: Bloomsbury Academic.

Young, M. (2008) *Bringing Knowledge Back In: From Social Constructivism to Social Realism in the Sociology of Education*. London: Routledge.

Conclusion

Education – what's the point?

Anne O'Grady and Vanessa Cottle

We all have an assumptive understanding of the concept of education; after all, we are all likely to have experienced it in one form or another. Our perspective of education is organic – it builds over time, and is determined and influenced by our interaction with it – either as a student, educator, parent, leader, researcher or policy maker. Most often, however, we tend to view education in terms of the familiar compulsory and post-compulsory structured and formal processes. The point is we all use the term *education* assuming a common understanding of its purpose. We hope this book has provided the space for you to stop and ask 'what is the point of education?'.

As educational professionals it is increasingly important for us to consider the point of education. The questions that surround the value, purpose and role of education for contemporary societies are not new. In fact, these questions are probably some of the most constant and commonly asked questions about education – and they are certainly addressed in this collection of essays.

It is interesting to observe that education within this collection is often discussed without a link to learning. Education is discussed and explored at a macro level as a structure, which you can see from some of the policy discussion about how education is provided. At a micro level, analysing the way in which pedagogy happens is uncovered in our section on theory. Finally, at the meso level the intersectionality and interface of education are considered in our practice section.

Asking 'what is the point of education?' is crucial for us as members of the education community to establish how we view education, and our role in it.

Education, and educational opportunities, in this country are often determined as much by *whom you know* as much as *what you know* (Bourdieu, 1997). We have argued elsewhere (Atkin and O'Grady, 2006) that in the country's race to be economically competitive, framing education within a model of individual accountability and responsibility puts us at risk of losing sight of the importance of education for social responsibility, in turn creating social fragility, rather than social cohesion, within our society.

Over the decades, authors have commented on the drive for education with often differing and conflicting opinions: for example, John Dewey (1963, 1966) for democracy; Paulo Freire (1993, 1994) for emancipation; Pierre Bourdieu (1977, 1990, 1993, 2003) for social engineering. More recently, sociologists such as Frank Furedi (2009) have suggested that education – schooling – is not fulfilling its role of actually educating our society, if we accept the fundamental premise that education is the space to develop an educated people and society.

Most often education is discussed within the context and structure of compulsory education, referring to the formal framework through which children and young people are guided to specific outcomes. There are some discussions regarding what happens 'post-compulsorily', but these are often simplistic and 'cinderella-esk' (O'Grady, 2013). Griffiths (2009) asserts that education should be for joy and justice. Engagement in education, and indeed lifelong learning, we contend, should provide a space for hope and a space to dream, and enable all to continue to be curious about the life in which they are engaging.

What we hope, through this collection of essays, is that we have provided a space for you to consider our English systems and practices of education. For example, there have been arguments put forward in this collection which suggest that, whilst a system of education is theoretically available for all – through statutory requirements to provide education and attend education – what is actually provided is very narrowly defined and determined. The types of knowledge that are shared are centrally controlled via national curricula; the expected learning outcomes are often determined through examination curricula, and increasingly there is a focus of learning on economic imperatives (there are further arguments to be had here about whether knowledge is delivered or co-constructed). Whilst one can eloquently argue for the value and location of an economic determinant in education, this seems to some, us included, to miss the point. By having such a narrow agenda, with such a strong focus on 'work skills' with associated individual accountability and responsibility, there is a risk to society of what can be termed 'social fragility'. This type of agenda leads to an approach which limits the opportunities for education to encourage learning as a community endeavour, where ideas are shared, hope exists and there is the inspiration and dream of a society which is socially just, creating space for social mobility and community cohesion. Some of our contributors have considered whether the education system can be refocused to hold a primary ambition of social justice and civic responsibility, rather than driven by an economic frame. The inherent and pervasive nature of cultural capital (Bourdieu, 1997), however, seems to have the last say as the determinant to ensure that our society experiences education in such a way as to ensure its reproduction, reflecting the 'status quo' and ongoing power and privilege of the dominant minority in our society.

Opportunities and challenges are laid at the door of our contemporary education system. Our observation is that it is *sagging at the seams* with the demands being placed upon it, targeted with *constructing* socially responsible citizens who are economically purposeful (or economically purposeful citizens who are socially responsible!).

Education – schooling – is a system; a structure. It is a framework through which our populations are socialised into the working mechanics of our society. It is also a learning space. However, whilst it cannot be held responsible for changing all that is wrong with our society, it does have the potential to shape the societies of the future – by supporting lifelong learning through a social justice model that recognises the manipulation of the space. We have to remember what the point of education is for us as educators who are the guardians of this space, and we hope that this collection of essays supports this ambition.

We hope that by engaging in this series of essays, you have been provoked to consider your position within the system we all so readily call education.

Education is for life – it is lifelong learning. It cannot always be measured or quantified, but its worth is infinite in our pursuit of our 'self'.

References

Atkin, C. and O'Grady, A. (2006) 'Devaluing social networks in the race to compete', *The International Journal of Learning,* 13, 6: 165–171.

Bourdieu, P. (1997) 'The forms of capital' (Nice, R., Trans.), in Halsey, A. H., Lauder, H., Brown, P. and Wells, A. S. (eds.) *Education, Culture, Economy and Society* (46–58), Oxford: Oxford University Press.

Bourdieu, P. (1990) *The Logic of Practice.* Cambridge: Polity Press.

Bourdieu, P. (1993) *Sociology in Question.* London: Sage.

Bourdieu, P. (2003) *The Social Structures of the Economy.* Oxford: Polity Press.

Bourdieu, P. and Passeron, J.-C. (1977) *Reproduction in Education, Society and Culture* (Nice, R., Trans.) (2nd ed). London: Sage.

Dewey, J. (1963) *Experience and Education.* London: Collier Macmillian.

Dewey, J. (1966) *Democracy and Education: An Introduction to the Philosophy of Education.* London: Collier Macmillian.

Freire, P. (1993) *Pedagogy of the Oppressed.* New York: Continuum.

Freire, P. (1994) *Pedagogy of Hope: Reliving Pedagogy of the Oppressed.* New York: Continuum.

Freire, P. (1996) *Pedagogy of the Oppressed (20th anniversary edition).* New York: Continuum.

Furedi, F. (2009) *Wasted: Why Education Isn't Educating.* London: Continuum.

Furedi, F. (2013) *The Philistines have Taken Over the Classroom,* Spiked online, Available from http://www.spiked-online.com/newsite/article/13497#.VAcjtaNwa70, Accessed September 2014.

Griffiths, M. (2009) *Justice, Joy and Educational Delights,* Inaugural lecture, University of Edinburgh.

O'Grady, A. (2013) *Lifelong Learning in the UK: An introductory Guide for Education Studies.* London: Routledge.

Index

Printed in Great
Britain
by Amazon